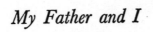

My Father and I

JOSEPH SCHILDKRAUT

My Father and I

AS TOLD TO LEO LANIA

THE VIKING PRESS · NEW YORK · 1959

First published in 1959 by
The Viking Press, Inc.
625 Madison Avenue, New York 22, N.Y.

Published in Canada by
The Macmillan Company of Canada Limited

Library of Congress catalogue card number: 59-6738

Printed in U. S. A. by American Book-Stratford Press

For Marie

ILLUSTRATIONS

The illustrations are in two sections, following pages 118 and 182.

My Father and I

Chapter I

THIS IS MY LIBRARY. Here are my books, my recordings, my desk, my favorite chair. Through the open door I can see Marie in the living room, busy as usual, writing and reading, keeping my life in order. Over there in the corner our two babies, Boychick and Cheety, two little Chihuahuas, one black, the other blond, are fast asleep. How familiar all this is, and still, today, so different.

It is late. No sound comes from the street, except the rustling of the elm trees in front of the house, and occasionally the barking of a dog far away, or the whizzing of a jet plane in the night sky overhead. Living in this part of Beverly Hills is like living in the country.

The scent of orange blossoms drifts through the open windows. It is heavy, intoxicating. I am sleepy and at the same time wide awake, tired and yet unable to sit still.

Tomorrow I can sleep as long as I want. No studio call in the morning. Neither tomorrow, nor the next day, nor next week. I have finished my work for *The Diary of Anne Frank.* Today was the last day of shooting. It is August 1,

1958. We started the picture on March 3. Up at six-fifteen, to the studio, to the make-up department, into the clothes of Otto Frank, on to Stage 14, and into the character of Otto Frank. Now it's finished.

I have known this feeling before—a kind of emptiness, a psychological letdown, as it were. Suddenly all the excitement is gone, the exultation that makes you forget everything but your work, and what remains is doubt and a nagging feeling of inadequacy. Have I succeeded? Was I faithful to Anne Frank? What will the public say? And the critics?

After the completion of each picture throughout the years I have had the same qualms. And yet this is different. I have played the part of Otto Frank one thousand eighty-six times. After the New York run I toured the whole country from coast to coast. I did not miss a single performance in twenty-eight months. On Saturday, March 1, 1958, I was on the stage of the Walnut Street Theatre in Philadelphia and on the following Monday I reported to Twentieth Century–Fox studios in Hollywood for costume and make-up tests. That was a little over five months ago. Only twice before did I work in a film for such a long time. The first time was in *Orphans of the Storm,* under the direction of D. W. Griffith. That engagement lasted even longer—eighteen months. The second time was under Cecil B. de Mille in *The King of Kings,* fourteen months.

George Stevens, who produced and directed *The Diary of Anne Frank,* reminds me so much of Griffith, that great pioneer of the American film; he has the same dedication, the same urge for perfection, a complete mastery of the motion-picture medium, and, above all, a deep insight into the characters he recreates and into the psychological make-up of his actors. What sensitivity in this giant-like body! It was a wonderful experience working with him.

It was a wonderful experience to win so much praise and honors for my work in *Diary*. There have been twenty-seven awards and citations, Brandeis University has dedicated a new library in my name, and just the other day I received news from Israel that "in recognition of Joseph Schildkraut's performance as Otto Frank his name has been inscribed in the Golden Book of Jerusalem together with the great names of Lord Balfour, Gandhi, Schweitzer, Einstein, Toscanini." I look at the little oil lamp in my hand, over two thousand years old, unearthed from the sands of the Judean hills, that was presented to me as a token of appreciation by the Israel Bond Organization. But even the thought of all these great honors fails to dispel my gloom tonight.

For close to three years I have lived in another world, in another period of history. Tomorrow I shall start letting my hair grow again, and soon the bald part of my head which I shaved off to resemble Otto Frank will be covered. But will that help me to step out of the character of Otto Frank back into my own personality? One thing is sure—I will never again be the man I was three years ago.

These three years were probably the most important and decisive of my whole life. Because I did not merely act a part, but had to live as Otto Frank through the whole terrible and shattering experience of an era which can never be erased from the memory of my generation.

I have gone through many periods in my life, as most men do. Today I feel there was a definite pattern in the many lives I lived, to the seemingly chaotic years of my artistic struggle and emotional wandering. It was, I believe firmly, not accidental that the *The Diary of Anne Frank* became the culmination of my professional life.

What is this pattern?

I cannot describe it without starting from the beginning. And that means that first of all I have to speak of my father. Our lives were indissolubly intertwined. Our relationship was more than the usual biological tie that binds a father to the son he loves and the struggling youngster to the man he admires and hopes to emulate.

One of the leading theater critics of Germany wrote after

my father's death, "Rudolf Schildkraut could be devil and hero, fool and sage, beast and Philistine, because this man of unusual temperament had more than talent—he was a man of genius. And his greatness manifested itself unforgettably when he acted the part of a father. Loving, majestic, kind and cheerful, helplessly crushed and frightening in his anger—always a father. This actor from a little village in Romania put his indelible mark on the German theater because he could rise to the highest levels of his art—whenever called upon to create the character of a father."

As for me, if it had not been for Father I would, of course, not have been born. If it had not been for what my father was and wanted to be, there would have been no pattern and no deeper meaning to my life.

So let's start from the beginning.

Chapter II

1

He could not sleep. He lay on his back, with his eyes closed, and shivered. It was not the cold that made him shiver; the air in the little room was heavy with the scent of lilac and the sharp smell of smoked meat, stale beer, and dung, which drifted in through the open window. The eiderdown was too warm for that time of the year. But he would not dare throw it off; he hardly dared to breathe. He opened his eyes, just for a moment. In the light of the full moon the room looked strange—table, chairs, the huge cupboard, seemed to sway, as if they were alive, as if they wanted to leave the room and steal down the staircase to the big saloon of the inn, where the miraculous performance had taken place.

Not that he was afraid. There were nights when he awoke trembling, and fear lay on his chest like a heavy stone, for someone was standing in the corner of the room, in the shadow of the cupboard, watching him. It was a huge man without a head, for the man was dead and, as is well known, a dead man has no head; the moment he is buried the worms eat it up, and what remains is a white skull with deep holes and big yellow teeth. The apothecary on the main square had such a skull in his window, where it had an honored place between two big decanters, one filled with a red liquid and the other with blue. The man in the corner must have a skull in the place of his head, and that was why Rudolf was afraid. He was afraid to look, and at the same time he had a terrible longing to rush up to him, to throw himself into the man's arms.

The dead man was his father. He had never known him. He had died long ago when Rudolf was a little boy. Now Rudolf was a big boy—eight years old.

An eight-year-old knows that a dead man can never return—except maybe at night when he sneaks into a house and stands in a dark corner and looks at his son because he's sorry for his boy and wants to help him against the bad and cruel stepfather. And if he, Rudolf, were not such a coward, he would jump out of his bed and take the dead father by the hand and run off with him. But then where could they go? To the graveyard? He was afraid of the graveyard and he would never dare look at the father who had a white skull instead of a head. Tears welled up in his eyes, tears of sorrow and pity—for the father and for himself. Thus he fell asleep again.

But tonight he was not afraid and he did not want to sleep. Hours ago the music and laughter had stopped. The drums were mute, tambourines and balalaikas no longer sang, the house did not shake any more to the rhythmic stamping of the dancing feet. Yet this silence was even more mysterious and exciting. It gave him a chance to hear and see more clearly what had actually happened in the big saloon. He lived through the whole performance over and over again.

It had all started days ago when the stepfather had told Mother that a group of wandering Greek players would come and give a performance here at their own inn, and that the elevated podium in the rear of the saloon, where the notables of the city of Braila—the apothecary, the lawyer, the doctor —used to gather for their wine and brandy on Sunday morning after Mass, was to be turned into a stage. There would be not just music and dance—there would be theater.

"What is that—theater?" Rudolf asked his stepfather.

"Some bloody nonsense you can hardly make money with," the stepfather had said.

Mother smiled. "They will put on a play," she said. "There will be Bengal lights and torches and real actors and a real villain."

"A play?"

"A story—a fairy tale."

"Then why is it called a play? And why do we need a stage? And why—"

"Stop asking foolish questions!" the stepfather growled.

But later on Mother explained, and the boy's sister Regina, two years older, supplied more information—how each actor would speak his own part and bring to life what are otherwise words and sentences between the covers of a book. Imagine, actually to see the knight slay the dragon, to hear the orphan cry for help, to witness the girl's rescue and the torture of the villain!

The players arrived. They came in a green painted wagon drawn by two dray horses. The wagon was like a magic box: you stole a glimpse through the curtain and saw sheets of colored silk, and rugs, and gleaming sabers and silvery armor. Splendid costumes were hanging there, and on a little table stood what looked in the shadow like a couple of heads. Rudolf's heart stopped, but in the next second he realized those heads were not the skulls of dead men. They had a lot of hair, beautiful hair, and the skin of the forehead was soft and pink. "Wigs," Regina whispered.

The actors were a strange and mysterious kind of people. The men wore suits that were no less shabby and ragged than those of some poor functionary or clerk, but they had big diamonds in their neckties and clean-shaven faces, not beards like the peasants of Braila. The women had red cheeks and sparkling eyes and smelled like flowers.

With every hour Rudolf's excitement grew. The more bitter was his disappointment when he was told by his stepfather that he was not allowed to attend the performance. Theater was not for little children, and he had to be in bed by eight o'clock as usual.

When Mother came to his bed to kiss him good night he turned his head away and buried his face in the pillow. He had been crying and he was ashamed of his tears.

"Are you still angry with me?" asked Mother in her deep voice, which was like a caress. "Don't be so stubborn. You don't miss anything, darling, really. Nothing but a lot of noise and shouting, that's what theater is. I will be glad when that crowd leaves tomorrow morning—a bunch of tramps!" She kissed him on the forehead. "You aren't getting sick? I think you have a cold coming on. You have a little fever." She tucked him under the eiderdown. "Keep warm, that's the main thing."

He followed her with his eyes when she left the room. How small she looked; she had never looked so small and helpless to him before. And never had he felt so strong and so superior. "Nothing but noise and shouting!" What did she know! "A bunch of tramps!" How blind and silly some grownups are!

For hours he lay motionless and listened to the sounds that drifted up to the room from the saloon. No, he need not be there to see the performance. All the stories he had ever heard, all the fairy tales the cook had told him were mixed up with the bits of dialogue he had picked up during the rehearsal, and behind his closed eyes he saw the whole drama unfold; he himself was part of it. He was the knight and he was the dragon, he was the orphan crying for help, and he was the mean villain with the black wig and the waxed mustache— "He-he-he," he laughed sardonically. But then he entered as the hero—blond and tall, with a voice like thunder. "Stop!" he shouted. He raised his arm. "Out you go!" And the villain slunk away.

He acted this scene over and over again, embellishing it; the hero's part became bigger and bigger, the villain's part more and more shocking. His silent, sardonic laughter chilled his blood.

An early dawn looked through the window. The room swam in a misty light. He crawled out of his bed and tip-toed to the window. The street he knew so well seemed different. It had a ghostly look; the walls of the house opposite had the color of bleached bones.

Utter silence. Then a cock crowed, a dog barked far away, another dog answered, and you could hear the horses move in the stable to the right.

Softly he crossed the room to the door and very cautiously opened it. No sound. In the room across the little landing his parents were fast asleep. Regina slept in the room to the left, the door ajar; now she sighed in her sleep and for a few moments he grew stiff with fright. Silence again. Softly, softly he made his way down the staircase.

When he entered the saloon a strange sensation overwhelmed him. While his eyes grew slowly accustomed to the twilight, picking out the tables, the stage, the scenery, an exciting perfume enveloped him. He sniffed and inhaled it with an almost painful delight. It was a magical perfume— this mixture of make-up, sweat, painted scenery, dust, and grease paint.

The garden on the stage, now touched by the first rays of the new day falling through the high window, was not a painted canvas, but an enchanted island of flowers and trees; he entered it with awe. He touched the costumes still lying around, and some of the props. Behind a tree there was a murderous-looking instrument. What was it? A rack, he decided, evidently used to torture the villain.

He could not contain his curiosity. Here was a hand crank; he touched it, started to turn it.

A terrific noise shattered the silence. The curtain fell down, enveloping him in its folds. Panicky, he tried to extricate himself from this mass of cloth and ropes.

A strong hand grabbed him. The stepfather!

He struggled to his feet, but a vicious blow struck him and he staggered. Another blow and another. He raised his hands to protect his face, but the attack had been so unexpected and the blows came so fast that for a few moments he was dumfounded, he did not feel anything. An excruciating pain shot through his head. Through a mist of tears he saw Mother, Regina, the cook. He tasted something very salty. His head grew bigger and bigger, a balloon ready to explode. It exploded.

He lay in his bed, every inch of his bruised body hurt, hardly daring to move his arms and legs. He moved his head instead; it felt as if it did not belong to him, as if it were too big for him. It did not hurt very much; it was just that he felt as if one side were quite different from the other, or as if he had water in his right ear. A funny feeling.

The doctor came, a little gray-haired man with a little gray beard and two twinkling eyes, carrying a little black bag. He gave him a red candy which was hard like a rock.

"Something wrong with his right ear," the doctor told Mother. "The eardrum must have been injured. Nothing serious. Thank God we have two ears and it's not so important to hear every single word. With all this damn nonsense people are chattering all the time, the less you hear of it the better off you are. Right, Rudolf?" He laughed heartily. Rudolf smiled in spite of his pain. He liked the doctor, and the candy was delicious.

2

The boys stood in a closed circle around a little ball, and when the name of a nation was called the one who had chosen to represent it had to grab the ball quickly while the others scattered in all directions. If you could hit one of the running boys with the ball you won a point. That was important. More important, however, was first to decide on the nation you wanted to stand and to fight for.

Nobody wanted to be a Romanian, for that's what everybody in Braila was called anyhow. Nobody wanted to be a Turk, either, for the Turks were the "enemy"; the principality of Romania was still in vassalage to Constantinople. You would not like to be a slave of the Sultan, would you? Hungarians were enemies too, for they claimed a province that rightly belonged to Romania; on the other hand their hussars wore a beautiful uniform, and some of the richest men in Braila were Hungarians. Most of the boys wanted to be Russian, with Germany second in demand. Russia was a most powerful nation: the Czar supported the Balkan peoples against the evil Sultan, Russia had defeated the great Napoleon, and the Cossacks were terrific. Germany had just won the war against France and the picture of the Kaiser was in every stationery shop. In his helmet and with his beautiful mustache he was quite a man. And Austria—

"I want to be Austria!" shouted Rudolf.

That was Mother's influence. Mother loved Austria. "Vienna—that's the city where I would like to live," she used to say. In Vienna a Jewish boy could become even a doctor or a lawyer if he was bright enough. Vienna had everything— in fact, Vienna was more than a city, it was a promise and a dream. "For us Jews there is no better place," Mother said.

Stepfather scoffed at this idea. "Jews are in trouble everywhere, always," he said. "Braila or Vienna—there is not much difference as far as a Jew is concerned."

But Mother, usually so subservient and never daring to contradict her husband, for the first time did not give in. "There is no future for Rudolf here," she insisted. "And he should learn German."

That settled it. Stepfather agreed that German was im-

portant; there was no more useful language if you wanted
to get ahead in the world, no matter whether you lived in
Braila or Budapest or Vienna.

"One day you will go to the *Gymnasium*, darling," Mother
said. "You will learn to speak a beautiful German—not the
Yiddish our people speak here—you will be a real gentleman,
an Austrian, a subject of the great Emperor Francis Joseph—"

"—and they will still call you a dirty Jew!" the stepfather
jeered.

Rudolf looked, bewildered, from one to the other. He
didn't mind too much being a Jew. The kids in school often
called him *Zsido* (Jew) and sometimes threw stones at him,
but that was nothing. He was strong and quick, he could take
care of himself in any fight, all the boys respected his fists, he
was on the best of terms with the worst rowdies. The name-
calling, the brawls and fights, were all part of the game.

He liked the school. He liked the life in Braila, which
was full of excitement, especially on the day of the weekly
market, when the peasants in their sheepskin furs and the
women in their multi-colored skirts invaded the town and
the big square was a turbulent whirlpool of shouting people,
neighing horses, mooing cattle, squeaking pigs, and cackling
fowl. What a gorgeous, wonderful racket! He liked his home
and the inn, where something interesting was going on all
the time. He would never tire of exploring the stable and the
kitchen; the old cook had an inexhaustible store of tales and
stories. By now he knew them all by heart, but that was the
beauty of it: he knew the outcome of each story, and he listened to the monotonous mumbling of the old woman as if
to a favorite melody. Her cackling voice conjured up scenes
and dramas and on the long winter evenings populated the
cozy, dim kitchen with a host of characters, standing in the
shadow of the room, waiting for his command, to laugh or
cry, to suffer and die. On Sunday afternoons, in the abandoned quarry where the boys met to play "Nations" or

"Robbers and Gendarmes," he made them play "The Sacrifice of the Janissary" and "The Search for the Hidden Treasure." He always got the biggest part, and the quarry became a favorite hangout for him and his chums.

For a thirteen-year-old, life in Braila was wonderful. There rarely was a day when he did not come home limping, with a bloody knee or a torn sleeve. He could not help getting into brawls, for he had a violent temper, and, since the stepfather had sworn to "make him behave" even if he had to "beat the life out of him," the scars earned on the honorable battlefield alternated with bruises inflicted by the beatings of the stepfather. Rudolf accepted this punishment stoically, as one accepts the inclemencies of the weather, having learned how to protect himself against the worst blows by starting to cry heartbreakingly even before the blow struck, bringing Mother and cook to his rescue, and always carrying for emergencies a schoolbook in the seat of his pants.

Yes, he liked his life in Braila, though he did not like *heder,* which he had to attend for two hours every afternoon. His parents were not orthodox Jews, but a Jewish boy had to go to heder, had to learn Hebrew, the Bible and the Talmud, and to be prepared for his *bar mizvah.* Rudolf had little trouble with Hebrew—the Bible had a lot of good stories in it. It was just that he had to sit in heder while his non-Jewish friends could play "Nations" and someone else was acting his part in "The Search for the Hidden Treasure." In Vienna he would not need to go to heder. He wanted to be an Austrian.

3

It all started on the way to heder. Turning into the narrow street which led to the *schul,* the synagogue, Rudolf heard a miserable whining and yowling in the back yard of one of the dilapidated houses in this poor neighborhood. He ran there and caught a glimpse of Isaak, a fellow student from heder, who rushed out of the privy. The pitiful howling of the dog seemed to come from there. Rudolf opened the door to the outhouse, lifted the lid, and saw a puppy dog squirming desperately in the excrement, unable to save himself. The stench was overpowering, but without a thought Rudolf pushed his hands into the filth and grabbed the puppy. He ran home, quickly washed the dog and himself—there was no time to change his suit—and returned to heder.

To be late was bad enough. Entering the heder without a *yarmalka* (skull cap), which Rudolf in his excitement had forgotten to put on, and bringing a dog into the schul were worse. But before the teacher could give vent to his outrage, something even more shocking happened. At the sight of Isaak, who was standing there in his *talles* (a prayer shawl) and *twillen* (prayer straps on his wrists and forehead), and holding the Bible in his hands, a picture of religious devotion, Rudolf was seized by fury. He dropped the dog and threw himself at Isaak with clenched fists and gnashing teeth. He knocked him down, jumped on him, hammered his head against the floor, choked him. The other boys, at first stunned, now joyously joined in the mêlée; prayer books flew in all directions, the dog barked happily, the teacher yelled, grabbed a cane—the most important symbol of his authority—and rushed to the rescue of Isaak, whom Rudolf was about to kill.

That was Rudolf's farewell to Braila.

When the teacher brought him home, to give emphasis to his complaint about the boy's outrageous behavior, Mother nearly fainted at the sight of her son. His face, hardly recognizable, was smeared with blood, the nose broken, the lips swollen, the right eye closed; his suit was torn, and he walked in a cloud of sickening stench.

For the first time the stepfather was at a complete loss for words to scold. One thing was clear: no normal punishment could fit this crime. Beatings were useless; the boy was unmanageable. Bar mizvah was, of course, out of the question. Rudolf had to leave the house. He must go to a boarding

school in Hermannstadt, a town across the border to the
north. Let the stern and experienced Austrian teachers find
out what they could do with this kind of boy.

4

The town had two names: Hermannstadt was its German
name, Nagyszeben the Hungarian. It belonged to Siebenbürgen, which was also called Transylvania; the principality
had been until recently in vassalage to the Turkish Sultan;
the Hungarians claimed it, the Austrians got it; there were
a lot of Romanians living there but all the "better people"
were Saxons. They lived in neat, whitewashed houses; they
had brought their German efficiency and cleanliness and
craftsmanship to this land. Across the border were the Balkans—dirt, illiteracy, perpetual turmoil. Beyond, Asia began.
Siebenbürgen was still Europe. The people spoke half a
dozen languages and dialects, belonged to different religions
and sects, were different in appearance and dress, but had
one thing in common: they were all Austrians, subjects of
His Apostolic Majesty Francis Joseph of Hapsburg, Emperor
of Austria, King of Hungary, King of Bohemia, Protector of
Jerusalem, Prince of Tyrol, Earl of Kraków, Grand Duke of
Siebenbürgen—only the students of the Gymnasium could
quote all his titles.

A Gymnasium was more than a school of higher education;
it was like a religious order, bestowing upon its students a
distinction no other secondary school could provide. There
the boys studied Latin and ancient Greek; they were not
trained for some profession or job so that they might eventually be able to earn a living; a Gymnasiast belonged to a
higher category of humanity. Let the ordinary people be concerned with practical matters—business, handicraft, farming
—the Gymnasiast had a loftier ambition: after eight years
he could enter the University and finally become a "Herr
Doktor." That was not just a degree, it was a title—nay, a
patent of nobility. It marked one as a member of Society.

If a boy was not lucky enough to be born an aristocrat, through the Gymnasium he could still make his way into the ranks of the intelligentsia. The aristocrats served the emperor, the priests were the defenders of God, and the intellectuals were the keepers of "Culture."

Even the fourteen-year-old Rudolf realized that Culture was something very important and precious, though he would not have been able to explain what it was. Ordinary people did not have it, it simply did not belong to them; neither did it belong to the various nations that formed the monarchy—the Czechs had no Culture, and even the Austrians had none. Only the ancient Greeks had it, and the Romans. Whenever one used the word "culture" one added the adjective "classical" or "humanistic."

Culture was a treasure hidden now for centuries in libraries and the classrooms of the Gymnasium and the University. Culture was nominative and ablative, strong and weak conjugations, *"Gallia est omnis divisa in partes tres,"* the Peloponnesian War, and the difference between Corinthian and Dorian columns. Modern history was part of Culture too: students had to learn by heart hundreds of dates, the birthdays and deaths of kings and emperors, of the battles they fought, and twice a week were led through the genealogical labyrinth of the Hapsburg dynasty. That was called "National History." Geography was not part of Culture, nor was physical science; those subjects were taught at random. That same stuff could be learned in all secondary schools; it was of no more than practical value. Algebra was something altogether different. Rudolf hated it and it had to be beaten into his head. He did not object. The beatings, the harsh discipline which excluded music, play, and physical training, had to be endured in the interest of Culture.

The subject Rudolf loved more than any other was German literature. He had picked up a smattering of German in Braila, and his Yiddish helped. He had a natural gift for languages, a sharp ear, and a fabulous memory for words and the rhythm of speech. In a couple of months he spoke German fluently. He spoke it with a peculiar foreign accent, but, since everybody in Austria spoke German with some kind of accent or special intonation, it didn't matter. There was a musical, strangely guttural tinge in his German that both the teachers and the fellow students found fascinating. His broken nose had not mended quite properly, and often his wonderfully resonant voice would sound slightly hoarse and nasal, giving his speech an additional personal distinction.

German literature was, of course, Goethe, Schiller, and Shakespeare. Shakespeare was, to be sure, an Englishman, but thanks to the masterful translation by Schlegel and Tieck he had become a German poet. You were not a man of Culture unless you could quote from *Hamlet* and *King Lear,* from *Faust* and *The Robbers.* To Rudolf those quotations meant more than just the expression of some great thought. He was passionately in love with the sound of the words. They intoxicated him. When he was ordered to recite a poem or to read a dramatic monologue he felt as if he were soaring high into the heavens; the class, the teacher, the other boys were far away; the words he spoke were now his own, his personal lament or prayer, challenge or revenge. The audience sat flabbergasted.

Aside from the Gymnasium there was another cultural center in the town of Hermannstadt—the Municipal Theater. Since the boys had to be in their dormitory by eight o'clock, they could not often visit it. Rudolf solved the problem. Each of the students contributed a few *Kreuzer* for the purchase of a ticket, and with the help of a long rope fashioned from bed sheets, Rudolf climbed down into the back yard and over the surrounding wall and rushed to the theater. Two hours later he came back by the same way and repeated for his friends the performance he had just witnessed, acting out the entire play. He was given the nickname "the actor," he became the darling of the German teacher—and he was

thrown out of the Gymnasium. For one night his escapade
was discovered, and, what made matters worse still, the play
he had just seen was a French bedroom farce, not at all suit-
able for a fifteen-year-old boy. (As one can see, sometimes the
citizens of Hermannstadt had a different approach to Culture from the one advocated by the teachers of the Gymnasium, and even a municipal theater could not live by
Goethe and Schiller alone. Girls in various stages of undress
were, unfortunately, "better box office" than Shakespeare.)

5

"Put the wash away—the comedians are coming!" This cry
heralded the arrival of the green-painted wagon at every
hamlet and village. As soon as the peasant women caught
sight of it, they ran from the fields to take in the laundry
they had left hanging to dry, and chased geese and chick-
ens into the barnyard and their teenage daughters into the
kitchen. Only children and dogs were eager to greet the
wandering players—the children with joyous excitement, the
dogs with ominous snarling and barking. The dogs expressed
the sentiments of their masters. To the villagers, actors were
nothing but "gypsies"—mischief-makers, thieves, and a threat
to the virtue of every innocent girl.

Barred from the Gymnasium and afraid to face the wrath
of his stepfather, Rudolf decided not to return to Braila. He
joined the first troop of comedians he encountered in the
outskirts of Hermannstadt.

The director was a man in his late fifties, with a stentorian
voice and an imposing stature. He was the star, primarily,
though grudgingly, admired for his ability to consume huge
quantities of the native brandy without ever getting drunk.
It was known that he rarely needed help in handling heck-
lers and brawlers in the audience; he simply stepped off the
stage, picked them up, and threw them out as if they were
so many sacks of corn.

He was completely under the domination of his wife, **an**

overripe blonde of awesome proportions. No costume could contain the mass of her white, flaccid flesh; it spilled over the footlights, as it were; it dazzled the fathers and disturbed the sleep of the sons. She was the heroine, and, in spite of her forty-odd years, the ingenue. If there was no part for her in a play she was the prompter; sometimes she acted and prompted on the same bill. She also administered the finances of the theater and prepared the meals for the little group— two activities that demanded greater ingenuity than her most exacting dramatic part. The nightly receipts never amounted to more than a handful of kreuzer; to divide this pitiful sum evenly among the twelve members of the group was a major problem in arithmetic and to fill their empty stomachs was even more difficult.

During the summer months it was somewhat easier. At night the two or three younger members of the troop went on expeditions in the fields and stole a few ears of corn or some watermelons to supplement the next day's meager menu. Sometimes luck smiled on them and they caught a chicken or goose before the watchdog could catch them, even if it meant leaving parts of their pants on the barbed-wire fence.

Rudolf proved himself courageous and resourceful on these nightly expeditions, and the director probably had these gifts of his youngest actor in mind when he called him "a very talented boy."

Resourceful he had to be. The hostile world attacked Rudolf not only through his stomach. After a few months on the highways and byways of the Hungarian provinces, covered alternately with dust and mud, Rudolf's only pair of shoes was worn to pieces and beyond repair. He had no money for a new pair, and therefore fashioned contraptions out of straw and leaves and ears of corn, painting them over with a mixture of liquid tar and ink. This invention saved him from the shame of running around barefoot like a peasant; at least from a distance it looked as if he were wearing shoes.

Rudolf started as a lamp-lighter and as dresser to the other members of the troop. Little by little he advanced to small parts. The most important education he got from the directrice; his colleagues could give him professional advice, the director could teach him useful tricks to enhance his stage presence, but she made a man out of him. At her insistence he was given his first "real part" in a play by Kotzebue, a very popular author of comedies and melodramas of that period.

Rudolf's debut took place in a big barn in a small Hungarian village. The stage was made out of boards placed on wine barrels and Rudolf appeared before the duly impressed peasants in the role of a suave, distinguished Austrian aristocrat. To portray the character convincingly, Rudolf borrowed from one of his older colleagues a dressing gown with sleeves four inches too long that drooped over his fingers. Since he had no shirt, the directrice gave him her brightly knitted colored scarf, which she tied into an ascot. His tar-covered contraptions of straw and corn served as shoes. But even with a luxurious mustache, goatee, and monocle he looked too young for the part and therefore he affixed side whiskers to his face, which gave him the appearance of a young orangutan. Still not satisfied, he went to the director's dressing room—the corner that served as such in the rear of the barn—and borrowed his make-up kit. Putting on every color that the famous cosmetic firm of Leichner manufactured, he transformed his face into a strange mask; speckled, lined, and furrowed with the colors of the rainbow, it looked as if he had contracted some horrible disease. The peasants didn't mind. They had no better conception of a Viennese aristocrat than Rudolf had. They applauded violently.

That memorable evening marked the end of his first theatrical engagement. Carried away by his triumph, Rudolf felt prompted to broaden the base of his amorous operations.

The same night the directrice discovered him in her daughter's bed. The young girl was a pale, timid creature and had arrived just a few days before for a visit with her parents. She lived in Budapest with relatives, respectable people, who had agreed to care for her education and to watch over her virtue until she could be properly married off to a distant cousin; the man was much older but he had a steady income as an employee in the post office, a civil servant, no less! And now this dreadful thing happened!

"And you insisted on renting a special room for her!" the director said, reproaching his wife. "She could have slept quite comfortably in our room. But no, nothing is too good for her, and she must be protected from the vulgarities of our life, you said. Much good did it do. We could have at least saved fifty kreuzer!"

The mother bowed her head in contrition. She was not jealous of her daughter and not surprised at her lover's wandering sentiments. She would even have forgiven him. But when the two youngsters declared that they were in love and wanted to get married, her indignation was boundless, and in expressing it she rose to the heights of a truly dramatic heroine.

"You have robbed an innocent girl of her most precious treasure!" The words were out of the popular melodrama, *The Miller and His Child,* and she spoke them beautifully.

"I will marry her," Rudolf repeated with passion.

Instantly the directrice turned from the wronged wife of the miller into a haughty Mary Stuart. "Never! Only over my dead body," she shouted. "I will never permit my daughter to marry a penniless actor."

Whereupon the girl was sent back to Budapest and Rudolf was fired.

Since he was by now a veteran he immediately found a new job with another company. There were dozens of them touring the provinces.

6

Four, five years passed. His life hardly changed. One troop was like the other; he got bigger parts, sometimes he even appeared in a leading role, but the misery remained the same. The privations could not dampen his enthusiasm for the theater. He forgot them the moment the curtain went up and he stepped in front of the audience. The following two hours were worth the tiring march of the previous day and going to bed on an empty stomach.

There was something else that sustained him: a dream. It was elusive as all dreams are but it was also very real. The dream had a name: Vienna. Unattainable as the city seemed, he was sure that one day he would reach it. He would stand on the stage of a real theater and have the people of Vienna for his audience.

One spring the goal seemed close. His troop had reached the Austrian border. With Vienna only fifteen miles away, a colleague had given him the name of an agent who might be able to get him a job with a municipal theater. This chance had to be taken.

He had no money for a train ticket, he could find no one to give him a ride, so he walked. In his new and comfortable shoes he could make it to Vienna in four hours. He and a friend had pooled their resources to buy these precious shoes, and they wore them alternately. The friend was willing to stay in bed while Rudolf used them on his expedition.

This first visit to Vienna allowed him no more than a swift glimpse of the city of his dreams. He arrived just before noon and would have to leave at three o'clock in order to be back in time for the evening performance. But three hours, he thought, would be enough to call on the agent, to gain his interest, to sign a contract.

It turned out differently.

It took him an extra hour to reach the center of the city, where the agent lived. There he got lost in a maze of crooked streets and crowded alleys. The noise and the bustle, the huge palaces, churches, and monuments, the beautifully gowned ladies in handsome carriages, the shop windows full of treasures—it all made his head spin. Finally, exhausted, he arrived at the agent's office. When he opened the door he found himself in a waiting room furnished only with a few posters and a long wooden bench, where a dozen actors sat waiting—men of various sizes and ages but alike in their dejected appearance. They stared rather suspiciously at the newcomer and potential competitor. With difficulty he got a seat, the last one on the bench.

At that moment the door to the inner office opened and the almighty agent appeared, a weasel-like man with little clever eyes and swift movements. A bulky man was with him, superior and self-assured, unmistakably the manager or director of some theater; he stood in the doorway like a tired elephant, slowly moving his head from one side to the other. The weasel flitted around him, darted forward, and, pointing to the bench, said in a high quivering voice, "That whole bunch as you see it here—you can have them for fifty *Gulden* a month!" Quickly he counted: "Thirteen actors" (he had included Rudolf) "that's less than four Gulden apiece, what more do you want?"

Rudolf could not remember how he had left the office. The last houses of Vienna were already behind him; around him was the peaceful countryside—blooming fields and meadows, the twittering of birds, the humming and buzzing of beetles and bees. The sky was blue and the sun smiled— a perfect spring day. Rudolf saw only that scene in the waiting room, and heard again and again the words of the agent. His face burned with shame and his heart was cold with fury. Never in his life had he felt so insulted and so powerless.

He staggered along the dusty road; one would have taken him for a drunkard or a very sick man.

Four hours later he arrived home. He took off the precious shoes and threw them into a corner of the wagon. His feet hurt. It was time to get ready for the performance.

7

On Easter Sunday, according to the general custom of the region, the troop always staged a Passion Play. The director proved his versatility—and his sense of economy—by playing three roles: the Voice of God, Pontius Pilate, and the High Priest. His wife, a prematurely aged and bony woman with the slow movements of a good-natured pack horse, was the seductive Maria Magdalena. Rudolf had the part of Jesus.

They played in the open air on a rough stage erected on the main square of the village. Behind them was the old church, and farther in the background the hills of northern Hungary, gray and barren but aglow with light from the setting sun. The air was warm and breezy. One could smell the spring.

In front sat the peasants and their women and children in their Sunday best. Every seat was filled. They had been to church, they had celebrated the Resurrection with an especially good dinner and many glasses of the native wine, for the village lay in the heart of a famous wine region. The exaltation with which they followed the Passion of Christ was not entirely due to religious fervor.

The first act met with great applause. When the curtain went up for the second act, there was Rudolf standing in the center of the stage, a crown of thorns on his head, a scepter in his right hand, a torn cloak around his shoulders. He was about to address his tormentors when he became aware of a peculiar commotion in the audience. A whisper was running through the crowd, growing louder. What was going on out there?

He tried to concentrate on his lines but a feeling he had never before experienced on the stage almost paralyzed him:

it was like standing close to a towering wall that was ready to topple and bury him.

He tried to shake off the appalling sense of danger and started to speak. His first words were drowned in a loud cry: "Jew! A Jew!"

He still did not understand. He looked bewildered at the audience. Many were on their feet; he saw faces distorted with anger and scorn, raised fists—for a moment he thought they were carried away by their compassion with Christ's suffering and wanted to vent their revenge on the Roman soldiers who were to drag him to the cross. He raised his hand, pleading for quiet, for understanding; a stone struck his shoulder, another grazed his cheek.

"Son of a bitch! Clear out! Jewish bastard!" From all directions men and women were pressing against the stage— it was he whom they intended to attack.

He retreated, turned to the rear, jumped off the stage, started to run. The howling, stone-throwing rabble was close behind him. He ran faster.

The main street was deserted. Only the old people had remained at home, sitting on their porches, resting their tired bones. They saw a curious apparition: a man, barefoot, the crown of thorns aslant on his head, desperately holding up the end of his cloak in order not to stumble over it, deadly pale and bleeding, pursued by a rabid, drunken mob. "Jesus, Maria, and Joseph!" they mumbled and crossed themselves. Before they could recover from their shock, the man had turned the next corner and disappeared behind a cluster of barns and stables.

For hours Rudolf hid under the roof of a haystack. Gradually the shouting and howling subsided, the mob dispersed. At last he understood: the anti-Semitic peasants must have somehow learned he was a Jew—a Jew daring to play Christ! What an outrage! A Jew . . .

And for years he had not thought of himself as a Jew. Not since he had left Braila. When was the last time he had gone to a synagogue? An actor, that's what he wanted to be. No Romanian, no Austrian, no Jew—an actor!

He took off the crown of thorns, held it in his hands, and stared at it with unseeing eyes. His lips moved in silent prayer: "I'll still make it. In spite of everything. I'll make it." "It" was, of course, the theater of Vienna.

Later, at nightfall, he left his hiding place and, after sneaking through vineyards and fields, rejoined his troop in the green wagon.

8

This was the lowest ebb in his career. A few months later came the great break.

It was after a performance of *The Robbers* by Schiller, with Rudolf cast as Franz Moor. To play just once this greatest and most tragic villain in the repertory of German classical drama is to this day the dream of every young actor in Germany and Austria. How good, how convincing, was Rudolf in this part? From what happened after the performance he himself could not tell.

For immediately after he had taken the last bow, a well-dressed, impressive-looking man accosted him on his way to the dressing room. The man introduced himself as the manager of the Municipal Theater in Salzburg and without wasting any words offered him a contract. Think of it—a long-term contract for a regular theater in the city of Mozart! He was also to get an advance; after all, he had to buy the train tickets and he needed a decent suit. Rudolf was speechless. But then the man quite casually added, "Of course, you will not play any dramatic parts in my theater; but as a character comedian you will do nicely, I hope. We need young men with your talent for comedy and burlesque."

Was my Franz so bad? he wanted to ask. I am a serious dramatic actor, sir, and you speak of burlesque! That's an insult! On the other hand, why did the man offer him a contract?

Rudolf decided to keep his mouth shut. If they wanted burlesque, burlesque it would be.

And so he went to Salzburg. For the first time he played in a real theater with real actors and real scenery, and was paid a real salary—small as it was, he got it regularly every month; like most theaters in Germany and Austria, this one was subsidized by the city and was financially secure.

He played small roles, "funny bit parts" in popular comedies. Only occasionally was he permitted to substitute for a sick actor in a serious part, but according to everyone's opinion that was not his forte. "You're really not gifted for the drama," he was told. "Stick to comedy."

And yet it was a serious role—Mortimer in Schiller's *Maria Stuart*—that finally helped him to reach his goal. The director of Vienna's Raimund Theater saw him in that classic role and instantly engaged him—as comedian. "You'll be a success in operettas," the director assured him. "You can be very funny, I'm sure."

Rudolf heard one word only: Vienna! At last he had won his victory. The year was 1892.

The victor was an emaciated, hollow-faced man of thirty with eyes glowing in a strangely Asiatic face and with a wild bush of curly hair. Looking at a faded photograph that shows him in that period of his life, it is hard for me to believe that this is the same man I have always known as a rather stocky and powerfully built gentleman, meticulously groomed, elegantly attired in expensive suits. Only his eyes never changed; they remained the same throughout his life, burning with a fierce, magnetic power, and at the same time so sad, so kind, so wise. They were the eyes of a dreamer and of a truly dedicated man—passionate, intemperate, but ice cold in the pursuit of what to him was the very essence and meaning of his life. One of the greatest actors of the last century. The rage of two continents. Rudolf Schildkraut. My father.

Chapter III

1

THE FIRST TIME Rudolf saw her, she was standing in the midst of a small crowd waiting at the stage door for the appearance of their matinee idol. Rudolf was not the idol. The students, housemaids, and shopgirls were waiting for the dashing baron whose charm had just broken the heart of his lady-love and whose expert kisses had moved the audience to tears. Rudolf was only the comedian; he had broken nothing more valuable than china and furniture and he had made them laugh. They recognized him, they greeted him with applause, but autographs of "that funny man" were not much in demand.

Rudolf, nevertheless, lifted his hat eagerly and acknowledged the applause with a theatrical bow. Raising his head, he surveyed the crowd. A girl was standing close to the door. In the dim light of the gas lamp he could hardly make out her features. He had the impression of a modestly dressed young woman, slender, petite, wrapped, as it were, in the drab cloak of middle-class respectability. Her big black eyes appraised him half defiantly, half timidly. Instinctively he averted his gaze. The childlike innocence in those searching eyes scared him off. That was exactly the kind of girl he never wanted to be mixed up with. Nothing for you, my boy, an inner voice warned him. With her you'll only get into trouble.

As if reading his thoughts, another young woman stepped from behind the dark-eyed girl and offered him an alluring smile. She was older, blond, with a fully developed figure. But before he could decide on his next move she had taken the arm of the younger girl and led her away.

Rudolf started to follow them, then changed his mind, shrugged his shoulders derisively, and walked off in the opposite direction.

Behind him he heard the shouting and hand-clapping that greeted the appearance of the star. In front of him stretched a long and ugly street. Artisans and small shopkeepers lived there. The large tenement houses, with their doors locked and the shutters down, had an unfriendly look. His steps echoed loudly in the stillness of the night. It was like walking through the corridor of a barracks.

He should have followed the girls. Why didn't he? The blonde seemed an easy catch. It was not his habit to pass up such a chance. If he hurried, maybe he could still overtake them.

Yet he did not turn around. What was the matter with him? He felt tired and at the same time wide awake. His feet were heavy but his head was light. A strange restlessness had taken hold of him and he could not shake it off.

No, he could not stand the idea of returning to the furnished room he had rented from a little tailor in one of the older one-family houses on the other side of the Gürtel, the boulevard that separated the rural suburbs from the city. In comparison to his previous lodgings the room was heaven. He had his own bed and dresser, he could lock the door and enjoy a luxury he had never known before—privacy. Frau Krupka served him every morning a large cup of coffee with two delicious *Kaisersemmeln*. He had nearly forgotten what hunger means and he was a permanent member of a well-known theater. From bit parts in cheap operettas he had advanced to the leading comic roles in the popular comedies and fairy plays of the two masters of the contemporary Austrian theater: Ferdinand Raimund and Johann Nestroy. What more did he want?

The question had attacked him so suddenly that he stood still and stared with blinking eyes at a lighted window across the street. A horse-drawn omnibus rambled slowly by and blocked out his vision. He shook his head and continued on his way. Yet, the question did not leave him. What did he really want?

Money? Fame? He would have it sooner or later, he was sure of it. So what? Expensive suits, a luxurious apartment, a house of his own, maybe? Fine clothes he liked, but not so much as to make him really long for them. And a house—who needs a house? Women? Those he needed. But he had no trouble getting them—chorus girls, chambermaids, and waitresses. He was fully satisfied with what these women of easy virtue had to offer; tiring quickly of his partners, he changed them frequently. The greatest passion never lasted for more than half a dozen nights. Would it be different with some high-class society dame or a nice girl from a good family? Would he ever fall in love?

Maybe there was no such thing as love in real life. These all-consuming agonies and ecstasies of love existed only on the stage. That made them, of course, not less real. Was it that he wanted? To be the handsome young idol whose romantic love-making no girl or woman could resist? No, he didn't aspire to these parts and he felt no envy for his famous colleague who strutted across the stage in tights or splendid uniforms.

He liked his own parts much better. He loved to play these ludicrous servants or misanthropes, the wronged husband, the rejected father; the more pitiful they were, the

more he loved them. They were *real* people. The audience
laughed at their rantings and tears, for the Viennese burghers never identified themselves with these nasty characters
on the stage; they didn't want to believe that their famous
Gemütlichkeit and kindliness was sham and self-deception.
Raimund and Nestroy showed them their true nature, their
foibles and selfishness, but to make the truth palatable they
had to turn it into a joke. The two authors had classical
stature. Raimund was gentle, a romantic at heart; Nestroy,
more perceptive, biting in his social criticism, a kind of Austrian Molière. Their contemporaries, however, regarded
them as "not serious writers"; their comedies were not "literature," just entertainment.

Rudolf felt akin to the two playwrights. He had no ob-
jection to acting the clown—provided the part was meaty
and gave him a chance to create a real character. And still
he could not overcome this nagging feeling of restlessness
and frustration. Why?

Rudolf was no introvert; he was never given to analyzing
his inner feelings. He looked upon life as an adventure, a
gamble. He was successful, he had good health, and no bad
dreams troubled his sleep. Life had to be lived—that was
all there was to it. And all of a sudden he found himself a
stranger lost in a fog. The familiar street looked foreboding;
every lighted window seemed a mocking eye. The night was
cool and clear, a gentle wind tugged at his hat, the air
smelled of dead leaves, winter was not far away. The moon,
a silvery sickle, balanced precariously on the top of a church
spire; the stars seemed very close and bright. It was a night
made for a game of billiards or cards with friends in a smoky
café, for dozing in front of a fire in a cozy room. He had
such a room and he could easily light a fire in the little iron
stove. He had friends. What was he doing alone, brooding
in this deserted street?

Had his performance been bad? No, it was not worse than
on any other day, and he had heard the usual laughs and

applause. It was just—"No good," he said half aloud, and listened to the echo of the two words. But if anyone had asked him what he meant, what it was that he thought "no good," he could not have found an answer. "Everything," he would have said. "It's just no good."

If I could only play King Lear! The thought was like a blinding light. Involuntarily he raised his hands to his face and shaded his eyes. It was not that he felt unhappy in playing comic roles or that the Raimund Theater didn't offer him serious classical parts; besides, he had played Lear before. What he meant was to play Lear the way the great Friedrich Mitterwurzer played the role, whom he had seen for the first time a few days before in the Imperial Burg Theater. The evening had been a revelation to him, but it had taken him three days actually to assimilate this new experience. Now he understood why that performance had affected him so deeply.

I could play that part as well or even better, he thought, if I only knew what he knows. I feel I can do it and at the same time I know that there is something I lack—not the talent, not the understanding of the part—something he has and I have not. What is it? How can I ever get it?

For the first time he dimly understood the cause for his depressed feeling. He was a self-made man. He had never really studied, never worked at his diction or his gestures and movements. He was a natural actor; in fact, success had come to him all too easily. Now he felt like an artist who is bursting with an idea he wants to express and painfully realizes that he does not know how to use a brush or a pen properly. Three months I've been here, he thought, and what have I achieved? Three months from today I will be on exactly the same spot. Just no good. I will have to start studying to become a real actor.

And with this decision the fog lifted. He took a deep breath. How wonderful the air was. From farther down the street music drifted up to him—the tinkling of a piano, a popular drinking song, men's voices singing in the silent night. Still time for a game of cards, Rudolf thought, and quickened his steps. Tonight luck would be with him. That's what he now wanted most—to win. After all, next to playing King Lear a card game was the most exciting challenge.

2

Her name was Erna Weinstein. She was the daughter of an orthodox rabbi from a small town in Hungary near the Slovakian border, the youngest of eight children.

The father, busy with the study of the Talmud, could not be bothered with such an unimportant matter as how to feed and clothe his family, and he left the solution of this vexing problem to his dearly beloved wife. He spent his days in prayer and the mother needed many hours of the night also to do her housework; between marketing, cooking, scrubbing, washing, ironing, and sewing she found no time for rest. One day she had to lie down to a good long sleep. She never awoke from it.

Erna was ten years old then. She realized very early in her life that as a girl she belonged to the inferior sex. At the dinner table the brothers got the bigger portions; they went to heder and she had to fawn upon them to make them lend her a book or a pencil. What does a girl need a book for? She should stick to thread and needle. One day the boys would go out into the world to become rabbis and doctors and shopkeepers. A girl had to stay behind in the ghetto waiting for some *bocher* to grant her the favor of serving him the way she served father and brothers.

Erna had one advantage over her sisters. She was the youngest in the family and unusually pretty. She had also a nice voice and a musical ear. While the elder girls were busy in the kitchen she was often permitted to run out and spend an afternoon with Lucy.

Lucy was the daughter of a wealthy widow whose husband had put the finishing touch to his successful career as a

peddler by opening a store in the *goyish* part of town. ROBES
& MODES was written in big golden letters across its windows.
The widow was rightly proud of this enterprise but even
prouder of the piano her husband had given her as an anniversary present just before his untimely death. Though she
was not an accomplished pianist, she loved to play the popular tunes, and she could not wish for a more appreciative
audience than little Erna. She grew very fond of the mother-
less child. Lucy and Erna became close friends.

Erna was eighteen when her father died. And shortly
thereafter Lucy's mother, too, passed away.

If it had not been for Lucy, Erna would never have dared
make the fateful decision that brought her out of the ghetto
of the little town of Verbo and changed the course of her
life. For it was Lucy, worldly and adventurous, who suggested that since there was nothing to hold them in their
home town they should go to Vienna—all alone—and seek
their fortune in that fabulous city. Lucy had inherited some
money; it would last both of them for a while.

Whereas Lucy had initiative and boldness, Erna, although
two years younger, was the more practical. If it had not been
for Erna, Lucy would probably have soon been lost in the
big city like so many of the warmhearted and inexperienced
girls who flocked there daily from the provinces. It was Erna
who suggested that they invest the money in a business. Thus
they opened a modest kosher delicatessen store. They needed
no help, for Erna was an expert cook. Soon her sandwiches
became the rage of the neighborhood. She had an acute business sense, a talent for making every kreuzer count. Lucy,
on the other hand, gave the shop glamour, a certain "atmosphere."

The combination of excellent salami and two pretty girls
proved especially attractive to the actors of the Raimund
Theater, which was located across the street. Most of them
dropped in for their second breakfast between rehearsals, or
for a snack after the performance, and one evening Rudolf

followed the example of his colleagues. Hungry and exhausted, he had not a single glance for the two girls behind the counter. The rich assortment of sausages, pickles, and corned beef commanded his full attention; avidly he sniffed the spicy aroma; it brought back childhood memories of his mother's kitchen in Braila. His mouth watered. What should he order?

"Half a pound of the Hungarian salami," he finally decided, and eagerly watched a woman's hand pick up the sausage and cut it slowly and carefully into thin slices. It was a small and soft hand, childlike, with short stubby fingers. The girl seemed quite capable, though the meticulous manner with which she went about her work irritated him. "You don't have to slice it *that* fine!" he growled. The hand fumbled, the knife slipped—she had almost sliced off her finger. The knife clattered to the floor.

He picked it up. Handing it back over the counter, he looked for the first time at the girl's face, and recognized immediately the dark eyes he had seen at the stage door a week or so before. The girl's face was flushed; her luminous eyes now had a hurt and painful expression; the mouth quivered, as if she were going to cry. He mumbled an apology.

The blonde had rushed to the assistance of her friend, "Why do you have to holler? You see how upset she is!" Lucy's reproach was belied by a coquettish smile. Erna tried to hide her embarrassment behind a superior frown.

After that evening Rudolf became a steady customer. He came night after night for his salami snack and a chat with the girls.

To be sure, the salami, fine as it tasted, was not the real reason for his daily visits. On the other hand, it was certainly not love at first sight that drew him to Erna. He liked her; she was so different from all the other girls and women he had known—but love? She was much too simple, too inexperienced to arouse in him the kind of passion he regarded as the real sign and prerequisite of love. A nice comradely feeling he had for her; nothing more.

Strangely enough, this feeling made it impossible for him to accept the advances of Lucy, who obviously would not have objected to an affair with him. Normally he would not have hesitated, and often he chided himself for not taking up with Lucy instead of courting Erna, who would not even allow him a kiss. But how could she? They were never alone. As "modern" as Lucy was, so far as Erna was concerned she was an old-fashioned and very strict mother from the ghetto of Verbo. And, wiser in the ways of men than such a mother could ever be, she protected Erna's virtue with effective diligence.

The winter passed. There were visits to restaurants on Sunday evenings, and to some of the old wine cellars where they listened to the sweet and fiery music of gypsies. Spring came, and they took the bus to the outskirts of the city, to wander through the Vienna woods or picnic on the bank of the Danube under the blossoming apple trees. Rudolf felt romantic; he recited love poems by Goethe and Heine and racked his brains as to how to entice Erna to his apartment. But first he would have to get rid of Lucy. He never could.

The disappointment made him moody and even insulting. Lucy had to marshal all her cleverness and natural humor to smooth things over. Only Erna seemed unconcerned and altogether happy, and that exasperated him still more. This is the last time I take the girls out, he decided; I will never see Erna again.

The next evening he came again for his salami and the next Sunday they went on another excursion—the three of them together.

One of their favorite spots on a Sunday afternoon was a café in the Prater. You sat in a little enclosure under old chestnut trees and watched the procession of elegant carriages and smart fiacres of exquisitely gowned ladies and officers in splendid uniforms. A band played the latest

Strauss waltzes, the violins sobbed, the flutes trilled, the kettle drum boomed, the cymbals clashed, and the crowd rocked and swayed. Even the horses seemed to trot in three-quarter time.

"Come on!" Rudolf shouted, and before Lucy could intervene he had pulled the bewildered Erna from her seat and carried her off to the dance floor.

But they did not join the dancers. Making sure that the dense, whirling crowd protected them from Lucy's view, he kept on pushing his way to the exit, holding Erna with a firm grip. She did not resist, did not even show surprise, and followed him obediently out of the café, across the broad bustling *Allee* into the peaceful meadow on the other side. Beyond it the woods began.

Presently they entered an emerald grove where century-old oak and beech trees stood guard against any intruder, and a thick carpet of moss silenced their steps. The air was heavy, hot, and intoxicating.

He took her in an outburst of frenzy, without a kiss, without a single caress. She did not defend herself. Whatever she felt—a little pain, a fleeting fear, and sorrow for her torn new dress—was dwarfed by her astonishment over Rudolf's strange violence. He was such a nice boy—why did he have to do that? What pleasure could he possibly derive from it? Such a filthy, ugly business! Everyone made such a big to-do about it—why? Was this really all there was to it?

When they came out of the woods a gray mist drifted over the meadows, dusk settled over the allee, the crowd was on the way back to the city. There was little laughter and singing any more. The pedestrians, dusty and tired, threw envious and malevolent glances at the passing carriages; the women thought of the supper they had still to cook; children cried and wanted to be carried. Sunday was over.

It was quite a walk to the bus station. They did not speak a single word on the whole way.

Next evening Rudolf did not show up in the delicatessen

store, nor the next day. He was very busy, what with the rehearsals for a new play, and, after all, he had some social obligations too; he had neglected his friends and colleagues long enough. The truth of the matter was that he had, for the first time, a guilty conscience. He was afraid of Lucy's reproaches, and he feared still more Erna's silence.

And then something happened that put Erna out of his mind. A new theater had been opened in the heart of the city—in the Praterstrasse—and the manager, the noted Franz Jauner, wanted Rudolf, in fact he needed him right away, and offered a very advantageous contract: higher salary and leading parts only. The Carl Theater had the great Strauss as its patron saint, *The Bat* was to be the opening play, and Rudolf's first role would be the Frosch, an excellent part for a comic. He could clown, he could sing and dance, he could even get drunk. That scene could not miss.

Rudolf signed up immediately.

The Praterstrasse was quite a distance from the Raimund Theater. Rudolf gave up his furnished room and moved into better quarters closer to the Carl Theater. Now there was half the city between him and Erna's delicatessen store.

During one of the final rehearsals an usher approached him. "A young lady to see you," the man said.

Rudolf knew instantly that his caller must be Erna. Suddenly he felt very good, gay and lighthearted, like someone who had been on a long journey and at last was returning home. And at the same time he wondered, Why do I feel that way? It's finished between us anyway.

Erna had not changed; she had the same slightly drab air of respectability, the same beautiful eyes. She was not embarrassed—he was—and her greeting was friendly and natural.

"Excuse me, please, if I disturb you. But I must speak to you." There was no trace of coyness in her words, and no threat either. She had certainly not come to make a scene.

He tried a little banter, complimented her on her looks.

Where had she been hiding all the time? Why had she not called before? Or had Lucy kept her safely locked up?

She smiled but remained very matter-of-fact. "Can we not sit down somewhere? I will not keep you for more than a couple of minutes."

He took her to the little café next door.

Only after the waiter had brought the coffee and gone did she speak. "I'm pregnant, Rudolf," she said.

He stared at her dumfounded. She had not raised her voice, nor lowered her eyes; she seemed not a bit abashed; there was no reproach and no hysteria.

"Pregnant?" he muttered.

"Yes. I thought I had to tell you."

His head swam. What am I going to do? What does she expect from me? After all . . .

Her eyes, big and searching, did not leave his face. The hurt and painful look in them was gone, they looked rather proud. Proud and confident.

She got up. "I guess you must go back to your rehearsals," she said softly.

At last he found his voice. "You mean— Are you sure? You'll have a baby? Our baby?" He had jumped up and nearly overturned his chair. The startled guests at the neighboring tables looked up from their newspapers. He did not care. He grabbed her hands, held them, hugged her tightly. "But that's wonderful! Isn't it? We must get married right away."

They were married the next week. Lucy was a very proud bridesmaid, Erna sweet and composed, Rudolf torn between conflicting emotions. Did he actually love her? Or had fate tricked him into a marriage which as a struggling actor he could hardly afford? On the other hand, she was a nice girl, the daughter of a rabbi; it was the only honorable thing for him to do.

And—what was most important—he was going to be a

father! How could he forget that? A father! Wasn't that
simply marvelous! Of course, he was happy. He must be.

3

It was an exciting year for Rudolf.

After *The Bat* the Carl Theater presented Strauss's *Gypsy
Baron,* and Rudolf as the amorous and thieving cattle
breeder became the talk of the town. When he played General Kantschukoff in Suppé's *Fatinitza* his popularity grew.
The press hailed him as one of the most talented young
comedians of the contemporary stage, and the public elevated him to the status of a local celebrity.

It was then that his secret wish was fulfilled. Friedrich
Mitterwurzer appeared in his dressing room. He had seen
Rudolf in his latest roles, and came to make him an offer.
How would Rudolf like to become his student?

"I have never had a student before, I don't know how
good a teacher I am," Mitterwurzer said. "I just think you
can do better. You are making it too easy for yourself. Of
course, if you are satisfied with the laughs and applause you
get every night . . .! In fact, you don't need me to secure
your popularity; the Viennese are loyal to those they have
once taken to their hearts. So you will stay famous and make
money. On the other hand, what can you lose by accepting
my offer? A little of your time and some of your self-assur-
ance." The big man, every inch the majestic hero of the classical drama, towered over the slim, hollow-cheeked clown,
shaking his wild grayish mane. "I just think you can do
better."

In a period when the German stage was dominated by
the romantic and declamatory school of acting, Mitterwurzer
was one of the few exponents of the nascent era of realism.
He had started an artistic revolution by speaking the famous
verses of Goethe and Schiller as if they were written in every-
day language, thus forcing the audience to listen to the
meaning of the words instead of being intoxicated by their

melody. The audience, first stunned, then enraged, was finally captivated by the actor's overpowering personality.
Where they were used to the mask, the costume, the beard,
they suddenly perceived a human being.

When Rudolf appeared for his first lesson, he was informed that Mitterwurzer was preparing himself for the part
of Mephistopheles in Goethe's *Faust*. Rudolf was to cue him.
To get some personal benefit out of this job, the new student
had to make up and actually play each part in the drama as
they went along. In turn Rudolf had not only to be Faust,
but also Martha—an excellent part for a middle-aged com-
medienne. And thus Rudolf presently found himself to his
great surprise in a wig and skirts and apron, a bonnet on his
head, cooking utensils in his hands, slipping into the character of the pandering widow. He had certainly never
dreamed of dramatic lessons of this kind. But how much fun
it was!

"The Carl Theater is not the right place for you, Rudolf,"
Mitterwurzer assured him a few months later. "The Burg
Theater, that's where you belong. It will not be easy to get
you there, for many reasons. You are a Jew, your foreign
accent will sound strange on that hallowed stage, and, worst
of all, you are stamped as a comic, a knock-about, highly
gifted but still a clown. It will take time to overcome the
resistance of the courtiers and bureaucrats who run the Imperial Burg Theater. I'll try my best, I promise you."

In the meantime Rudolf had another and bigger worry.
He was plagued by money trouble. It was strange, inexpli-
cable. The more he earned—and his salary had risen rapidly
during this last year—the less money he had, and the more
he needed. Erna was certainly not the cause for his financial
difficulties. She spent practically nothing on herself, she was
an excellent housekeeper, and in spite of her advanced preg-
nancy she insisted on doing all her marketing herself and
would never dream of letting the maid prepare the meals.
The actual living expenses were not difficult to meet. There

were the "incidentals," however: his wardrobe got more expensive from month to month, there were the after-show card games with his cronies and the Sunday visits to the race track—an irresistible passion recently acquired.

Money simply ran through his fingers. He could not hold it. He was paid his salary the first of every month. Since he was under a long-term contract he could ask for an advance whenever he was short of money. Unfortunately, very soon his advances exceeded the amount he was supposed to receive on his next payday. The first of the month arrived and Rudolf found not so much as a Kreuzer in his pay envelope. He borrowed against his salary for the next and for the third month. The baby was expected any day now, and he simply had to get some money. But director Jauner, for the first time, remained adamant. Rudolf begged, protested, ranted—all in vain.

The company was in the midst of rehearsals for a new play in which Rudolf had an important part. One morning, two days before the opening, with all the actors on stage and Jauner supervising the rehearsal from the pit, there was a big commotion in the corridor. The door burst open. Police!

In walked a member of the local courts with four uniformed gendarmes. "Is the actor Rudolf Schildkraut in the house?"

"Here!" Rudolf came forward to the footlights. He was calm and composed.

"You are under arrest."

With impressive calm Rudolf started to climb down from the stage. "At your service, gentlemen."

But Jauner exploded. "What is the meaning of all this? What has he done? What is the charge?"

"Unpaid debts." The official presented the director with a document. "Here is the warrant, sir."

Jauner fumed. "But we are to open the day after tomorrow. You cannot do that—"

The official smiled sardonically. "You are wrong, sir. Of

course we can do it. Either the debts are paid, and right away, or we take him to jail."

Rudolf, contrite, shrugged his shoulders. "I guess that's it."

Jauner held him back. Schildkraut in jail—that meant postponing or even canceling the performance. Where would he get a substitute? How? No, if he wanted to save the performance, those damned debts had to be paid. "How much is it?" he asked.

"Five hundred *Kronen*."

"Five—hundred?" Jauner nearly choked but he had no choice. "I'll pay," he growled.

"If you wish," said Rudolf; then he bowed slightly and returned to the stage. He was the only one in the theater who showed no excitement. "Can we go on with the rehearsal, Mr. Jauner?"

What the director never found out was that the party of arrest were all close friends of Rudolf, actors from another theater, whom he had bribed to stage the whole scene. Their uniforms, their make-up, the warrant—every detail was very convincing. It was an expert job, as was to be expected, since he had personally supervised and rehearsed the performance.

The five hundred Kronen lasted, after he paid off his friends, for another two weeks. But in the meantime, on Easter Sunday of that year of 1896, the baby was born. It was a boy. They called him Joseph.

Chapter IV

1

I SPENT ONLY THE first four years of my life in Vienna. Later on we moved to Germany. I went to elementary school in Hamburg, to the Gymnasium in Berlin. And yet, in my childhood memories Vienna plays a most important part, for even when our home was in Germany, every summer Father insisted on taking his vacation in the Austrian Alps, mostly at one of the lakes in the Salzkammergut near Salzburg, and on every trip we stopped in Vienna for a few days, sometimes for a couple of weeks.

When I think of the Vienna of my early childhood, I think of a top-hatted, grinning Negro with a large cigar in his mouth. The Negro stood at a street corner which I passed daily on my way to the kindergarten with Mother. She gave me a kreuzer and I was permitted to put it in the slot of that intriguing automat. Out dropped a chocolate cigar. I still think it was the finest chocolate I have ever tasted.

When I remember Vienna I think of being awakened by a tickling sunbeam. The tiny golden thread grew rapidly into a broad ribbon, became a sparkling shaft, dissolved, and became a little river. I jumped out of bed and bathed my feet in the rippling golden flood. I ran to the window and peered out into the courtyard. Two men were sprinkling gravel on the cobblestones; women, barefoot with their skirts tucked high, were washing tables and chairs; waiters brought in the "garden"—two oleander and three laurel trees in large tubs. The Happy Viennese, Kieselhofer's outdoor restaurant, was opening its summer season.

All windows were wide open, draped with pillows and blankets. And now, as if an invisible conductor had lifted his baton, a rhythmic beating began; the maids were in full attack against carpets and mattresses. Clouds of dust drifted across the courtyard. You could hardly hear your own words.

When you came out on the street, everyone seemed eager to join the concert. The coachmen cracked their whips, a hawker chanted the praise of his wares, two young chimney-sweeps, pitch black, looking like pieces out of a toy box, passed by, whistling a military march, and the conductor of the tramway rang the bell without interruption.

On the tram Mother found a seat inside while Father took me out to the platform and I stood behind the conductor. Holding firmly to Father's hand, I swayed and jumped with the jolting car. I felt like singing.

Here was the Ring. The dark green of the chestnut trees was already a little dusty, decorated with tiny emerald green balls; in two months, after our return from the country, the balls would be lying on the ground, their thick prickling shells half open, and I would carefully extract the brown gleaming kernels that felt liked polished ebony, and fill my pockets with them.

In front of the Opera flower girls offered the passers-by big bunches of lilac. The girls were grandmothers, but the bright red of their kerchiefs and the coquettishness of their laughter belied their age.

The tram crossed the Danube. I caught a glimpse of a garishly painted steamboat with its big wheels. The water ran swiftly; it had a mean and greenish color—I have never seen it blue.

Last stop—the Prater. High above the trees rose an immense Ferris wheel. The iron spokes were a net of filigree, and the windows of the little cars glistened in the morning sun. The wheel turned slowly, like a gigantic toy.

To the right was the Hauptallee, with equipages and fiacres, riders on horseback, dignified retired officers and court officials enjoying their constitutional—nothing exciting. We turned to the left, to the Wurstelprater.

What would have Vienna been without the Wurstelprater? Just another city. With its merry-go-rounds, Punch and Judy shows, shooting galleries, with its barkers and freaks, giants and midgets, clowns, acrobats, magicians, sword-swallowers, fire-eaters, with its infernal noise and strident music, this was a veritable fairy land. And I was permitted to enter it!

I did not skip a single carousel; I rode on horses and elephants, on swans and camels. I paid a visit to the most famous merry-go-round, dominated by the enormous figure of a wooden Chinese whose black pigtail reached his heels, and while his strange head nodded to the rhythm of the music his slit eyes followed me all the time.

Finally came the biggest thrill. I took a seat in a little car and drove through dark tunnels where skeletons and devils and dragons suddenly appeared in a phosphorescent light and beckoned to me. I was scared stiff, and proud as never before: Father and I were braving dangers that no woman or girl could face. He was sitting next to me, his arm around my shoulder; I was safe and strong. Poor Mother had to wait patiently outside for our return from the underworld.

Father and I, with Mother on the outside—that's how it always was. Oh yes, Mother took very good care of me; she never failed me when I needed comfort and warmth. But she was "every-day." Father was "Sunday." He was fun and laughter and Wurstelprater and presents—and more presents. He spent money lavishly on his girl friends, card games, horse racing—how could he be niggardly toward his son? Of course his hobbies were expensive, but that did not worry him. Mother did the worrying. She worried about how to save a krone here and a krone there and how to pay the bills. She worried about my health, which she thought was threatened by the candies and chocolate that Father never stopped bringing home for me; she worried about my being spoiled. Mother was the home, Father was the great world. The home was always modest; whether we lived in Vienna or Berlin or Hamburg, regardless of Father's skyrocketing fame, Mother always remained what she had been in the ghetto of Verbo: a conscientious, hard-working housekeeper, serving unselfishly husband and son to the best of her ability.

My first recollection of Mother is of a soft and kind woman in a simple dark dress. I felt comfortable in her lap, listening raptly to her melodious voice singing Hungarian folk songs. She smelled of kitchen soap and onions. Father was an impressive gentleman in a silky suit, rather stout and rotund —one year of Mother's rich Hungarian food had changed his silhouette radically—and smelling wonderfully of eau de Cologne.

Mother never dressed up. Once Father bought her as an anniversary present two very expensive gowns, all silk and lace. The next day Mother took them back to the store and asked for the money back. What did she need these fancy costumes for? Better save the money for next month's rent.

2

In those early years in Vienna the atmosphere of the theater never penetrated our home. No colleagues of Father came to visit us, and I had no notion of his professional and social life. Only twice was I touched by the stormy world in which my father lived.

During our last year in Vienna, just before we moved to Hamburg, I was four years old, and though I could not understand the excitement that swept our home, I felt its shock.

Never before had I seen Mother so desperate; her tearless grief terrified me. What I learned from the bits of conversation I overheard was even more sinister. There was talk about a knife Father had drawn against someone; ugly words swirled around me: blood—kill—prison. What had Father done?

The complete story I learned much later.

A few times a week Father played poker with his friends at the Actors' Club. One day a newcomer joined the party. Father soon realized that not just luck was responsible for the man's constant winning. The others shared Father's suspicions; they were ready to quit and to forget the unpleasant incident, in a gentlemanly fashion. Not so my father. He insisted on continuing the game, but at a given moment, just when the man was laying down his cards, Father drew a knife out of his pocket, and, while the others watched in horror, drove it with all his force through the back of the man's hand, nailing it to the marked cards on the table.

But for Rudolf Schildkraut's popularity and for the loyalty of his friends and colleagues who protected him against adverse publicity, the case might have had very disagreeable consequences for him.

Mother, however, was not so much concerned about what the people in general would say or think; she was shocked at her husband's unbridled temper. She abhorred violence, and she was afraid Father would fall into still greater trouble.

The second affair was of another kind. It affected her more directly and she felt it much more personally.

It all started with a horse, and the drama unfolded in the beautiful setting of the Freudenau, Vienna's fashionable race track.

Father had found a congenial friend to share his passion for horses and the races—the actor Louis Treuman, the first and perennial Prince Danilo in Lehar's *Merry Widow*. Thanks to this role, Treuman had become not only the most popular operetta star but also the personification—in fact, a symbol—of Viennese nobility. While to the average theater-goer, and especially to the feminine element, this son of a poor Jewish tailor seemed to embody all the elegance and charm of a true aristocrat, the aristocrats themselves hastened to copy his speech, his suavity and mannerisms, in order to live up to the image that he had created. Slim, of sallow complexion that gave him an air of decadence, his black hair plastered to his narrow skull, he looked like the most authentic count or baron.

Rudolf Schildkraut and Louis Treuman were the joint owners of a box at the Freudenau; no important race was without their illustrious presence.

Another friend of Father's at the race track was an English jockey who rode the horses at the Freudenau and who, in exchange for passes to the Carl Theater, provided Father with inside information on the chances of the various favorites.

One day the jockey had great news. At the races on the following Sunday a particular horse was certain to win. Its name was Mabel Move a Penny. If the weather should be bad and the track muddy, the chances for Mabel would be doubtful. If, however, the weather was as good as could be expected and the track fast, Rudolf Schildkraut would have a unique opportunity. "Take the advice of a real friend, Maxl." (His intimate friends, like Mother, always called Father by the diminutive of his middle name, Maximilian.) "If you are short of cash, borrow, beg, or steal a few hundred kronen and put everything on Mabel. You cannot fail."

And that's what Father did. He borrowed money left and right and then spent every free hour of the week praying for good weather for the following Sunday. His excitement had to be shared, and so for the first time he even took Mother into his confidence. She never cared for horses or cards, but this time Father's enthusiasm proved infectious. If there was so much to be won, she too wanted to be in on it. Out of the proverbial stocking in which she kept her savings she pulled ten kronen. "Well, if this horse is so sure to win put these ten kronen on it for me too, Maxl."

Father gave Mother his most benign smile, took the money, and promised to watch over her investment. Little did she know how much bigger his own stakes were, though she must have had some suspicion, for she had not seen her husband as enthusiastic about a horse for a long time.

Sunday came and it was a perfect summer day. Father's prayers had been answered. Impeccably attired in his elegant race-track outfit, wearing a gray top hat on his head and binoculars around his neck, and twirling a malacca cane with a golden handle, Father kissed me good-by, gave Mother an affectionate hug, and departed in a fiacre for the Freudenau.

After an hour or so Mother got worried. How was the race going? She could not afford to lose her ten kronen. Besides, what if in his excitement Father went on a spree and spent her winnings in the company of his no-good cronies?

A decision was quickly reached. She herself would take a look at what was going on in the Freudenau. A fiacre was, of course, out of question. She took the tramway to the race track.

On her arrival she was told that Mabel had not yet run; the great event was still ahead. She bought the cheapest ticket and presently found herself pushed and pressed against the barrier that separated the track from the cheering crowd.

Since horse racing was a complete mystery to her, she inquired among the bystanders about the fabulous Mabel Move a Penny, and was informed that the horse belonged to Baron Rothschild and was a big favorite, and that an English jockey was riding her. His colors were gold and purple and he had a big black 9 on the back of his blouse. She began to feel like an expert.

A few minutes later the race was on. And there he was—jockey number 9 in a resplendent gold and purple blouse.

Mother's heart was in her throat, but it sank immediately into her stomach. Mabel had dropped behind, was now the third—no, the fifth; more horses overtook her—"Mabel! Mabel!" In agony Mother watched the whole field go away from number 9. In a race of fourteen Mabel limped in the fourteenth.

Mother was thunderstruck. She could not know that on the night before Mabel had injured her right front ankle and that Father, informed just in time of this incident—he could always count on the loyalty of his friends among the trainers and jockeys—had switched his bets to another horse.

Convinced that Father must have lost a lot of money—and her hard-saved ten kronen to boot—Mother was at first desperate. The next minute, however, her despair turned into cold fury. Someone had played her a dirty trick: that jockey number 9! She caught sight of him, leading his horse back to the paddock, at ease and smiling. That did it. She crawled under the barrier, ran onto the track, and threw herself against the flabbergasted jockey. Screaming and brandishing her parasol, she began beating both the jockey and the horse.

Guards and policemen came running. Arrested and asked to identify herself, she explained that she was Mrs. Rudolf Schildkraut. The policemen, who knew the famous actor quite well, scoffed at her. This ordinary, hysterical woman the wife of Rudolf Schildkraut? Ridiculous!

"But Mr. Schildkraut is in his box over there. I saw him just a while ago," one of the policemen volunteered.

"So call him," Mother said.

In a few minutes Rudolf Schildkraut appeared on the scene, imperturbable, every inch a man of the world. And behind him was Louis Treuman, a true aristocrat from monocle to patent-leather boots.

The moment Mother saw her husband she tried to break away from the policemen. "Maxl!" she yelled. "Maxl! Look what they are doing to me!" The policemen kept their grip on her arms.

For a few seconds there was a complete silence. The crowd hardly breathed. Every eye was on Father.

Then Rudolf Schildkraut raised himself to his full height, slowly lifted his top hat, and shook his head.

"Pardon me, gentlemen, but I have never seen this lady before."

Then he put on his hat, turned, and departed, with Louis Treuman at his side. It was a magnificent exit.

When, years later, Mother told me this story in all its details it had become a Viennese legend, and Mother could laugh at the recollection of Father's performance and her own plight. But that evening when she came home from the Freudenau she was heartbroken and in tears. I was not moved or impressed. I felt annoyed. Why could Mother not be as gay and funny as Father was?

It was so often that Mother cried.

3

Friedrich Mitterwurzer was dead. Father heard the tragic news when he came on stage for a rehearsal. Surrounded by the whole cast, a young actor was telling his colleagues how the night before the great man had mistaken a poisonous liquid for his usual mouthwash; after swallowing a few drops he had died instantly. Being the center of attention, the young actor obviously enjoyed the opportunity of finally playing an important role and he was making the most of it.

Father was violently shaken. To him Mitterwurzer was not only a revered colleague and teacher but also probably his closest friend; more than anyone else he had helped him to find himself and to broaden and deepen his talent. Father needed minutes to grasp the magnitude of his loss. Tears came to his eyes. As if through a mist he saw all those faces, none reflecting the great sorrow that he felt. How could all those people stand there and listen to that no-good, vain, untalented bastard? In a rage Father pushed through the crowd and, crying, "A Mitterwurzer has to die and this vermin lives," he slapped the young man hard in the face. Then he stormed out of the theater.

It took Father days to regain his composure. He did not want to see anyone, he refused to talk to Mother, he stayed away from rehearsals. He locked himself in his study, determined to drink the cup of bitterness and despair to the last drop. There was an intoxicating poison in this drink—wrath. He poured it out upon the theater, on justice, mankind, and God.

Exhausted, he cried out for Mother. When everyone failed him, there was only Mother left.

4

Mitterwurzer's death seemed to mean an end to Father's hope of making that great jump from a popular comic to a serious dramatic actor and of landing on the coveted stage of the Imperial Burg Theater. Who else had that kind of faith in him? Who was willing and influential enough to help him realize his burning ambition?

There was such a man. His name was Baron Alfred von Berger. This Viennese nobleman, cultured and erudite, had dedicated his life to the theater. To him, unlike most of his contemporaries among the wealthy and noble, theater was not merely an enchanting mistress whom one kept and made love to on the side; he respected and revered it as his truly legitimate spouse. He wrote essays and novels and had an intense interest in literature and art, but theater was an entirely different matter; it was, in Schiller's words, "a moral institution—the stage that encompasses the whole world."

That was the year 1900. Whereas in republican Paris the Comédie Française remained the symbol of the past, keeping the splendor and spirit of the *ancien régime* alive with Racine and Corneille, in Imperial Vienna the Burg Theater under the banner of Goethe, Schiller, and Lessing radiated the ideas that had sparked the struggle of Central Europe's middle class for its liberation and power. In this regard the Burg Theater was more representative of the nineteenth century than the Comédie Française, but not less isolated from the ideas and the spirit of the approaching twentieth century.

The Burg Theater was not a national or a state theater. It was, like the Vienna Opera, the property of the emperor, subsidized out of his privy purse, administered by officials and courtiers of his choice. In general these men were Catholics first, Europeans second, and last of all German nationalists. They were not even Austrian patriots, only servants of the house of Hapsburg, and since they had been brought up in Vienna, its cosmopolitan and mellow atmosphere had made them weary of principles and causes. They thought of themselves as liberals, mistaking their lack of conviction and their cynicism for tolerance and worldliness.

All around new forces were stirring. The problems of the rising industrial working class were reflected in the literary works of the new realistic school; from Norway, Russia, and Germany came strange and powerful voices. In Vienna, too, a new literature emerged; its language was German but its flavor and spirit distinctly Viennese. There were no unemployed weavers, no tramps and social outcasts in the plays of Arthur Schnitzler and Hermann Bahr. In their comedies one was in the respectable company of genuine aristocrats and the sons of rich industrialists. The superintendent of the Burg Theater was nevertheless much opposed to producing plays in which young men of fine background seduced shopgirls, or countesses betrayed their noble husbands with lowerclass salesmen. He was not narrow-minded—certainly not, such things happened—and there was no harm in presenting a drama of shocking passion if it took place at the court of a seventeenth-century English king or in a medieval German city, and was couched in the poetic language of Shakespeare or Schiller. The new young Austrian playwrights, however, wrote in the every-day idiom, the men and women they described could be met daily on the Ring or Graben, and, what was worse, they had an ironic disrespect for morality. No, the Imperial Burg Theater must not become the sounding board for the atheistic revolutionaries from abroad and their Viennese disciples.

Baron Berger was an exception among the men of his caste. He had convictions and was ready to fight for them. As the artistic adviser of the Burg Theater he was in charge of the repertory, and on his recommendation the emperor's lord chamberlain engaged the actors and actresses. For years he had been in line to become the next director general of the "Burg." When, because of intrigues and the opposition of the superintendent, his promotion failed to materialize, Berger disgustedly decided to turn his back on Vienna.

Hamburg was his destination. As a theater center this city was second only to Berlin. Quietly Berger had laid the groundwork for the foundation of a new theater. In the fall his Deutsches Schauspielhaus was to open. He had already engaged most of the cast for his permanent repertory company when Mitterwurzer's death reminded him of the latter's interest in that gifted and popular comedian from the Carl Theater. He went to see him. Schildkraut was appearing as matchmaker in Franz Lehar's *Rastelbinder,* a current hit. Berger was impressed. He returned on another evening to watch Schildkraut's performance as Frosch in *The Bat,* and a third time when Father played his famous role in Suppé's *Fatinitza.* The next day Berger sent him a congratulatory note and an invitation: Would Schildkraut be good enough to visit him in his villa in the Cottage?

5

Around the turn of the century the Cottage, Vienna's garden suburb at the foot of the Kahlenberg, ceased to be merely a geographical term; it was rapidly becoming the city's intellectual and artistic center. Ten years later its fame had spread to New York, Paris, and Constantinople, and its influence made itself felt throughout Europe. The Cottage came to mean Arthur Schnitzler's psychological dramas and the birthplace of his "sweet Viennese girl," the music of Gustav Mahler and Arnold Schönberg, psycho-analysis, and modern painting.

If it was Vienna's role to fuse all the intellectual and artis-tic strains of the various nationalities of the monarchy and to blend the refined decadence of the nobility and the uni-versalism of the Catholic Church with the natural artistic gifts of the common people into a unique culture, so was it the mission of the wealthy Jews to be the catalytic agent in this process. The Cottage was their stronghold.

At a time when one needed either money or a great name to be socially accepted in Berlin, London, or Paris, the Cot-tage recognized artistic achievement, with or without fame. Whereas in other European capitals the ruling class ran after high-sounding names, in Vienna both the nobility and the bourgeoisie ran after talent. To be sure, in its insatiable hunger for art and intellect, Viennese society was by no means free of snobbery, but it was gifted with a great toler-ance, and relatively free of religious and national prejudices. This was the major influence of the Cottage. The upper class knew how much it owed to the Jews for their alert percep-tions, their sense of values.

6

Rudolf Schildkraut approached Baron Berger's villa with a trepidation he had rarely felt. He had left his fiacre at the outskirts of Grinzing, where he had gone to visit a sick col-league, and decided to walk the rest of the way to the neigh-boring Cottage. It was a beautiful summer day. The air will clear my head, he thought, and give me a chance to plan my conversation with Berger.

But there was another reason for his nervous tension, one that he himself could hardly fathom. He was no stranger in these surroundings. He loved this part of the city—the nar-row crooked lanes with their dainty houses tucked away behind hedges and flower beds, the vine-clad taverns famous for their *Heurigen,* the new wine of the season; every turn

offered another enchanting view of the rolling hills, covered
with vineyards and orchards. Over there was the house where
Beethoven had lived and worked; in that little garden
Schubert had played for his friends.

The streets turned and twisted and led finally into a broad
avenue of modern villas and beautifully kept gardens. Here,
too, he had been before. But never had he been admitted
behind the wrought-iron gates. Oh, yes, he knew many of
these noble and rich people who lived here, he met them
at the Actors' Club or at the café, but he had never been invited to their homes. If he had been a Mitterwurzer or Kainz
it would have been another matter; as an "Imperial and
Royal Actor to the Court" he would have been socially ad-
missible, not merely because he was a state official but, more
important, because he would have been a respected champion of culture and art. Popularity as a comedian was not a
substitute for that distinction.

Rudolf Schildkraut cared next to nothing for social standing and was never impressed by wealth or rank. The invitation to Berger's home excited him not because Berger was an
aristocrat, an imperial official, but because he was one of the
few men whose knowledge of the theater Schildkraut truly
respected. Berger's accolade was not needed to bolster his
ego—he never lacked self-confidence—but it was conclusive
proof that he had arrived at a turning point of his life and
career. In crossing the threshold of Berger's villa he was entering a new world. He was sure he belonged there. But how
far would Berger go to support his claim?

From somewhere came the ringing of a church bell. Twelve
deep notes. He quickened his steps.

A few minutes later he was ushered into Berger's study.
Furnished with exquisite taste, it was clearly the work room
of a creative man: there were comfortable chairs, an enormous desk, books everywhere. Spacious as the room was, it
seemed too small for the towering six-foot figure of the host,
bursting with a very un-Austrian energy. His speech had the

soft Viennese melody, Viennese was the eloquent gesture of
his long hands, now underscoring a point, now twirling his
short mustache, the ironic smile never leaving his wise and
weary eyes.

After the first few words Schildkraut felt as if he had
known Berger all his life. This was a man he could trust
completely, always.

" I have engaged all the actors I need," Berger said. "However, I want you too. Mind you, my Hamburg theater can
do without you, but not the German stage. I offer you a
contract under two conditions: First, you will stay with me
for at least ten years. And second, I will present you primarily
in the classical dramatic roles, as our mutual friend Mitterwurzer suggested. I am sure he was right. Start preparing
yourself for Shylock and King Lear. I had my secretary draw
up the contract. You can sign it straight away."

Indeed, there was little of that famous Viennese Gemütlichkeit in Berger's make-up.

When the newspapers announced Berger's plans, Vienna
greeted his idea of starring Rudolf Schildkraut in the great
tragic repertory of the classics with mocking laughter. Who-
ever heard of such a thing: a little Romanian Jew, a comedian whose main assets were his funny accent and his talent
for burlesque, as King Lear? Now everyone knew why the
superintendent had opposed Berger's appointment to the
post of a director general of the Imperial Burg Theater: the
man had no respect for the classics, no appreciation of the
serious drama.

For once the critics, the colleagues, and the public agreed.

Chapter V

1

I HAVE MANY FOND memories of Hamburg: my teacher in the elementary school, the awakening of my interest in music, my first visit to the theater. Over all hovers that peculiar smell of the sea, the salty tang of which I was probably never really aware, but which I associate with Hamburg because Father constantly complained about the climate: the humidity and the fog affected his nose and throat. I keep seeing the city through the eyes of my father. Its climate is not *that* bad; it cannot have been foggy and rainy every day during the five years we lived there.

They were years of triumph for Rudolf Schildkraut. His King Lear was hailed as a milestone in the history of the European theater. "Probably there were other great actors who had a more regal appearance but no one could have ever shown us the *father*, make us feel his sorrow, his suffering as vividly as Schildkraut does," a Hamburg critic wrote. "He has the majesty of grief and the majesty of a kind and noble heart." Later one of the leading critics of Berlin, Alfred Kerr, who was regarded throughout Germany as a supreme judge in all matters pertaining to the theater, said about him: "Rudolf Schildkraut is overpowering. The most original genius of the German theater. Unforgettable. Others have shown us Lear as a choleric king, Schildkraut's king is a melancholy man. A virtuoso? Maybe. However, there are virtuosi one admires, and that's all. Schildkraut's Lear makes your soul tremble, you cannot help crying your heart out."

Vienna was stunned. Baron Berger had been right, after all.

"Do you now understand why I insisted on such a long-term contract with you?" Berger asked Schildkraut after the opening night. "In a few years I will return to the Burg Theater. They will call me back. And when that happens I will not go alone. We will go together."

During the following years Schildkraut stormed through the whole classical repertory from success to success—from Euripides to Molière, from Shakespeare to Lessing. In between he starred in the plays of the then modern dramatists: Gerhart Hauptmann, Hermann Sudermann, Arthur Schnitzler, Bernard Shaw. Next to Lear, Shylock became his most famous role. Every few weeks there was a first night at the Deutsches Schauspielhaus, and every time it was Rudolf Schildkraut's night.

He was Berger's special pride and his major headache. Their personal relationship presented no problem—the respect and affection they had for each other was sincere—and they could cooperate artistically, too, without great difficulty. Berger was no innovator, no founder or champion of any particular "school." While in Moscow, Paris, and Berlin Stanislavsky, Antoine, and Otto Brahm led the revolution for a new theater, Berger stood aloof both from the new naturalism and the traditional classicism. In an essay on the histrionic art he explained why he felt "uncomfortable" in the presence of Eleonora Duse, much as he admired her. Like the great art of Dostoevski, she left him "shattered and exhausted." The clinical probing into human sentiments "debased somewhat the real mission of art." The mission of art, so Berger concluded, was "not to copy life but to reveal its deeper meaning." Not dedicated to any particular style, he gave his actors freedom to seek their own approach to the characters they were called upon to create, insisting only on a strict discipline and selfless devotion to the spirit of their common work. The theater was an order and each performance a religious service, the whole more important than any one part. Rudolf Schildkraut's very nature rebelled against conformity and discipline. He had always been the pet of his colleagues and the horror of his directors. With Berger it was not different. That this sensitive man, who regarded self-control both in life and art as the most essential quality could appreciate and admire Schildkraut's wild genius is astonishing.

There was a law Berger had decreed at the opening of his theater; it was scrupulously enforced. In each dressing room and in the corridors backstage posters proclaimed it in big black letters: *In my theater extemporizing is strictly forbidden. Baron Alfred von Berger.*

Each evening, watching the performance from his special box, Berger made sure that no actor deviated from his text, did not change a single word in his lines. Blessed with a phenomenal memory—he knew most of the classics by heart—he had earned the nickname of Kaiser Wilhelm Gedächtniskirche (Emperor William Memory Church), an allusion to an imposing and not too graceful landmark of Berlin.

On the opening night of Schiller's *William Tell* Rudolf Schildkraut was playing the role of Count Gessler, the Austrian tyrant. The famous scene when Géssler orders William Tell to shoot an apple from his own child's head seemed to Berger too melodramatic for a modern audience, and he had therefore conceived the idea that Gessler should appear slightly drunk: the villain was to be "humanized," his cruel order made less improbable, and to heighten the effect of the scene Gessler was to make his entrance on horseback.

Father eagerly accepted the suggestion of playing Gessler in a state of intoxication, but the idea of acting the whole scene on the back of a live horse did not appeal to him at all. "A Jew should sit in a coffee house, not on a horse," he declared. Berger remained adamant. He had set his heart on this spectacular entrance, and the only concession he was ready to make was to have two actors, dressed as soldiers, lead the horse by the bridle. "Besides, it's an especially nice horse," he assured Father. "Nothing to worry about, really."

When Schildkraut made his entrance its scenic effect fully justified Berger's idea. The audience was impressed. The tension mounted. It affected even the horse. At the famous words of Gessler, "I don't want your life, Tell, I want that shot," the horse lifted its tail and let nature take its course.

Schildkraut did not lose his presence of mind for a second. Before anyone in the audience could react he turned around and addressed the mare's rear in the character of a drunken tyrant: "In this theater extemporizing is strictly forbidden!"

A howl of laughter shook the theater. But in the next minute the audience was again in the grip of the drama, the incident forgotten.

Called to account by an irate Berger, Father explained that if he had ignored the incident the audience would have continued to snicker and giggle all through the rest of the scene. With his remark he had cut the hilarity short and led the public back to the drama. Berger grudgingly admitted that Schildkraut was right, and then sent him an affectionate note congratulating him on his performance.

Berger wrote my father a number of such letters and notes. One of these, picked at random, illuminates quite well their strange relationship. It was written during a summer vacation.

"You talented monster," the letter starts. "I am sitting here in a little arbor of my country home, and every day I read the Bible, a chapter here, a chapter there. How many wonderful parts for Schildkraut! Old King David and Solomon, Saul and Absalom—and many others.

"I hope that during the coming season you will give me only as much trouble as your temperament absolutely needs to make you feel happy. Is it really so difficult for you to subordinate yourself as a member of a company to its general discipline, or is it, I wonder, part and parcel of your character to be a lone wolf—just as your unique ability is a sort of lone-wolf talent on the contemporary German stage? I wonder. . . ."

2

I led a sheltered life. The world where my schoolmates played and fought their battles I seldom saw. I had no friends, no playmates. Father was my playmate. He read to me, helped me start a stamp collection and a library of my own books, he taught me to play chess and billiards. Together we explored the old port of Hamburg and went to the zoo. Summers he taught me how to swim and to row, and organized little excursions just for the two of us.

Every one of my childish whims was satisfied. He showered presents upon me and guarded me jealously, his personal property. Not even Mother was permitted to cross the charmed circle which he had drawn around the two of us.

Sometimes I realized how lonely I was and that there was a life outside of home and classroom, the every-day life of the children of my age. Instinctively I searched for a substitute.

I found it in music. That was Mother's private domain. Father's interest in music was rather superficial; he loved Johann Strauss, Jacques Offenbach was his favorite composer, and now and then he would listen to a symphony by Beethoven or Mendelssohn. With Mother it was different. Busy from morning to night with knitting, sewing, cooking—I rarely saw her idle—she never found time and never had the urge to read a book, seldom glanced at a newspaper. She could not compete with Father, and never attempted to, when it came to satisfying my growing intellectual curiosity. Music, however, created a new bond between us. The moment I became infatuated with the piano it was she who stimulated my interest.

As soon as Father noticed that I had come under the spell of music he insisted on hiring a professional teacher. Was he motivated by his consideration for the development of my musical talent or by his jealousy of Mother's newly won influence on me? However it may have been, he immediately decreed that I was going to be a musician, probably a conductor, maybe a composer. If anyone believed the exciting stories he told about me, they must have thought I was a child prodigy. At any rate, thank God, I would never become an actor. And how much comfort Father drew from this thought!

Practicing the piano and the violin took up much of my time. At my father's insistence I also had to take dancing lessons. I disliked them heartily, though I had an excellent sense of rhythm and was one of the best pupils in my class.

My aversion for these lessons dates back to an incident which I did not dare divulge to my parents or teacher, and which to this very day is one of my strongest childhood memories. During one dancing lesson I slipped and fell on the highly waxed parquet floor, dragging my partner down with me. For a moment the little girl's scented hair touched my face and I experienced a new sensual urge. Helping her up from the floor I felt embarrassed, ashamed, torn between excitement and guilt.

My sensitivity to odors has remained very strong. To me the fragrance of a flower, of a perfume, the scent of a woman's skin, the odor of a particular place is not merely enchanting or distasteful, as the case may be; it always is a smell that unlocks some hidden recess in my mind, starts a chain of visual associations and brings to life faces, places, and scenes of the past.

And equally strong remained my aversion to stepping on a dance floor. I am a great fan of the ballet and I often fell in love not because I was attracted by the beautiful face or figure of a girl but by the grace of her movements and gestures. I myself, however, have never danced in public, only on the stage or in films when my part called for such a performance.

It was Mother who took me to the theater the first time. It was a Christmas matinee, the dramatization of a fairy tale, *Little Elsie in Search of Santa Claus*. My father played the king of the dwarfs. Neither the play nor my father's acting made any strong impression on me. The only scene that excited me was Elsie's departure from the kingdom of the dwarfs where she had failed to find Santa Claus. The king, having been moved to tears by Elsie's parting, wiped them off his face and flung them with a kingly gesture on the floor where they exploded like firecrackers. This trick impressed me so much that I could have done without the rest of the play.

Without telling Father, Mother took me to a dress rehearsal of *King Lear*. At first I followed the performance with only a perfunctory interest, but gradually I became incensed by Goneril's and Regan's treatment of my father, and sobbing bitterly and shouting at the top of my voice I berated the two actresses for their meanness and cruelty. I nearly wrecked the rehearsal. My first encounters with the theater were not propitious.

Concerts and opera became my great passion. I was thrilled by Engelbert Humperdinck's *Hänsel und Gretel* and Carl Maria von Weber's *Freischütz;* their mixture of the romantic and the gruesome made a deep impression on me. My first experience with Verdi, on the other hand, was disappointing. The opera was *Il Trovatore* and I loathed it. I have retained my original aversion to Verdi until this day, with the exception of his Requiem and two of his operas, *Falstaff* and *Otello*. In later years I came to appreciate his genius but he has never meant much to me; his music strikes me most often as vulgar, a kind of hurdy-gurdy melody.

Today three gods reign supreme in my musical heaven: Mozart, Gustav Mahler, and Anton Bruckner. In fact, my devotion to Mahler has grown into a form of mania. I know all his scores by heart, I own the records of all his works and every book about Mahler that has been published in German or English. I have a complete collection of his photographs from his baby pictures to his death mask. Next to Mozart it is Mahler, this last romanticist, standing at the threshold of our modern age, who touches me most deeply.

3

Aside from Father, Mother, and the head of my school, Herr Fritz Brehmer, the most understanding teacher I ever had, there was a fourth important figure in my childhood world: Appolonia Klotzek.

We called her Polka. She was our housemaid, and Mother had imported her from her native Ruthenia. Barefoot, cross-eyed, and, because of a broken and badly mended hip, afflicted with a heavy limp, she was a sight to behold when she alighted from the train at the Hamburg station where Mother and I had gone to meet her. It was her first trip away from the little mountain village where she had been born and raised, but, bewildering as the big city must have appeared to her, she was not going to be overwhelmed or even impressed by it. She was induced to wear shoes, but otherwise she adapted herself to the new surroundings only superficially.

She was a hard and efficient worker, obedient and stubborn, with an instinctive mistrust of anything that was unknown or strange to her. For months she could not be made to understand what Father's profession was. When she was told that the photographs of so many different men that adorned the walls of our apartment were actually all pictures of my father in his different roles, she simply laughed. She never believed it.

And so one day Mother decided that Polka must go to the theater and see my father perform. She received elaborate instructions. She would enter the theater, then turn to the right, where she would see a box with a man behind the window. She should give him her name and receive a ticket, then go to the cloak room across the corridor, leave her coat, show the ticket to a man in uniform, and be led to a seat. There she must stay until the end of the play.

"And how do I know when is the end?" Polka wanted to know.

Mother explained. "A curtain will come down, which depicts a beautiful garden, young men playing all kinds of instruments, some girls in veils dancing to their tunes. When the lights go on and you see that curtain—that's the end."

Polka departed. Half an hour later she was back.

What happened? Why didn't she stay for the play?

"But I saw it," Polka insisted. "It was beautiful."

"What? What did you see?"

"The garden, the young men with the instruments, the dancing girls—just beautiful."

At last Mother understood. Polka had arrived early, and, seeing the curtain, she had remembered Mother's instructions. The lights were on, the curtain down, so she came home.

Polka was told to go back. It was only a ten-minute walk, and she could still see a good part of the play.

At first we could not find out what impression the performance made on her. But Father came home bristling with anger. Never in his whole professional career had he endured such a shattering experience. The moment he came on stage Polka jumped up and greeted him excitedly. "That's Herr Schildkraut!" she shouted. "My boss. That's him all right!"

The audience laughed and stamped their feet; ushers made her sit down and told her to keep quiet. But at Father's next entrance Polka was again on her feet, shouting and gesticulating. "That's him! You cannot fool me, Herr Schildkraut!" The audience became indignant. When she was at last calmed down and satisfied with having identified her master, Polka kept on disturbing her neighbors; every few minutes they had to get up to let her pass.

"Where did you go all the time, for God's sake?" Mother asked.

"To the cloak room. I wanted to make sure my coat was still there. With these city slickers, you never know."

It was the first and only time Appolonia Klotzek went to the theater to see Father.

4

In the summer of 1901 Father decided that we should use his vacation for a visit with his parents. At that time they lived in Buenos Aires, where they had found refuge from the growing anti-Semitism of Romania.

Father had not seen them since the days of Braila, although he had kept in touch with them by occasional letters. The visit was probably motivated not so much by his filial sentiments as by the urge of proving to the family that at last he had made good; the boy given up as a delinquent was now one of the great and famous actors of Europe. It was a kind of revenge he must have had in mind. Once the thought had struck him the plan was immediately put into operation.

I was five years old then, and I have only a vague recollection of our trip. I remember that Father suffered from seasickness and during the crossing hardly left his cabin. Mother, on the other hand, was gayer and more lighthearted than I had ever seen her in Hamburg. Deprived of Father's company, and with no children to play with, I soon got bored. The excitement of the first day when I was busy exploring the ship, watching the maneuvers of departure and the spectacle of the ever-changing sea, gave way to a feeling of lassitude. And then I too became seasick and for long hours I had to stay in bed.

Buenos Aires was just another city to me. The street where my grandparents lived was not much different from our street in Hamburg, but their apartment was quite exciting. It swarmed with animals. There were dogs and cats and parrots and turtles. That was fun. Grandfather was some kind of businessman, stern and old. I did not like him. But Grandmother was sweet. She had a strange, deep voice and her love for her many pets immediately brought us close together. She permitted me to play with them, to feed them, and told me a lot of funny stories about them. I felt as if I had been accepted into a kind of fraternity which consisted only of Grandmother, the animals, and myself. There was also Aunt Regina, Father's sister. She was quiet, always smiling. I liked her smile. And then I came down with the measles and that was the end of our trip.

We returned to Buenos Aires the next summer for another visit. It marked my debut as an actor. The German Theater in Buenos Aires had asked Father to give a guest performance and he had consented to appear in *The Daughter of Mr. Fabrice,* a melodrama in which he had starred in Hamburg a few months before with great success. Why and how it came about that I was to appear on the stage with my father I don't know. Probably his wish to show me off to all his admirers in that foreign country was greater than his aversion to exposing me to the dangerous attraction of the theater.

I was cast in the part of my father's grandson and I got my first notice in the local paper: "Little Joseph Schildkraut, a handsome, curly-haired boy, full of vitality, shows promise as a future actor; it seems he inherited his father's gift."

I suspect these remarks were not merited by my acting, but merely intended to flatter my famous father.

The second episode that made this trip memorable occurred the morning of our departure. We were sitting with my grandparents and friends around the breakfast table when we heard the long and piercing hoot of a ship's siren. Mother pricked up her ears. "That's our ship!" she exclaimed. "It's ready to leave. We must hurry."

Father smiled indulgently. "You with your sharp ears! That's not the *Cap Roca*. I know her siren."

"If we miss our boat you will never make Hamburg in time for the rehearsals," Mother insisted. "Remember how Captain Langerhans begged you to board the ship not later than nine o'clock. It's ten past already."

"Don't worry, please. We have plenty of time. Langerhans will not leave without us. That's what friends are here for —to wait for you."

And on we went with our good-bys, exchanging pleasantries and good wishes.

A few minutes later the same siren sounded again. "It's our ship, all right," Mother warned. "Let's go."

But Father was not to be hurried. "I tell you, it's another boat. Why are you so nervous?" And he went into a long dissertation about his traveling experiences, boasting that he had never missed a train. Mockingly he said to Mother, "You think because you have a good musical ear you can distinguish between the sirens of different ships."

At last the final adieus had been said, the last kisses exchanged, some tears shed, and we were off.

When we arrived at the dock we saw the *Cap Roca* moving out to sea. And there on the captain's bridge was Langerhans, wringing his hands in despair.

"Langerhans! Langerhans!" Father yelled. "Wait for me in Montevideo—Monte-vi-deo!"

The ship slowly disappeared in the distance.

Everyone was trying to give us advice. Father was unperturbed. A few hours later he had hired a small tender and the three of us raced all night through a choppy sea to Montevideo, where we arrived more dead than alive. But we caught up with Langerhans.

"I told you there was no need to worry, my dear," Father said to Mother when we finally boarded the ship. "We made it all right, didn't we?"

5

During the next two years a marked strain appeared in the relationship of my parents. I was now old enough to notice it. I had known of Father's interest in horse racing and that he spent many hours playing cards at the Actors' Club and in cafés. Now I began to understand that there were other reasons, too, why he failed to show up for dinner or why he often returned home in the morning just when I was leaving for school. There were quarrels; Father shouted, Mother cried, and there was always the name of some female in their arguments. It was women that caused all this trouble. Mother complained about the huge sums of money that Father squandered while she had to pinch and scrape—and the grocery bill of last month was not yet paid. I would have liked to sympathize with Mother but I resented her tears and lamentations. Why could she not leave Father in peace? If he wanted to have some fun, was that not his right? After all, she did not work, she could quietly sit at home and chat with Polka and bake and cook—wasn't that what she liked best? Or did she expect Father to be interested in her little afternoon parties at which some dowdy ladies sat around the coffee table, knitting and gossiping? I, too, hated them. Father's friends were in a different class—witty, elegant. No wonder he preferred them to Mother's company, and I was proud when he took me along to meet them. But I must admit I loved the cookies Mother served at her *Kaffeeklatsch*, and her apple strudel.

During rehearsals, and especially the day of an opening night, things got really bad. Father was in an ugly mood, one moment terribly depressed and the next minute exploding, making Mother responsible for every little thing that went wrong. But on these days she never remonstrated with him, never argued. She suffered and kept quiet.

Hours before Father went to the theater he lived, no, he *was* the character he represented on stage.

A very bad scene occurred after the last rehearsal of *King Lear*. Father came home for lunch; as is the custom in Central Europe, it was a full course dinner, served at two o'clock, and on that day Mother had prepared it with special care. That was a prerogative she never relinquished. No servant was permitted to cook our meals, part of the reason being Mother's insistence on keeping a kosher house. She was not religious, she went to the synagogue only twice a year on the High Holy Days, but not to attend these services was as inconceivable as to transgress the dietary laws. Father had no feelings in the matter, except that he was all in favor of Mother's cooking. Sometimes, just to tease her, he announced that he was taking me to a good restaurant for roast pork, a declaration of culinary independence which Mother accepted with a shrug, and which was invariably followed on our return by his assurance that no restaurant in all Hamburg could compete with her cooking, and as far as her boiled beef was concerned, it was simply out of this world. To mention it in the same breath with roast pork was sacrilegious.

And so it was boiled beef that Mother had prepared as the main course for that particular dinner.

Father was late. I had already eaten and was ready to leave for my afternoon classes when he arrived. He hardly noticed me. He was a different man, awe-inspiring, frightening. Though he had left his costume and beard in the theater he was still the king, royal in every gesture.

In majestic dignity he sat down at the table. He surveyed the dishes—boiled beef?

He rose to his feet. "Is this the food for a king?" he thun-

dered. And while Mother and I stood petrified he picked up
the dish of boiled beef and threw it out the window. As if
this was all that was needed to kindle the flames of his rage,
like a madman he seized all the other dishes, glasses, and
silverware and hurled them through the window to crash on
the street below.

I trembled, terrified. I was sick. I vomited in the middle of
the dining room—boiled beef and spinach, my whole dinner.

6

Our financial troubles were the recurrent topic of our talk
at the dinner table. I found it boring. I could not grasp the
seriousness of the matter, for we lived very comfortably and
no luxury was denied me. We were rich, weren't we? At least
that's what I had to believe when I compared my clothes
and toys with those of most of my schoolmates and when I
gradually came to understand how famous my father really
was. The Kaiser himself had come to Hamburg to attend a
command performance at the Schauspielhaus—it was a comedy, *Master Flaxmann,* by the popular writer Otto Ernst—
and after congratulating Father the Kaiser presented him
with a gold ring set with three large diamonds. Such a ring
must be worth a lot of money, all the children in school
agreed.

As for Mother's reproaches about Father's lady friends, I
must admit that the more often I had to listen to them, the
less interesting they became. Therefore I certainly did not
mean to criticize Father one evening when I interrupted an
altercation between him and Mother. He had just kissed me
good night and was ready to leave, dressed with his usual
elegance, from the top hat set at a rakish angle to his precious cane.

"And when will you be back?" Mother asked. The sarcasm in her voice must have angered him.

"When I'm back, you'll notice it," he replied curtly.

"Probably by tomorrow morning, when I go to school," I pertly interjected.

Father raised his cane and struck me. The blow cut my body like a knife, but I was too surprised really to feel it. He lifted his cane again, and now the blows came fast on my back and shoulders. As if in a terrible nightmare Father's distorted face swam before my eyes and I awakened only when I saw him standing there sweating and panting. The cane was broken; its gold handle was all that was left in his hand. Only then I sensed the pain and ran out of the room.

I threw myself on my bed. Why had he done this to me? My stupor was so great that I even forgot the pain. Then Mother came and kissed me and comforted me, and at last I cried.

That was the only time Father ever struck me. I bore him no grudge. Maybe I sensed that he was angry not really with me but with himself. I had always looked up to him as my idol, never doubting him, never questioning his actions, and now through his own fault he had destroyed this image and allowed me to see him with the eyes of Mother.

When I came home from school for lunch the following day I found a little box next to my plate. It contained a beautiful watch and chain. And it was a "real" watch, the kind only grownups carried, and real gold! I felt proud as never before: now I was no longer a child; Father had accepted me as his equal. I rushed to him, but then I did not throw myself into his arms as I always had on similar occasions. I stretched out my hand and said very solemnly, "Thank you, Father." He looked at me puzzled, then, embracing me and holding me tight, he kissed me on the top of my head. He understood.

7

In November 1904, the visit of a gentleman from Berlin created quite an excitement in our home. He was Felix

Hollander, a noted writer and the first assistant of the famous director Max Reinhardt.

Reinhardt had started out as an actor. Not until he founded his own theater, Das Kleine Theater, where he stunned Berlin with his production of Oscar Wilde's *Salome,* did he attract wide attention. This "daring" drama immediately aroused a violent controversy between the intelligentsia and the respectable citizens of Berlin. The clamor gained in intensity after the presentation of Frank Wedekind's *Erdgeist,* a battle cry against middle-class morality, a paean to the elementary power of sex. It was followed by Hugo von Hofmannsthal's adaptation of *Electra* and then Maxim Gorky's *Lower Depths.*

Here in Reinhardt was a new voice, a new force in the European theater, heralding a new era. After the pseudo-classicism of the Königliches Schauspielhaus (Royal Playhouse) and Otto Brahm's somber naturalism, Max Reinhardt ushered in a new baroque, as it were, an ecstasy of color and movement, theater in the imperishable tradition of the *commedia dell'arte.* Imperial Berlin, intoxicated by its role as the capital of the richest, most vital and rapidly expanding nation on the European continent, took Reinhardt to its heart, showman in the true sense of the word, a magician who transformed an average audience of bankers, shopkeepers, industrialists, and intellectuals into a glittering *society,* with himself as master of ceremonies.

In 1904 Reinhardt had acquired the Neues Theater, where he produced Bernard Shaw's *Caesar and Cleopatra* and finally scored his biggest hit with *A Midsummer Night's Dream.* His revolving stage, the first of its kind in Europe, became the rage of Germany. From all countries people flocked to Berlin to see Reinhardt's forest turn like a merry-go-round; a schoolbook classic had been restored to its rightful place as one of the great visual and poetic spectacles of all time. But Reinhardt's fame did not rest merely on his

technical innovations. He had gathered around him a group
of unusually gifted actors; he knew how to direct them to
high accomplishments.

Now he was ready for a new venture. In the fall of 1905
he was going to open his third and biggest theater, Das
Deutsche Theater. And Felix Hollander had come with a
special and urgent offer from Max Reinhardt himself: if
Rudolf Schildkraut would leave Hamburg and join Reinhardt's company he would get the best possible contract, star
parts, a much higher salary than his present one, and a sub-
stantial advance. Reinhardt was smart enough to know
Father's need for money.

The offer was tempting indeed. There was, however, an
obstacle: the contract with Baron Berger. It had many more
years to run. And Berger would never dream of letting
Schildkraut go. Father pleaded, argued, begged, threatened
—the answer was no. Definitely and positively no.

The more adamant Berger showed himself, the stronger
grew Schildkraut's determination to win his freedom. And
so the war was on. From month to month it became more
and more bitter and ruthless.

At first Father tried the usual tricks. He played sick, he
played hoarse, he bombarded Berger with doctors' certifi-
cates attesting to his incapacity. Berger did not budge. He
sent his own doctor to examine the "ailing actor," and
Father had to get out of bed and perform.

Berger had just acquired the rights to a one-act play by
Maurice Maeterlinck. *The Intruder* was not much of a play,
but the world premiere of a work by an author who, thanks
to his *Monna Vanna* and *The Life of the Bee,* had gained
great popularity and was hailed as one of the most important
writers of his generation, would be a great event for the
Deutsches Schauspielhaus.

Father had read the script. It had an interesting part and
the temptation was too great. Regardless of his conflict with
Berger he had to play that part. He swallowed his pride and

asked Berger for an appointment. It was immediately granted.

Berger greeted him with extreme politeness and Father pretended not to notice the ice-cold formality in the baron's attitude.

Father explained the reason for his visit. "It's about *The Intruder* I came to see you, Baron Berger."

"Yes?"

"The part of the grandfather. It's just the part for me. I want very much to play it."

"H'm. Do you?"

"Yes."

Berger's face was inscrutable. He stroked his chin. "Well, Mr. Schildkraut, that's interesting." A long pause. "But somehow I see this grandfather lean, tall, and lanky. Not your type at all. No, I cannot imagine you in this part. Sorry."

"I see—lean, tall, and lanky," Father repeated. He bowed and left.

Berger brought a new actor from Vienna to play the part. He was Josef Giampietro, very tall, slim, aristocratic-looking, sporting a monocle and a shaved head. A few years later he gained great popularity as a star of the Metropol Theater, Berlin's cradle of musical comedies and operettas.

The premiere of *The Intruder* was a complete flop. The first-night audience disliked the play and rejected Giampietro.

After the final curtain Berger and the cast assembled in the green room of the theater. Nobody dared to speak. Everyone watched Berger pace up and down the room, biting his lips, cracking his knuckles, unable to control his agitation.

Suddenly Father approached Berger. With the mischievous smile of a little boy he looked up at the director who towered over him and said sweetly, "Lean, tall, and lanky he must be!" and left the room.

There were many more such incidents. The atmosphere in the theater became insufferable. An explosion was inevitable.

It came when, at his wits' end, furious about Father's rebellion and deeply hurt by what he regarded as a betrayal of their former friendship and a black ingratitude, Berger decided to teach Schildkraut a lesson.

Presenting *William Tell* once more, Berger took away from Schildkraut the part of Count Gessler in which he had scored a great personal triumph and cast him in a bit part, as one of the two soldiers guarding Gessler's hat. In the course of the play the tyrant orders this hat to be put on a flagpole as a symbol of his personal power, and the two soldiers have to make the townspeople pay reverence to it.

Berger himself conducted the rehearsal. When the scene of the two soldiers came, the whole cast, assistants, stagehands, and prominent guests held their breath.

Schildkraut came on stage, stumbled, mumbled some incoherent words.

Berger exploded. "Mr. Schildkraut, you don't know your lines!"

Father remained calm. Sweetly he said "How should I know them? I didn't learn them."

Berger, controlling himself, not raising his voice, said, "Someone will give Mr. Schildkraut a script, please. He will read the lines. Scene from the beginning, please."

But now Father lost his temper. He started to read. "Why should we not pay reverence to a hat since"—and here he left his place at the flagpole, walked down to the footlights, and yelled the rest of the sentence into Berger's face—"since all of us so often pay reverence to a hollow head."

Berger stopped the rehearsal. The next morning Father had his release. He was free to sign the contract with Max Reinhardt for the coming season.

And yet the war was not over.

In the fall of 1905, when Father was about to make his

debut on Reinhardt's stage, Berger took his revenge. Three days before the opening night he sued Rudolf Schildkraut for 100,000 gold marks and demanded an injunction against his appearance in Berlin unless Max Reinhardt was willing to pay 1000 marks for each time he put Schildkraut on the stage. Reinhardt paid. In fact, he paid a total of 30,000 marks until he got a ruling from the Supreme Court in Leipzig—having used his far from negligible influence and personal connections with the Berlin courts and the Department of Justice—that declared Schildkraut not guilty and condemned Berger to repay the 30,000 marks and to sustain all court costs, which were considerable. Baron Berger never recovered from this blow.

The epilogue to this drama of a great friendship turned into violent hatred came a few years later. In 1908 Berger at last achieved his greatest ambition; he was appointed director general of the Imperial Burg Theater in Vienna. And he failed miserably. He was by then a very sick man, and bitterness and frustration hastened his end.

On his death bed he dictated his last interview:

"It all came too late. Since my boyhood, through all my life, it was my dream to stand some day at the helm of the Imperial Burg Theater. My appointment came too late, at a time when my health gave way, when I had drained the cup of constant disappointments to the dregs; when the one man, my only really great artistic discovery, around whom I had planned my entire repertory in Hamburg and whom I had hoped to have as the mainstay of my repertory here in Vienna—when this man, Rudolf Schildkraut, cruelly and in utmost ingratitude deserted me for the artistic and financial fleshpots of Max Reinhardt in Berlin."

As soon as the newspapers with this interview hit the street Felix Salten, the noted Viennese novelist and later world-famous author of *Bambi,* a close friend of both Berger and my father, took the night express to Berlin. He arrived at our apartment very early in the morning. Father was still asleep. Salten rushed into his bedroom and awakened him.

My father needed minutes to understand what had happened. He had never seen his friend, usually so calm and correct, in such excitement. Waving a newspaper in front of Father's sleepy eyes Salten shouted, "Berger is dying! Look, this interview appeared yesterday. Berger must not die without shaking your hand. You were his discovery, you were his great artistic love and his greatest disappointment. Maxl, you must come at once. Do it for my sake. For your own sake."

Two hours later, granted a leave of absence for three days, Father left in Salten's company for Vienna.

Immediately upon their arrival they drove to the Sanatorium Loew, a private hospital where Berger was staying.

While Father waited in the corridor Salten went into Berger's room to announce Schildkraut's visit. The door had been left slightly ajar and Father could hear Salten's soft voice and then the shout of Berger. It sounded like a curse: "Schildkraut? I don't want to shake his hand. I never want to see him again!"

Father closed the door and left. The same day he returned to Berlin. The same night, Berger died.

Although I never felt like criticizing Father's actions, which so often shocked people who lacked the deeper understanding of his wild temper and complex character, even I could never find a valid excuse for his break with Berger, and for the manner in which he treated him. I have the feeling that in later years Father himself might have given much to erase this whole episode from his life.

Chapter VI

1

RUDOLF SCHILDKRAUT FOUND a congenial director in Max Reinhardt. They were kindred spirits, much as they differed in their characters: one the bohemian, the other the patrician, Schildkraut bursting with vitality, Reinhardt the high priest of art, to whom the sacrificial rites were of greater meaning than the act itself. But both were sensualists.

The master of the Deutsches Theater, Berlin's most representative stage, was not a Berliner, not even a German. He was an Austrian like Berger and, like Schildkraut, he was a product of the peculiar melting pot of the monarchy. Born in a little provincial town in Moravia, he had no social background, was a self-made man and a Jew. His real name was Goldmann.

Young, ambitious, and determined to be an actor, he had come to Vienna. He had a modest allowance from his father, a small businessman, for his studies, but he spent the money to get himself a job.

There were beer halls and restaurants in the suburbs of the city where theater performances were staged on Satur-

days and Sundays. The innkeepers put their dining rooms at
the disposal of a troop on two conditions: the show had to
stimulate the consumption of beer and wine, and it had to
cost them nothing. The troop manager in turn had his conditions: for the privilege of appearing in his play he charged
every actor a certain amount. The more you paid, the bigger
was your part. Young Reinhardt's greatest wish was to play
Franz Moor in Schiller's *The Robbers,* but the price was too
high. He could afford nothing better than the part of one of
the robbers. In this role he made his debut.

What Reinhardt lost in money he gained in experience.
After a tour from one provincial theater to another he finally landed in Salzburg. From here Rudolf Schildkraut had
made the jump to Vienna. And at the very same Municipal
Theater Reinhardt came to the attention of one of the outstanding directors of Germany, Otto Brahm.

As a young journalist Brahm had led the fight for the
recognition of Henrik Ibsen and Gerhart Hauptmann. In
1883 he founded the Freie Bühne (Free Stage) which became overnight the most important theater for the new naturalists, the poets and dramatists who were using the drama
as a weapon for social reform. With *The Weavers,* an indictment of the exploitation of workers in Silesia, Gerhart
Hauptmann emerged as a German Gorky. Written in Sile-
sian dialect and using vulgarities that were shocking to the
ears of every respectable theater-goer, the play was immediately banned as subversive political propaganda. However, it
would not have kept its high place in European literature
had it not been distinguished by more than dramatic power
and passion for social justice. Its real merit lies in the wonderful realization of each worker as an individual character.
The common people, until *The Weavers* only supers standing faceless in the background of the drama, at best mere
foils for the deeds of noblemen and burghers, advanced into
the center of the stage—full-blooded human beings. Hauptmann's drama was not a political tract, not an exposé of

social conditions; it was, in Emile Zola's words, "human nature seen through the eyes of an artistic temperament."

Otto Brahm was more than a discoverer and promoter of the new naturalistic dramatists. He also developed a new style of acting and direction for the new kind of play. And although his approach to drama was not entirely his own, but much influenced by the French and Russian naturalists, he was unmistakably German, even Prussian, somewhat heavy and didactic; but on the other hand he was also a faithful servant of the author, admirable in his dedication to his work, honest, self-effacing.

The classics were not his forte. True enough, he liberated them from the pompous veneer under which their original vigor and freshness had become hardly recognizable; ripping off the declamatory straitjacket, he led the actor out of the maze of rigid poses and stilted gestures. Brahm lacked, however, the lightness of touch, the sense for color and music— elementary sensuality. His productions of Shakespeare, Goethe, and Schiller were austere to the point of drabness. They had grandeur but they were hardly enchanting. Neither was Berlin. Terribly busy, it had no time for dreams and no urge to escape reality.

When in 1894 Otto Brahm took over the management of the Deutsches Theater he was the ideal man for the position. The Königliches Schauspielhaus was no longer in tune with the new times; the Deutsches Theater was. While Vienna's Burg Theater and the royal, princely, and ducal theaters of Munich, Dresden, Stuttgart, and Weimar kept alive the traditions of the past, of German particularism, the Deutsches Theater reflected truly the spirit of the German Reich. It was representative of the new Berlin.

The other German cities envied Berlin its domineering position, its rapid growth and wealth; they resented its coldness and self-confidence, they accused it of being *nouveau riche*. The denunciations were only partially valid. Berlin, located in the "sandbox of Brandenburg," lacked the natural resources that made life in the south and west so much easier. It was the cradle of Prussia's militarism, but also of the labor and trade-union movement. In revolutions against the feudalistic order the Berliners had led the fight. This was the city of Wilhelm II, but here republicanism was stronger than in the capitals of any of the federal states. Exasperating and fascinating, never resting, young and vital, possessed by insatiable curiosity, always in search of something untried— and determined to try it out—Berlin was destined to become a laboratory for every new idea and movement in the fields of literature, art, music—not so much a creative center as a marvelous market place where every artist, writer, actor could win speedy recognition and fame if he only appeared more "modern" than the current idol.

In such a spiritual climate charlatans flourish. They flocked to Berlin. But so did the honest avant-gardists who could not find a hearing in the tradition-bound and paternalistic society of Vienna and Munich.

This was the Berlin that Reinhardt set out to conquer. In Brahm's theater he played with considerable success. His specialty was old men; the older, the more decrepit they were, the better he liked the part.

Under Brahm's direction Reinhardt discovered two things: the limitations both of his own acting talent and of Brahm's directorial style. Schall und Rauch (Sound and Smoke), a kind of intimate vaudeville theater, which Reinhardt founded, was primarily an escape from Brahm's rigidity.

Dozens of similar "cabarets" had sprung up all over Germany. Young actors, composers, painters, and poets banded together to defy the reigning concept of morality and conformity, striking out for the right to laugh to scorn everything that respectable citizens held holy.

Max Reinhardt was less interested in causes than in the fun of slicing off good-sized pieces from contemporary life and serving them with all the dash and gusto of a refined gourmet. The sketches and playlets he presented had action,

color, music. He found in modern painters such as Emil
Orlik and Lovis Corinth the inspiration for scenic designs
that had stunning visual appeal to an audience.

That Max Reinhardt could succeed Otto Brahm as director of the Deutsches Theater was more than a personal triumph. It signaled an artistic revolution.

In view of what happened thirty years later a pamphlet
written in 1906 by Dr. Ernst Bergmann, a noted Berlin
theater critic of those days, is of more than historic interest.
That gentleman saw in Reinhardt's accession to the management of the Deutsches Theater a blow to the Germanic
spirit, "the invasion of Oriental sensuality into the realm of
the native culture." Bergmann did not yet ask for the physical extermination of the Jews, but he denounced them bitterly for "holding leading positions in all the arts." Max
Reinhardt was an outstanding example of their "corruptive
influence"—this was "the fall of Berlin."

There was a distinct difference between the anti-Semitism
of Vienna and that of Berlin. In Vienna anti-Semitism was
a prerogative of the lower middle class, the "Socialism of the
idiot," as Viktor Adler, leader of Austria's labor movement,
called it. It was not fit for good society. Emperor Francis
Joseph was no anti-Semite. He had Jewish advisers. One of
his closest counselors was Mendel Singer, editor of the influential *Wiener Tageblatt,* and the Archbishop of Olmütz
bore the name of Cohn. In a Catholic country a baptized
Jew immediately became a full-fledged Christian. Aristocrats
married the daughters of rich Jewish families. Every college
graduate who was drafted into the Army had the right to
enter officers' candidate schools and get a commission. He
might not rise to a high rank, but in most cases he left the
service as a lieutenant in the reserve. And as for the cultural
and artistic life of Vienna, it could not have existed without
the active participation and the contribution of the Jews.

It was different in Wilhelminian Berlin. Here anti-Semitism manifested itself primarily in social discrimination. The

lower classes, especially the workers, were free of anti-Semitism. But in all the finer regiments Jews could not become
officers. An aristocrat would never admit a Jew to his social
circle, his club, or his home. Even when baptized a Christian, he was still a Jew. To the Viennese anti-Semite a Jew
was a member of an abhorrent religious faith; to the Berliner
he was a "foreign element."

The emergence of Berlin as a metropolis of Europe
changed the status of Jews, at least in that city. The old
Jewish families who over centuries had established themselves as a kind of patrician enclave—the wealthy business-
men, bankers, manufacturers—were now reinforced by the
influx of Jewish intellectuals and artists. They, more than
any other group, were responsible for Berlin's cosmopolitan
air which, in the short period of two decades, from 1910 to
1930, transformed the capital of Germany into a cultural
center of Europe. What Berlin still lacked at the turn of the
century was a homogeneous society of both Jews and Gentiles, aristocrats and middle class. Reinhardt's Deutsches
Theater became their meeting place. His first-night audience
was now the "society" of Berlin.

Was it boldness or shrewdness that prompted Max Reinhardt to open his new reign in the Deutsches Theater on
November 9, 1905, with *The Merchant of Venice,* the most
"controversial" play in the classical repertory, because it can
be so easily misunderstood as an indictment of the Jewish
people? Or was he so sure that Rudolf Schildkraut would
succeed where so many very great actors had failed: that he
would break down the barriers of mutual mistrust, of national resentments, of religious prejudices through the mere
power of his acting?

That first offering of *The Merchant of Venice* was Max
Reinhardt's greatest gamble, Rudolf Schildkraut's greatest
victory, and Berlin's baptism as an artistic center of European liberalism.

2

"Max Reinhardt's production of *The Merchant of Venice* is a perfect blend of the classic and the modern. It centers not at all on Rudolf Schildkraut and yet one would be very much afraid to see it without him." Thus Siegfried Jacobsohn, the editor of Berlin's leading literary weekly and a noted critic, wrote in his review about that memorable evening.

Reinhardt had drawn on the support of all his collaborators; even in the smallest parts he had cast his best actors. Emil Orlik designed the scenery, Engelbert Humperdinck wrote the incidental music. Agnes Sorma had the role of Portia, Alexander Moissi was Gratiano—every actor on that playbill became in the next ten years a star in his own right; together they represented the golden age of the German theater. Its legend has survived two world wars and the thousand years of Hitler.

About Rudolf Schildkraut's Shylock, Jacobsohn wrote, "Edmund Kean and Ludwig Devrient, the two most famous actors in this part, were heroes of revenge. The first one— a broken old man; the other—manly, powerful in his resistance. Mitterwurzer—the third of the great Shylocks—turned him into a fabulous monster, frightening, grotesque. Schildkraut resembles not one of them. His Shylock is entirely and completely his own creation. He does not ask for pity and allows no laughter to rise. Suffering is a heritage of his tribe —he confesses this truth neither in hate nor in sorrow but in the tone of a factual report."

In his reserve, his simplicity, his art of "underplaying," as we would call it today, Rudolf Schildkraut was twenty years ahead of his time. For that matter, he was as timeless as the character he recreated and as all great art is, defying classification and transcending the confines of style and school: naturalist in his minute observation of detail, classicist in his respect for form, expressionist in his relentless drive for the essential, ultramodern in his search for the hidden truth behind the façade of sham and illusions. He was a rare combination of wild passion and self-discipline; much as he lacked discipline in his private life, on stage it was his most important asset. None of his creations could be reduced to a formula, for he presented each character in all its complexity and inconsistency. On that basis even King Lear and Shylock were brothers under the skin—*ecce homo:* Rudolf Schildkraut.

After the curtain fell that night, the audience sat for a minute in complete silence, stunned. Then pandemonium broke loose. The cold Berliners shouted themselves hoarse. The curtain rose and fell, over and over again.

Finally the iron curtain came down, which in case of fire shuts off the stage from the house. The public refused to leave, calling for Reinhardt and Schildkraut. The lights went out, and still no one left his seat. And so the lights had to be turned on again, and for the first time in Berlin's theater history the little door in the iron curtain that is never to be opened except in emergency was unlocked, and Reinhardt and Schildkraut appeared once more in front of the cheering audience, arm in arm.

Schildkraut's dressing room was packed with celebrities, well-wishers, friends. At last they left and only Mother remained. That was a custom Father observed scrupulously: after a first night no lady friend, not one of his many mistresses, could count on his company. That night always belonged to Mother, and to her alone.

But there was still a visitor outside in the corridor who refused to leave and insisted on paying his compliments to Schildkraut.

"Let him come in," Mother pleaded. "It's really touching to see how excited he is. And he is an old man."

Father sighed. "All right."

The man who entered was toothless, bald-headed, seedy-looking. "Master!" he exclaimed. He grabbed Schildkraut's hands and kissed them. "I thank you, I thank you for this evening! My name is Siegwart Friedmann."

Schildkraut withdrew his hands. For a few seconds he stared at the man. His look hardened.

Siegwart Friedmann—was it fifteen, twenty years ago? The days of the green wagon—yes, it must have been just a few months before the manager of the Salzburg theater picked him up in that God-forsaken Hungarian town and gave him his first contract. As if through the wrong end of binoculars Schildkraut saw the scene—far away and very clearly etched.

In this very same theater, on the first-floor corridor, had been a brass name plate on the door: *Professor Siegwart Friedmann*. It was Felix Hollander's office now. And he, Rudolf Schildkraut, had paced up and down the corridor, waiting to be received by the great man. How hungry he was and how tired, after that terrible twenty-hour ride on carts and trains! In his old-fashioned Prince Albert, shabbily freshened up with black ink on the spots where it was gray, he had really looked like a tramp. And the ridiculous Lavallière cravat he wore to give himself an artistic air! He had stiffened his hair with sugar water to make it stand up and lend impressiveness to his head. His feet burned—as usual the shoes were not his, he had borrowed them from a friend.

Hours passed. What torture! And then—what luck! The professor condescended to see him.

He entered the room. Behind the big desk sat the professor. "What do you want?"

He never forgot that bored, arrogant voice. And after he had stammered the purpose of his visit, the pause seemed endless. He watched the professor toying with his pencil. Will he let me read for him? What shall it be? Shylock?

Friedmann took the pencil and scribbled a few lines on a piece of paper, folded it carefully, handed it to him. "Give this to the gentleman in the third office to the right."

When Schildkraut left that room he was walking on air.

Here in his hand he held the key to his career. This little
slip of paper, granting him an audition, meant the end of
years of frustration and misery. He would become a member
of the Deutsches Theater. He was so excited that he did not
even look at the paper. He ran to the indicated door. *Office
of the Accountant.*

Accountant? Then he unfolded the paper and read it:
Give this man five marks.

He would never know how he reached that bridge. But
there he was, staring over the railing into the murky water
of the river, and a voice ceaselessly whispering into his ears:
Let yourself fall, and it's over. Nothing to it. You'll never be
a real actor. Nobody wants you. Nobody believes in you. You
will never make it. Never. Never. Jump. Jump.

"Professor Siegwart Friedmann?" How long had the man
been standing here? To Schildkraut it seemed like hours.

"Yes, sir. My name is familiar to you?" The man blushed in
pride.

Schildkraut's face was inscrutable. Slowly he turned, and
very slowly he walked to the clothes rack in the corner of
the room, took his gold watch out of the pocket of his coat,
opened its back lid, and extracted a yellowed slip of paper.

"We met once before, Professor Friedmann. And this you
gave me at that time." His voice was soft; it sounded tired
and yet chilling.

The professor looked puzzled. He took the slip of paper.
He read it. He still did not understand. He started to read
it again, aloud. "Give this man . . ." He looked up and recoiled as if under a blow.

Schildkraut's face was a mask of cruel triumph. A smile
twisted his lips; his eyes glittered dangerously.

Friedmann instinctively raised his hands to his face as if
he could not stand the sight. No, that was not an actor who
confronted him, not Rudolf Schildkraut—Shylock! Shylock
demanding his pound of flesh.

Friedmann broke into a cold sweat and staggered out of the room.

3

We lived in the Weimarerstrasse. In the course of the next six years we moved frequently from one apartment to another, in the same neighborhood in the western district of the city, a residential section which at that time had a distinctly suburban character—wide streets, little traffic, front lawns, and trees. The small apartment buildings had an elegant air, as if they were trying to look like private villas.

The main thoroughfare, the Kurfürstendamm, was a symbol of Berlin's newly acquired cosmopolitanism. The few shops catered to a discriminating clientele, the cafés with their big terraces attested to the leisure and opulence which the hard-working Berliner was slowly learning to enjoy. The main shopping center was still downtown, and so was the theater district. The old aristocratic families and the rich lived in the Tiergarten in their own mansions, or had new villas built in the Grunewald at the outskirts of the city. Berlin West was the domain of the upper middle class, the new intelligentsia. To them the Kurfürstendamm was the equivalent of Vienna's Ring or a Parisian boulevard.

Alas, the style was missing. Or rather, it was the style of the eighties and nineties, the years of the building boom, that this avenue and its side streets displayed: almost every house was adorned with Roman and Greek columns of false marble, with caryatids and elaborate classic, Gothic, and baroque ornaments. No house was considered "fine" that did not have an abundance of balconies, ledges, cornices, gables, buttresses, and curlicues. The big church at the lower end of the Kurfürstendamm was a monstrosity.

Downtown, Unter den Linden, the old part of the city, still kept its eighteenth-century charm, but for this past the new Berliner cared very little. "Modern" was the slogan of

the day and the Wilhelminian era equated it with pretentiousness and ostentatious luxury.

I was too young to know the difference. I liked the cleanliness of the streets and the comfort of our apartment, and
was impressed by the efficiency and order in Berlin. And the
climate was wonderful; Father never tired of praising the
dry and invigorating air, so different from the humidity of
Hamburg and the dust and wind of Vienna.

I went to the Mommsen Gymnasium, a junior high school
noted for its high scholastic standards and its curriculum in
Latin and Greek. I disliked the school. I was very good in
German literature and composition, not so good in the classical languages, and a complete failure in mathematics. As I
was going to take up a musical career, I could not understand
why I had to cram my poor head with Cicero and the theo-
rems of Pythagoras and Euclid. In this matter, however,
Father was pitiless. "You never know, perhaps you will not
succeed as a musician. In that case you can become a lawyer
or a doctor. What else could you be? A businessman?"

That settled it. I would never sink that low. A businessman was nearly as bad as a locksmith or a carpenter. The
idea that I might follow in Father's footsteps occurred neither
to him nor to me. In spite of his own bohemian life and the
success and wealth it had brought him, he had an abiding
faith in the blessings of bourgeois respectability and an unwavering respect for what was generally accepted as the
standards of "culture." The nomadic life of the green-wagon
days had never erased the memories of his few years in the
Gymnasium of Hermannstadt.

Our Gymnasium was run like a military school. I didn't
mind the harsh discipline; everyone accepted it as a matter of
course and even took pride in the authoritarian order; it
attested to your manliness. You were not a kid any more, and
only a sissy, a mother's pet, would complain. To be different
from the other boys meant you were queer, and earned you

the mistrust and hatred of all. The few who distinguished themselves by good marks paid a high price for the preferential treatment the professors granted them: they were ridiculed and scorned by the other boys. In order to be popular you had to conform, and popularity—being hailed as a "regular guy"—was the most important goal. The sons of the rich and noble worked doubly hard to meet that test.

In Hamburg the fame of my father had given me a definite distinction among my schoolmates. In the Berlin Gymnasium it made me very uncomfortable. Probably that was my fault; my self-consciousness and previous isolation from children of my age made it difficult for me to establish a friendly contact with the other students. My shyness was taken for arrogance.

Yet there was also another reason why I felt excluded from the games and secrets of my schoolmates. It had been hidden from me for quite a while. I discovered it one morning during one of our Greek lessons.

The night before, Father had appeared in a new production of *Lysistrata*.

"Schildkraut!"

I rose.

The professor beckoned me to the blackboard. I walked the few steps with a pounding heart. What did he want from me? There were no examinations scheduled for that day. And there was something in his manner that frightened me. He was leaning against the desk, cracking his ruler like a whip. He surveyed me from head to toe, a nasty gleam in his cold, hard eyes. He did not speak. I waited.

"Your father played in *Lysistrata* last night?"

"Yes, sir."

"The part of Kynesias?"

"Yes, sir."

"I didn't know Kynesias was a Jew. Did you?" The question was not addressed to me but to the class. He asked it with an exaggerated naïveté. Realizing the reaction expected from them, the boys laughed. And, seeing the grinning face of the professor, they laughed louder and louder.

My face burned. I trembled. I was torn between shame and fury. Shame won out.

"You may go," the professor said with a little sarcastic bow. The bow was the epitome of mockery.

I could hardly find the way back to my seat.

At home I did not tell Father or Mother about that incident. I sat for hours in my room, before my unopened textbooks, staring at nothing.

Why was I a Jew? What did it mean to be a Jew? I had hardly been aware of my Jewishness. I had never received any religious instruction, never visited the synagogue, not even on the rare occasions when Mother went there. I knew Jewish history, and some of the stories of the heroic struggle and martyrdom of the Jews through the centuries made me very proud. Yet Father, who had told me many of these stories was, after all, a German actor, one of the greatest. Everyone said so. I was a German, wasn't I?

I could never hide my troubles from my father for very long. When I finally told him what had happened he seemed, to my surprise, more worried than angry. "I don't want you to stay in the Mommsen Gymnasium," he said softly. "I don't see why *you* should suffer from anti-Semitism. That's much too high a price to pay for being a Jew. One religion is as good as the other. I don't believe in any—a lot of superstition. But if people are that stupid, it's no use fighting them. One day you may decide to become a freethinker or a Protestant or Catholic—that will not make you a better or worse person. And if it made your life easier . . ." He paused and concluded, "I think I'll put you into the Lutheran Gymnasium. There everyone will take it for granted that you are a Protestant by faith. You will have to attend their services—so what? At least, nobody will bother you."

Just a few weeks after I had enrolled at the Lutheran Gymnasium in Steglitz a message arrived from Vienna. We were at dinner when the maid brought in the telegram. Father opened it; it took him a long time to read it.

Mother and I watched him anxiously. "What is it?" Mother asked finally. "Anything wrong?"

He passed the telegram to Mother. I, too, read it, looking over her shoulders:

OFFER YOU FIVE YEAR CONTRACT BURG THEATER AS LEADING
CHARACTER ACTOR SAME SALARY ARRANGEMENTS YOU HAVE IN
YOUR PRESENT POSITION STOP LEADING CHARACTER PARTS IN
CLASSICAL REPERTORY GUARANTEED IF AND WHEN THOSE PLAYS
WILL BE PRODUCED STOP CONDITION YOU ARE PREPARED TO
UNDERGO CATHOLIC OR PROTESTANT CONVERSION STOP PLEASE
WIRE RESPONSE REGARDS SCHLENTHER

Paul Schlenther, the new director of the Imperial Burg Theater, was Baron Berger's successor. The Burg Theater! Imperial and Royal Actor to the Court—that was the ultimate goal Father had struggled for all his life, hoping, despairing. Now it was within reach. Young as I was I knew what that offer meant to him. The condition? A mere formality. Gustav Mahler had to become a Catholic before he got his appointment as Director General of the Vienna Opera. Bruno Walter had accepted conversion. Nobody took exception to this regulation; it was the Kaiser's wish and had to be respected as such. Certainly Rudolf Schildkraut was not more pious or Jew-conscious than they were.

"What are you going to do?" Mother asked.

The maid entered. "The boy from the telegraph office wants to know if there is an answer."

"Let him wait a few minutes," Father said, and a broad, mischievous grin spread over his face. "Fetch me a piece of paper and a pencil, Pepi."

Mother could not hide her solicitude. "You don't have to answer immediately, you know—you can—"

He raised his hand in a calming gesture. Then he took

the pencil and wrote with deliberate pace, not once pausing in search of a word.

"Here!" He passed the paper to Mother.

HIS EXCELLENCY DIRECTOR GENERAL IMPERIAL BURG THEATER
VIENNA PROFESSOR DOCTOR PAUL SCHLENTHER KISS MY ASS
RUDOLF SCHILDKRAUT

"But Maxl—" Mother gasped.

He took the paper out of her hands. "Here is the answer, Polka," he said to the maid. "Give it to the messenger."

Since there was no censorship in the telegraph office, the message was delivered to Director Schlenther as sent.

4

While continuing my studies at the Lutheran Gymnasium I entered the Royal Academy of Music. I majored in violin and piano and studied harmony, counterpoint, composition, and conducting. I was twelve years old when, as a birthday gift to my father, I played for him Wieniawski's D-Minor Violin Concerto. I must have been quite good, for my teachers predicted a great future for me when, three years later in 1911, I graduated with honors from the Academy. For my graduation piece on the violin I again played the Wieniawski concerto, and my graduation piece on the piano was a Schubert sonata. I was the youngest in the class; all the others were between eighteen and twenty-one, young gentlemen and ladies. I still wore short pants.

During the intervening years I had suddenly been smitten by a new passion: the theater. It started around 1906 or 1907 and was actually kindled by the visit of Stanislavsky's Moscow Art Theater in Berlin. The general excitement of this event proved contagious. Father's triumphs had been too close to home, as it were; now I saw them in a new perspective. Theater became the great fashion of the day and I eagerly succumbed to it.

When my grandfather and cousin Nelly came from Buenos

Aires for a visit, I conceived the idea of surprising Father on his birthday with the performance of a play. It was *Puss 'n Boots*. I wrote the dramatization of the fairy tale myself and acted as star and director. The play was to be presented in the hall of our apartment the moment Father returned from the theater at night. The cast consisted of friends of mine, two young brothers, my mother, grandfather, and cousin Nelly, to whom I gave the part of the princess. She was very short, of almost dwarflike stature. The lace curtains I had torn off the walls served as her costume. She wore a corset in which she felt uncomfortable, her skin itched, and she kept beating her sides with her fists to overcome this irritation. I was the prince and therefore entitled to an especially colorful costume. Mother rented it from an establishment that supplied fancy costumes for masked balls; its glitter was almost blinding. The most important role of Puss 'n Boots was entrusted to our own Polka. Her German was still very poor; she spoke it with a heavy Czech accent. Her costume was made up out of the straw with which our wine bottles were covered; she also sported a tail which I had torn from a tiger skin that Father had received as a present from some South American admirer and that covered the couch in his library.

Puss 'n Boots' entrance was to be the most spectacular feat of my production. She was to crouch on top of an old-fashioned chest in our hall, and when Father entered the door she was to jump upon him and greet him with a violent meow.

All through the days of rehearsals I lived as if in a dream; I forgot school and music lessons, I could hardly eat or sleep. As director I treated my cast like a sergeant, imagining myself as Reinhardt and Stanislavsky rolled in one.

The evening of the great event arrived. At eleven-thirty we heard Father's footsteps on the stairs, I called "Places"; Father opened the door—and recoiled flabbergasted when a frightening creature jumped on him with a screech. With his thoughts still at the theater he had just left, he could not grasp the meaning of these strange happenings; in his confusion he retreated, murmuring, "I beg your pardon, I entered the wrong apartment." He closed the door and was gone. That was the end of our performance. The payoff was a terrific dressing-down that Father gave mother for catering to my "stupid whims." "No wonder that son of yours neglects his studies," he yelled, "when instead of school and music lessons he has nothing but theater in his mind." The next few weeks I had to practice violin with redoubled vigor; Father himself saw to it. Thus ended my debut as a director.

But no punishment could dampen my interest in the theater. As a twelve-year-old I was not permitted to see Stanislavsky's performances, but hardly a day passed when they were not discussed at our dinner table.

Among other plays Stanislavsky presented his world-famous production of Gorky's *Lower Depths* with himself in the part of Satine and the great Kachalov as the Baron. The play had been one of Max Reinhardt's biggest successes, the springboard to his career in Berlin. In the premiere of Stanislavsky's performance Father sat right behind Reinhardt, and after the last fall of the curtain, in the midst of the thunderous ovation, Reinhardt turned around, nodded to my father, and said softly, "Well, *this* we can't do."

The same evening Reinhardt introduced Father to the Russian master. It was the beginning of a life-long friendship.

Theater, drama, directorial styles—these were now almost exclusively our conversation topics at home. This was probably largely due to Mother's growing understanding of Father's work. Slowly, gradually, she had been drawn into his professional life. She was still the typical housewife, and had no part in his social affairs. His liaisons and love affairs she had finally accepted as inevitable. Of course, she suffered from them as much as ever, but she found comfort in the realization that Father needed her badly and relied more and more often on her advice and support. By now he insisted on her attending the important rehearsals, especially after Reinhardt himself had expressed more than once his appreciation of her criticism, her artistic instinct and common sense.

Father had to rely on Mother's help for another reason. In spite of the fabulous successes which in those years brought him the highest income of any actor in Germany, we were constantly in financial straits. The gambling and the mistresses became, so it seemed, more expensive from year to year. A few times, on my return from school, I found our apartment completely empty of furniture, carpets, curtains, and pictures. By order of the courts they had been taken away to be sold at auction in order to satisfy some of Father's many creditors. And then Mother always got together some money—her proverbial savings which she had cached away. She went to the auction and bought back the most important pieces.

More often Mother succeeded in out-talking the bailiff, and how proud she was when she could relate a victory she had won over the hard-boiled officials by plying them with promises, her wonderful cookies, and expensive liquor! This combination proved quite potent in many cases.

Her loyalty to Father never wavered. Regardless of whether he was right or wrong, she always took his side. Any unfair criticism of Father she took as a personal affront, and in answering such an insult she was as swift as Father himself— sometimes swifter.

The noted critic Norbert Falk, whose mean disposition was well known and much feared by every actor in Berlin, had repeatedly flavored his reviews with nasty remarks about Father's background and Jewish looks. Mother was enraged. Without informing Father, she went to the opening night of a play. During the intermission she had Falk pointed out to her in the foyer, walked up to him, and, disregarding all the prominent people around, she introduced herself. "Good evening, Herr Falk. I am Frau Schildkraut,"

she said with a charming smile. "I have a present for you,"
and, lifting her hand, she smacked him right across the face.
Before the perplexed critic could recover his composure
and as the other people stood aghast, she turned away but
stopped short and, looking back over her shoulder, added
with the same innocent smile, "You know what that's for,
don't you?"

5

A list of the parts Rudolf Schildkraut created and of the
plays in which he appeared under Reinhardt's management
fills a glorious page of the German theater. It is also a veritable index of the European dramatic literature during the
first decade of this century. Schildkraut moved back and
forth from the classical to the modern repertory, from Shylock, Lear, Malvolio, Richard III, and Falstaff, from Lessing
and Molière, Goethe and Schiller, to Henrik Ibsen and August Strindberg, Bernard Shaw and Maxim Gorky, Anton
Chekhov, Frank Wedekind, Herman Heyermans, Ferenc
Molnar, Henri Bernstein, Sem Benelli, Sholem Asch. In the
repertory of the Deutsches Theater every European country
was represented by its leading contemporary dramatist, and
each of these authors found, in large measure thanks to Rudolf Schildkraut, a second home in Germany.

The only time Father had to accept defeat was in Goethe's
Faust, in the part which had formed the first link between
him and his teacher and great friend Friedrich Mitterwurzer
—Mephisto.

Reinhardt conceived his production of *Faust* as a novel
project. The drama was to be given on three consecutive
evenings, each time with a completely different cast, different
sets, different music, and in a different style.

Father asked for the part of the witch. At first Reinhardt
agreed but then he changed his mind and insisted on casting
him in the role of Mephisto. Protests and arguments were
of no avail. When Father pointed out that his stocky, heavy

figure must prove a definite handicap and that his whole appearance contradicted the conventional concept of the devil, Reinhardt defended his decision with even greater determination. "That's it. Precisely because you will be an unconventional Mephisto I want you to play that part."

Schildkraut's strong doubts remained, but finally he acquiesced. He played Mephisto as a vulgar, filthy creature, smelling of brimstone, with no grandeur, no superior intelligence or agility—as the devil of medieval folklore. It was an interesting experiment, but it did not come off. The audience was at first baffled, then irritated. The critics panned him mercilessly. This was the only failure in his whole acting career, and he never played the part again.

In 1907 Reinhardt opened a new theater, next to the Deutsches Theater, the Kammerspiele, an intimate playhouse with only three hundred seats. It had wood-paneled walls, thick carpets, and luxurious club chairs, and was illuminated by real candles which were lighted by ushers in black *escarpins*. The stage, equipped with the most modern technical devices, was separated from the audience by only two steps, thus creating a still greater sense of intimacy. You had to dress formally and pay the then exorbitant price of twenty gold marks per seat if you wanted to qualify for admission. It was just what Berlin society wanted. Now even the first-nighters at the Königliches Schauspielhaus, all those nobles and courtiers, could not compete with the illustrious, elegant, and sophisticated audience of the Kammerspiele.

The theater opened with Ibsen's *Ghosts*. Alexander Moissi was a wonderful Oswald, the great Agnes Sorma an unforgettable Mrs. Alving. Rudolf Schildkraut as the slimy, hypocritical carpenter Engstrand was the talk of the town for weeks.

Then Reinhardt discovered a play by an unknown Polish author, Sholem Asch. *The God of Vengeance,* written in Yiddish, had its world premiere in Berlin with Schildkraut in the leading role, but playing the part in German. It was one of the greatest successes of the season and Father liked the part so much that he appeared in it more often than in any other play and toured with it in most European countries. In the United States he did the role in German, then in Yiddish, and finally, with triumphant success, in English.

By now Rudolf Schildkraut's fame had spread beyond the borders of Germany and Austria. He was invited for guest appearances in Switzerland and the Scandinavian countries, in England, France, Italy, and Holland, in his native Romania and Russia. Each year he went on tour.

From these trips he brought home medals and decorations, which—much as he pretended that he did "not give a damn about that stuff"—nevertheless flattered his vanity, and fascinating stories about his encounters with the great actors and writers of other nations: Strindberg and Ibsen, Molnar and Schnitzler, Lucien Guitry, whose fame was already dwarfed by his son Sacha's versatility as actor, writer, and lover; the "divine" Sarah Bernhardt and Réjane, her fiercest rival; Coquelin, the creator of Cyrano de Bergerac, and Yvette Guilbert, the incomparable *diseuse;* Eleonora Duse; Ermete Novelli and Ermete Zacconi, the stars of the Italian stage. I had known all these names, they spelled glamour and greatness, but now through Father's descriptions and anecdotes I came to know the living people behind the legends.

Father was not interested in abstract ideas, in social or esthetic theories; he always translated them into human terms and personal experiences. Maybe that is the reason why, in contrast to most of the young men of my generation, I was never attracted to politics. Whereas so many of my fellow students saw Ibsen, Strindberg, and Hauptmann primarily as the champions of social reform, as revolutionaries who had set out to charter a new course in sexual relationships, as liberators from the shackles of worn-out moral concepts, I admired and loved these dramatists only for the men and women they had created. In discussing those plays and their authors Father gave me an insight into their thinking and feeling, their outlook on life and love. My schoolmates got excited about these new writers because they "stood for something"; I, however, devoured their books and plays for the mere joy of discovering new friends. They were closer to me than any other friends I had.

Thus the theater acquired a new meaning for me. Nothing could be more exciting than tiptoeing into Father's library when he was studying a new part. He didn't mind my sitting quietly in a corner of the room. It was like attending a session of magic rites; words and gestures became weird, enchanting formulas, a vision materialized, some dear friend of mine suddenly stood there in Father's place, spoke to me, poured out his soul to me. In sharing his doubts, his grief, his joy, I found an answer to my own doubts and questions.

It was in those days that, at first subconsciously, I decided to become an actor like my father. At the same time I also acquired an instinctive understanding of his approach to acting. In describing the performances of the great actors he had seen abroad, he made me see what he himself wanted to achieve in the same parts. As he explained, the three actors who influenced him most were his discoverer and teacher, Friedrich Mitterwurzer, and the two Italians, Novelli and Zacconi. Zacconi's Oswald must have been a brilliant performance, although somewhat too clinical, a harrowing sexual pathological study. The part in which Father admired him most was Kusofkin in Turgenev's rarely played drama, *The Bread of Mercy*.

On the other hand, while Father certainly admired Stanislavsky greatly, neither the Russian master nor his two great stars Moskvin and Kachalov exerted any artistic influence on him as an actor. Not until many years later—in 1923 —when I saw the Stanislavsky ensemble in America, did I detect the reason for Father's attitude. The Russians were in style and technique very much like himself. They had nothing new to show him. From the Italians he gained a fresh and different point of view. Their art intrigued and excited him.

6

In 1910 Father found himself at his wits' end, and even Mother could not help him. He had lost constantly at the races, he had tried to recoup at the gambling table and lost still more, and he had fallen in love with a girl who not only needed expensive clothes and jewelry but wanted to be an actress to boot.

Did Father really believe in her talent? I doubt it very much. But to satisfy her ambition and to prove to her his sincere interest, he talked Reinhardt into giving her a contract and had her salary deducted from his own.

There were so many deductions to satisfy his creditors that in the end Father had not a mark left to his name. All of Mother's savings had also gone down the drain. The rent was many months overdue, and the bailiff was a daily visitor to our home. He had attached most of our furniture and refused to wait any longer.

Those were bitter days. Father and Mother hardly spoke to each other. He stayed away from home for days, and when I saw him he was sullen and gruff. Mother suffered without uttering a complaint. That was terrifying. I wished she would cry.

And then one day Father found a solution to his troubles. He took a six-month leave of absence from Reinhardt and signed a contract to appear in vaudeville. The decision struck the German press like a bombshell. Imagine, the great Schildkraut, the first actor of the German stage, as a half-hour stunt sandwiched between musical clowns, acrobats, and dancing bears! And in what kind of "acts" he performed! They were cheap farces or melodramatic sketches, the kind you could watch at the Grand Guignol in Paris.

Father shrugged off the clamor and criticism. He got

30,000 marks per month. Now at last he would get rid of his debts.

Unfortunately, even the 180,000 marks were only a drop in the bucket; after the six-month tour we were not much better off than before.

A year later the great miracle happened: America came to Father's rescue. The Irving Place Theatre in New York, the leading German repertory theater in the States, where many great German and Austrian actors had appeared as guests, offered Rudolf Schildkraut a one-month engagement. He was to appear in his most famous roles and to receive a fee of $35,000, a fabulous sum at that time, equaled only by the salary that Enrico Caruso commanded.

Of course, it would be hard work. Since there was only a limited audience for plays produced in the German language, Schildkraut would have to appear every second day in a new play. That meant constant rehearsals and three premieres a week. Actually he played fourteen different parts in that one month. But the prospect did not dampen Father's enthusiasm. He was ready to leave immediately.

Alas, when he decided to accept the American offer he overlooked an important detail: his contract with Max Reinhardt. And he did not take into consideration a man who, in contractual matters, was much harder to deal with than the great director. He was Max Reinhardt's brother Edmund.

To the outside world Edmund was practically unknown. His picture never appeared in the newspapers, he was never seen at the splendid gatherings where Max was lionized and feted. However, Max's triumphant career was made possible only by the untiring efforts, the selfless devotion, the perspicacity and financial wizardry of his brother Edmund.

Edmund's relationship with Max was more than a touching example of brotherly love. Here was a gifted, highly intelligent man, an outstanding organizer who could have made a fine name for himself in any business enterprise but who instead decided to give up his own personal aspirations

in order to serve the genius of Max. Max had to be free and
independent from financial worries, free to dream, to plan,
to squander money—and there were few producers in the
whole world who squandered money as easily as he did on
his lavish productions, sets, travels, and very expensive hobbies—free to live like a prince of the Renaissance, while he,
Edmund, sat in a little office in a corner of the Deutsches
Theater and sweated and scraped and invented ingenious
schemes to keep the money rolling in. For Max, everything:
wealth, glamour, fame. For himself, nothing—not even
credit or public recognition for what he did on behalf of
the German theater.

He was an unusual man, this Edmund Reinhardt, in his
way not less remarkable than Max. Along with his business
acumen he had a rare understanding of all the intricate artistic problems of the theater. Very often it was he who, with
his flair for knowing what the public wanted, drew up the
repertory. Many times he found the play that could show
off Reinhardt's directorial talents at its best, and there were
numerous young and unknown actors whom he discovered in
dramatic schools or in provincial theaters and brought to his
brother's attention. These discoveries were then invariably
hailed as proof of Max Reinhardt's artistic instinct.

For over thirty years, till the rise of Hitler, Edmund man-
aged the Reinhardt enterprises—half a dozen theaters in
Berlin and Vienna—and the world-wide tours of the Reinhardt ensemble with unfailing success. There were difficult
periods of inflation and financial crises, but Edmund weathered all these storms and had only one worry—that nothing
should ever trouble Max in his dream world and disturb
his luxurious life in his century-old castle of Leopoldskron
in Salzburg.

Edmund was a shrewd but certainly not a hard man. He
always understood the psychological and emotional problems
of actors and artists. He had granted Schildkraut a six-
month leave of absence when he realized how much he

needed the income from that vaudeville tour. But when Father asked for another leave of ten weeks to fulfill his engagement in New York, Edmund refused. Why? Probably he was afraid that Father's visit to America would be too big a temptation; realizing the opportunities of New York and earning a salary Reinhardt could never afford to pay, Rudolf Schildkraut might decide to turn his back on Germany once and for all.

Or was Edmund's antagonistic attitude caused by an incident that had occurred a few weeks before? Still hard pressed for money, Father had barged into the office of the financial manager of the Deutsches Theater and demanded another advance on his next month's salary. The teller, the type of German bureaucrat who, since he sits behind a grill, regards himself as a person of rank and all those who pass in front of his window as second-class citizens, explained with a malicious glee that Schildkraut's salary account was overdrawn for many months ahead and that he was not permitted to give him a single mark without Edmund Reinhardt's personal order. His arrogant manner enraged Father even more than his refusal. Incensed, Father raised his cane, smashed the glass window of the teller's cage, and threatened to kill him on the spot. The man did not wait to find out whether Father's words were meant in earnest. He ran for the police.

The incident had two consequences: one, of a more farcical nature, Father was to feel two years later. The other he experienced immediately. For the first time, Edmund, usually so conciliatory, was stubborn and angry and refused the leave of absence. Max, as always in similar cases, followed Edmund's lead.

Rudolf Schildkraut's contract had ten more years to run. It was torn up. The separation, "by mutual consent," was nevertheless very painful. Hard feelings were not soothed when Edmund refused even to lend Schildkraut the costumes for the classical parts he was supposed to play in New York. Father had to have them made at his own expense.

No, Schildkraut and the brothers Reinhardt were anything but friends when they parted.

Early in September 1911, Father left for America. He embarked with great hopes; in two or three months he would be back, a very rich man.

He was gone for three days and on the high seas when Mother received a cable from him:

FORGOT ALL COSTUMES STOP PACK EVERYTHING FOLLOW ME ON NEXT BOAT KISSES MAX.

Chapter VII

1

Now I was grown up. For the first time in my life I was away from home and parents, and with my fifteen years I felt like "a real man."

Before Mother followed Father to America she arranged with Paul's parents—Paul was a school friend of mine—for me to stay in their apartment. They were to take care of me in her absence; thus my freedom was somewhat limited. Nevertheless there was a decisive change. The maid called me "the young gentleman" or "young Mr. Schildkraut"; at home I had always been plain Joseph or Pepi to our servant. No one told me what suit to wear. I could manage my own finances, a weekly allowance, not just the pocket money that Mother used to parcel out to me from day to day.

It was an exciting winter, quite different from any I had experienced before. There was the usual snow and frost, but it seemed to me as if I saw the snowflakes for the first time in my life, and the beauty of the delicate ice ferns on the window panes touched me to tears. I would be restless, but then suddenly succumb to an overwhelming lassitude. I wanted to race with the wind, to shout, to throw myself into the snow, and then again I would sit in front of the big porcelain stove for hours and stare into the fire. The big lumps of coal disintegrated, formed fabulous creatures, monsters and nymphs, their contorted, quivering bodies arousing my horror and delight. My face burned and I shivered with cold.

Here in front of the stove I felt secure and could revel undisturbed in my explorations. I neglected my beloved books. No foreign lands were as interesting as the mysterious territory through which I roved, no hero in any drama as fascinating as the stranger whom I had met for the first time. The stranger was I myself.

I could not share my discoveries with anyone. Certainly my friend Paul would not have understood me, and it was good that Mother and Father were away; they would have been horrified to discover what a depraved person I was. They must never find out that, every day on my way to the Gymnasium, I had a tryst with a naked woman. Made out of bronze, she was lying in the window of an antique shop, stretched out on her back, her hands folded behind her head, her firm breasts erect. If only once I could have touched them, caressed her smooth thighs! I would gladly have given all the money in my pocket to buy that woman, but I knew I would never have the courage to enter the shop and to ask the price. That did not stop me from spending hours planning where to hide her when and if I could ever get her. At night she would sleep with me in my bed.

That was my secret. I was torn between the fear of being found out in my sinful desires and the pride of my vices.

Before leaving, Mother had given me once more a stern lecture on the dangers of women. I was too young to meet nice, decent girls; the ones I might get involved with would certainly be evil, carriers of all kinds of disease that would cripple me for life. Father had given me the same warning. It was not necessary. I was much too afraid of girls anyhow. When, on the Kurfürstendamm Bummel, the Sunday promenade, a girl or woman smiled at me I crossed hurriedly, with pounding heart, to the other side of the street.

Most of my schoolmates had love affairs. They carried letters and poems and photographs in their wallets to prove their romantic adventures. Some of the photographs were of cousins, or of some famous actress, but no one would have admitted that his affair was either purely platonic or merely worship from afar. Two or three of the boys could boast of visits to a brothel; they were looked upon in awe by the others, though we all pretended to be as experienced as they were. Sex had all the fascination of the forbidden. The female anatomy was an inexhaustible topic; it was discussed in whispers, alluded to in smutty stories, immortalized in crude drawings that passed from hand to hand in the washrooms during recess.

I reacted to these stories and drawings with a superior smile that cost me a lot of self-control but earned me the reputation of a boy "who knew his way around girls."

In the end I made myself believe that my reputation was well deserved. There was not only my affair with the naked woman of bronze. Already three years before I had risked a daring foray into the realm of sex.

It was during a summer vacation which we spent at the villa of the Goldners in a resort town near Vienna. The Goldners, relatives of ours, had three daughters. One of them, Steffy, was my age, and a very gifted musician. She played the harp beautifully and was the pride of her music teacher, a charming young lady named Vicki Baum, who predicted a great future for her. What Vicki did not foresee, however, was that she herself would one day become famous as a novelist and playwright, the author of *Grand Hotel*. Steffy, after playing with the Vienna Philharmonic, became the first harpist of the New York Philharmonic under Arturo Toscanini in the early twenties, and married the noted conductor Eugene Ormandy.

During our visit with the Goldners, I staged with Steffy,

her sisters, brother, and friends a one-act comedy in the garden of their villa. This event left a deep impression on me, not because of my part in the play, but on account of what happened one afternoon during rehearsal. It was very hot, and the girls decided to take a dip in the mountain brook that formed a little pool at the far end of the garden. It was a secluded spot, hidden from all sides by high rocks and a dense cluster of old trees. When the girls left I stealthily followed them. Hiding behind the trees, I watched them undress and jump completely naked into the pool.

With the passing of time that secret gained in importance. In front of my stove the memory of the nude girls in the pool blended into the picture of the woman in bronze, and suddenly my room was full of naked girls. They were at my command. Oh, I was very bold and invincible in my dreams. If I could ever find the courage to approach a girl in real life, to talk to her, to kiss her!

The most I dared was to sneak into the rehearsals of an Oriental dance pantomime, *Sumurun*, at the Deutsches Theater. I took Paul along. There were chorus girls, exotic dances, lavish sets. Our great thrill was to crawl into the empty prompter's box from where we could see the legs of the girls very close and their panties under the swirling skirts. How exciting that was and how depraved we felt!

The year before I had joined a *Wandervogel* group, a kind of Boy Scout organization. This entitled me to wear a cap with a black-red-gold ribbon, to take part in excursions to the Wannsee and picnics in the nearby forests. Twice a year we staged plays in the auditorium of our Gymnasium. The cap and the excursions did not tempt me, but the theatrical performances were definitely an opportunity I did not want to miss.

When *Alt Heidelberg* (*The Student Prince*) was chosen by our group, I got the part of the prince. For this great honor I was indebted to our counselor, a young man with a pasty face whose pallor was heightened by a big, reddish, puffed-up scar won in one of his many duels. I was his favorite.

I took delight in the friendship of such a worldly-wise man whom, though he was not yet thirty, I regarded as quite old. At the same time I could not overcome an aversion for him. His hands were always moist, and I hated to be touched by them. He always seemed to find an opportunity to stroke my hair or my cheeks. When we were on our excursions I had to march next to him and he would put his arm around my shoulder.

A week or so before our premiere the counselor, who directed the play, asked me to visit him at his apartment on a Sunday afternoon for a *Jause,* the Viennese equivalent of afternoon tea. When I arrived, he was wearing an elegant dressing gown of rich silk. He greeted me most affectionately and led me to a table loaded with cakes, sweets, liqueurs, chocolate, and fruits. I was the only guest. Through the open door I saw a part of the adjoining room where the bed was open.

I had hardly sat down to the delicious Jause when he suddenly came around the table and pulled me off my chair. Petrified, I stared into his eyes, which were watery and protruding like those of a frog. One of his moist hands slipped under my shirt, and he kissed me on the mouth. When he tried to open the flap of my pants I awakened from my stupor. I hit him with all my strength, broke loose, and fled.

The incident disturbed me greatly. For days I was upset. In my innocence I could not fully understand his intentions and felt somewhat guilty of having behaved badly. After all, it was not his fault that he had moist hands. And I had hit him—a much older man, a counselor! I decided to resign from the Wandervogel group. But what about the coming performance? How should I ever confront the man again?

Conveniently, a solution presented itself. It was a letter from Mother. She was on her way back to Berlin. Father

had decided to make our home in America, and she was re
turning to close our apartment for good and to take me to
New York.

2

My first impression of New York was mixed, more confusing than exhilarating. The skyline, the harbor, the piers, the
crowd—all these were exactly as I had seen them in paint-
ings and photographs. Reality was merely copying art. I felt
like the little boy who, seeing the ocean for the first time,
confessed sadly that he had expected it to be bigger.

The greatest thrill was the automobile that was waiting
for us. That splendid car belonged to Mr. Boris Thomashefsky, who had come with Father to greet us. We were
going to spend the next two months at his estate.

Boris Thomashefsky was the manager, director, and star
of the People's Theatre, and one of the great figures of the
Yiddish theater in America. After Father had finished his
one-month engagement at the Irving Place Theatre, every
one of the Yiddish managers in New York had approached
him with the most tempting offers. He had gained as much
praise and fame here as he had in Germany, and the leading
Yiddish directors and producers regarded it as a matter of
personal honor to claim the great Schildkraut whom the
non-Jewish world had taken to its heart as one of them.

There were a dozen Yiddish theaters in New York alone,
four or five of the first order. The competition was fierce.
Thomashefsky won.

3

The Yiddish theater of New York was born in Odessa,
Russia's port and trade center on the Black Sea. A young
actor and playwright, Abraham Goldfaden, is credited with
having founded the first permanent company of professional
Jewish actors. He started in a wine cellar of a little tavern
in Jassy, Romania, where he staged performances of his plays

and vaudeville shows, written in Yiddish. The year was 1876.

Long before, at the beginning of the eighteenth century, Yiddish plays had been performed in the ghettos of the towns and cities of western Russia, Poland, Romania. Amateurs put on the shows, mainly in celebration of the Purim festival commemorating the deliverance of the Jews of ancient Persia from the tyranny of an evil ruler. Esther, a Jewish Jeanne d'Arc who played an important part in that liberation, was anything but a mystic. She was more "little woman" than heroine, and her victory, a vindication of feminine shrewdness, beauty, and charm, gives this anniversary an air of gaiety and light comedy. The Purim plays reflected that mood.

Goldfaden and his friends drew their inspiration not only from the Bible but more and more from contemporary life. They put the troubles and joys of their fellow Jews on stage, their heartaches and their laughter. Much of the dialogue and action was improvised. The actor ruled supreme. Clown, troubadour, and storyteller, he became one of the strongest links between the glories of the past and the harsh reality of the ghetto.

Goldfaden's fame spread throughout the Jewish communities of eastern Europe. He moved to Bucharest, where Sigmund Mogulescu joined the company and immediately became its most beloved star. Two years later they arrived in Odessa. Here Jacob P. Adler, a born tragedian, became a member of the troop, and so did Boris Thomashefsky, who had started as a singer in the choir of a synagogue. They soon split, each forming his own company. Thus Odessa became the center of the Yiddish theater.

The 1880s brought important changes in the social and intellectual climate of Russia. The Muscovite empire was in ferment and the ghetto felt it too. Engaged in a bitter struggle for freedom and human dignity, standing in the forefront of the fight against the oppressive order of the Czar, the Jewish intelligentsia objected to the lack of literary merit of the cheap comedies and burlesques that dominated the repertory of the Yiddish theater. These intellectuals were champions of Western culture, of the ideas of Goethe and Schiller. Their hearts beat for Russia but Germany was their promised land, the country of enlightenment, "the home of poets and thinkers," and they demanded that the Yiddish theater reflect these ideas. The actors obliged. Goldfaden presented his adaptation of *Uriel Acosta* by the German dramatist Karl Gutzkow. The tragic conflict between absolute faith and the search for truth, between the rebellious mind and the stern rule of religious authority, struck a responsive chord in the hearts of Jewish youth. Jacob Gordin, the most prolific of the Yiddish playwrights, adapted Schiller's *The Robbers,* and his *Judah Maccabee* was both a reminder of one of the most heroic episodes in Jewish history and a call to action.

The Russian government reacted as could be expected. In the nineties, censorship was tightened, there were arrests and pogroms, and the Yiddish theaters were closed. Actors and playwrights had to flee for their lives.

Vienna, Berlin, London could not hold them. They loved the West but they loved their Jewish heritage even more. There was not enough *Yiddishkeit* in the life of those cities, not enough of the clannishness, the adventurous spirit and the mysterious soul of the East. In their quest for personal fulfillment they finally, after long and perilous journeys, reached the United States.

They brought with them the indomitable courage of their race, the intellectual fervor of Russia's revolutionaries, and Germany's preoccupation with social ideas. In contrast to the millions of emigrants who came to America in search of a decent life and material wealth, the Yiddish actors, poets, and playwrights came as missionaries. To them theater was not a profession but a way of life. In the new-found democracy they were true aristocrats.

4

Thomashefsky's estate at Hunter in the Catskills was the domain of a millionaire. Even the great Reinhardt had not yet achieved this style of living. Aside from automobiles, there were horses which I was permitted to ride, and a part of the spacious grounds had been set aside for an open-air theater with a capacity of eight hundred people. During the summer Father starred here in a one-act play that Thomashefsky staged just for the entertainment of his friends and colleagues.

What impressed me even more than the opulence of this household was its decorum; the great actors I met had the dignity and bearing of an exalted caste. It was inconceivable that these men should call each other by their first names, even though they had been close friends for half a lifetime. No one would have dared to speak of Jacob Adler's wife or to address her, even at rehearsals, without giving her the proper title of "Madame." The Adler children were brought up like those of a royal family, always kept aware of the prestige attached to their parents' name. Whereas I had never been forbidden to visit my father in his dressing room, they were never permitted to enjoy that privilege with their mother, though they were acting together in the same play. Stella and Luther were younger than I was, but they seemed to me much older, self-controlled, mature. I had never met children like them before.

My first contact with the Jewish world was a revelation to me. I had always thought of myself as a German, and I spoke only German. Communication, however, was not too difficult, since Father's friends understood the German language and very soon my ear got used to their idiom.

It was an exotic world, that Lower East Side where the People's Theatre was located. Custom and manners were not merely strange, they were full of hidden meanings—symbolic puzzles, as it were. The German milieu in which I had been brought up seemed flat and prosaic by comparison; it was as if after walking for many years on well-paved and clearly lighted streets I found myself suddenly in an Oriental landscape with its dazzling colors and violent dissonances; and at the same time a sad twilight seemed always to hover over it.

A world of contrasts, and yet I felt immediately at home in it. I had the impression that I had been here before— maybe in my dreams.

The Jewish settlement on the Lower East Side was not a ghetto, although it formed a distinct and separate part of New York. Somehow it blended harmoniously into the life of the big city, its influence reaching to all the boroughs.

And how self-confident and proud this world was! Its warmth captivated me. It bubbled with genuine excitement, it had an insatiable appetite for art, music, literature, it burst with life. Its center was the Café Royal on Second Avenue.

Here every one of the leading Yiddish actors had his own reserved table where he held court like a reigning sovereign. At one side sat Thomashefsky, the typical matinee idol, on the other side Jacob P. Adler, the tragic hero, over six feet tall, a truly majestic figure.

Thomashefsky was a very handsome man, as proud of his legs as of his melodious voice, and the unsurpassed star of the Yiddish operetta. When stepping close to the footlights to sing one of his sentimental tunes, serving up his little mannerisms as if they were special jokes he was sharing with the audience, every woman and girl felt his smile like a personal caress. He had a fabulous reputation as a lover, and when it became known that an aspiring actress, after auditioning for him, had refused to sleep with him, the public summarily discarded her as ugly, "a hopeless failure." He was married to a gifted actress, Bessie, who excelled in serious dramatic parts.

The dream of a wandering player came true: thirty-year-old Rudolf
had conquered Vienna (1892)

(*Above, left to right*
Father, Cousin Nell
Grandmother, myse
Grandfather, Aunt
Regina, Mother

Family reunion in
Buenos Aires (1901)

I was six

Mother

Father and I

Some of Father's famous parts:

in *The Mongrel*

in *The God of Vengeance*

in *His People*

as Shylock

. . . and as King Lear (Hamburg, 1901)

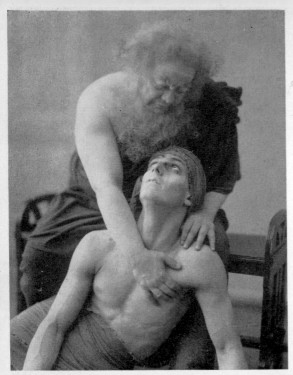

(*Left*) *The Prodigal Son* (Ber
1913)—the first time I was i
play with my father

(*Below, left*) My first appear;
on the stage, as young Frede
the Great (New York, 1912)

(*Below, right*) In *Don Ca*
(Vienna, 1920)

Liliom by Ferenc Molnar (New York, 1921)
Eva Le Gallienne and I became stars overnight

On a visit to the Universal Studios (1927): Bruno Walter, Conrad Veidt, Father, and I

Donald Crisp directs us in *Young April,* a Cecil B. de Mille production (1927)

Thomashefsky's end was sad, even tragic. Not able or not talented enough to make, as Father put it, the transition from a romantic idol to a character actor, he fought, in later years, a desperate battle against growing old, and lost. There came the day when not even make-up number 5—the strongest there is—could restore his youthful appearance, and the great lover became a pitiful caricature. The public turned its back on him. His fortune evaporated, and in the end he made a paltry living as a singer in a little Romanian café on the same Lower East Side where he had once been king.

One corner table in the Café Royal always attracted a big crowd. Here presided Sigmund Mogulescu, small, wiry, melancholy, probably the greatest comedian of the Yiddish stage. A master extemporizer, he convulsed his listeners with jokes —a potent weapon in the Jewish people's fight for survival for over two thousand years.

The center table was reserved for David Kessler, the greatest of them all. "The only real genius of the contemporary stage," Father called him. In comparison to his career even the fantastic life stories of the others seemed pale and commonplace. A vagrant from Russian Poland, later a banana peddler in New York, he was brought to the stage by his son-in-law, a theatrical producer by the name of Max Wilner. Kessler was an illiterate. He never learned how to read or write. He studied his parts by having a prompter, the noted Sam Weissman, confidant and adviser of all Yiddish actors, read his lines to him over and over again. Often he forgot them when he came on stage, but that did not matter. He created his characters as if in a trance; his acting was as natural as an elementary force. He had his own theater, called the Kessler, or Second Avenue, Theatre.

There was, of course, a Schildkraut table, too. For while the potentates were close friends, their respective followers would never mingle with one another. These disciples, devotees, and hangers-on were called "the patriots," and their loyalty to the chosen idol was as exclusive as it was fanatical.

To be for Schildkraut meant you had to place him high above anyone else. A patriot of Kessler regarded any follower of Adler as an ignoramus who should be barred from the theater for the duration of his life. And the heated debates about the merit of a particular performance or the staging of a play were conducted not only at the tables of the Café Royal. Many times after a first night the respective fans clashed in violent street battles. No soldier has ever fought for his country with greater conviction than a little shoemaker or tailor from the Jewish East Side for Schildkraut's concept of Shylock, or Adler's production of *Faust* which Jacob Gordin had adapted under the title of *Man, God, and the Devil.*

The Café Royal was under the guard and administration of a very important personality—Hymie, the headwaiter. He was bowlegged and cross-eyed, and he reeked of garlic. He was the trusted friend and professional adviser of each of these famous customers, a highly respected critic, and the "angel" to producers in search of money. Often it was thanks only to his financial investment that a new production could reach the stage.

Once Max Wilner wanted him to invest money in *King Lear*. The waiter refused. "There is no money in Shakespeare," he declared. "Who wants to see a mad English king?" Whereupon Wilner told him the story of Lear in terms of a Jewish family tragedy from Brooklyn: a rich banker, betrayed by his business associates, abandoned by his ungrateful and evil daughters. "That's it!" the waiter exclaimed. "That play will make money." And the deal was on. Later Jacob Gordin gained from this incident the inspiration for his "modern version" of Shakespeare's tragedy. The *Jewish King Lear* was the result. It had a resounding success.

While the Café Royal was dominated almost exclusively by men, there were, nevertheless, some women who shared in the reign of the Yiddish theater. Through all those years two of them vied with each other for the title of First Lady: Madame Sarah Adler and Madame Lipzin. Each had her own theater. And it was in Madame Adler's Novelty Theatre in Brooklyn that Father appeared in 1912 as her partner in a dramatization of Tolstoi's *Kreutzer Sonata*. Stella and Luther acted the parts of the children.

5

Father made his American debut in the People's Theatre on Labor Day, 1911. He chose as his opening play *The Inner Man,* a melodrama by the well-known Yiddish dramatist Abraham Schomer. Years later it was turned into a film and produced in Berlin under the title *Man and His Demon,* one of the most notable successes Father had in his career as a film actor.

To prepare himself for this part Father spent the summer vacation at Thomashefsky's estate studying Yiddish. With his natural gift for languages he mastered it quickly and soon was praised for speaking the purest, a "classical" Yiddish, different from other famous actors who spoke it with a distinct German, Polish, or Russian intonation. There were, however, two parts he never acted in Yiddish—Shylock and King Lear—although there were excellent translations of both plays available. Whenever these two plays were produced—and they were a mainstay of the repertory of the Yiddish theater—Father acted his part in German while the entire supporting cast spoke Yiddish. The audience at first was baffled, but in the end bowed to Schildkraut's "whim."

It was a heterogeneous audience. Non-Jews came from all parts of the city to enjoy an evening of "great theater." Foreign tourists "took it in" as one of the special attractions of New York. To the Jews from uptown who had achieved some social standing and wealth in this new country, a visit to the Yiddish theater was a nostalgic return to the land and traditions of their fathers. To the poor and hard-working laborers and artisans it meant glamour and exultation; it was as important as a service in the synagogue, and to many of them more rewarding. When Father left the theater they would rush up to him, old and young, men and women, crying, laughing, fighting for the privilege of kissing his hands or touching the hem of his coat.

The Saturday matinees, mainly frequented by women, were something else again. The housewives brought their babies along, leaving the prams outside in the foyer under the supervision of the doorman, who received a ten-cent tip for watching the little ones.

During a performance of *The Merchant of Venice,* in the Novelty Theatre in Brooklyn, the doorman suddenly rushed into the orchestra. The court scene of the fourth act had just begun, with Sarah Adler in the role of Portia and Rudolf Schildkraut as Shylock confronting each other. "Baby's crying!" the doorman yelled at the top of his voice.

Father froze in his speech. He could not have made himself heard anyhow, for, not knowing which of the babies was in need of attention, two dozen mothers jumped up and dashed out.

Father started again. But again he was interrupted by the same two dozen women tramping back to their seats. One of them had the baby with her. It was crying bitterly; the neighbors protested, and so the desperate mother quickly unbuttoned her blouse and gave the baby her breast.

At last there was silence. But in a minute the wailing started again, topped by the high-pitched voice of the frantic woman: "Hush, hush, darling! Take it, take it, quick! If you don't take it I'll give it to Schildkraut!"

Theater was never like this in Berlin.

6

After our summer vacation at Hunter we had moved into our own apartment on East 15th Street, opposite Stuyvesant Square. I had to go back to school.

Father insisted that I continue my musical studies. Ovide

Musin, the well-known French teacher, agreed to accept me as his pupil. I had different plans. Now, more than ever, I wanted to become an actor, and therefore I talked Father into letting me enter the American Academy of Dramatic Arts—not to prepare myself for an acting career, God forbid, but, as I explained, to study the English language. These studies would not interfere with my music lessons, and a private tutor would take care of my general education. Father accepted this arrangement. But my plan was not easily realized, since I was too young to be admitted to the Academy.

Help came from a new friend of Father's, the famous producer David Belasco. I first met him in Father's dressing room. With his clerical collar and long white hair, he reminded me of Franz Liszt. His appearance belied the stories about him that circulated around Broadway. He looked so benign, so sweet, so paternal, and yet he was supposed to be the most ruthless, tyrannical, and egocentric producer in America. But the stories were true, and so was his theatrical genius. He had started his career on the Lower East Side, a poor Jewish boy possessed by a love for the theater. According to the legend, he had written and produced fifteen plays before he had passed his fourteenth year. He had staged them in coal bins, funeral parlors, cellars. He had only one goal: Broadway. He advanced to it street by street, so to speak, from the Bowery to Times Square.

Thanks to Belasco's intervention my age was overlooked, and I was permitted to audition for the three luminaries of the Academy. Franklin H. Sargeant was the executive president, very Anglo-Saxon, correct and dignified. Emil Diestel, the executive secretary, was an artist whose sensitivity was reflected in his pale, translucent face; he suffered from a lung disease and his fragile body showed it. The third was Charles Jehlinger, one of the truly great teachers, much feared and deeply loved by all his students—by no one more than by myself.

To prepare me for the entrance examination at the Academy, Father engaged a lady whom he had met socially. She was a great fan of his, a gifted writer, though practically unknown, middle-aged. More than anyone else Cynthia was responsible for the rapid progress I made in learning to speak English correctly and with the proper intonation. (Incidentally, ten years later her efforts found public recognition in a special award that I received: the David Belasco citation for "the best and purest English spoken on the New York stage by any actor during the current season." That was during the winter of 1923-1924.)

I passed the audition successfully and was notified that I could enter the junior class of 1912. Until then I continued my studies in English.

Cynthia was an excellent teacher but she was also a charming woman. Sometimes the difficulty in communicating your thoughts in a language you don't know well is quite a blessing: eyes and hands take over and they can be very eloquent. Since I was a stumbling beginner, she provided the logical ending. Ours was a perfect liaison. I was in love with passion and she with me. We were both very happy.

When I entered the junior class I had lost my German accent, and my youthful doubts and frustrations as well. Six months later I graduated at what was then called the Carnegie Lyceum, a small subterranean theater in Carnegie Hall. The students had to appear in scenes from classical and modern plays, in costumes and make-up as if on a real stage.

Young actors and actresses, for some reason or other, always want to play a part that they either cannot play because they are not yet ready for it, or should not play because they are simply not the proper type. It was not different with me. And so I decided to play Lord Goring in Oscar Wilde's *An Ideal Husband*. If there was ever a role that needed an actor with the qualifications of a Leslie Howard or Rex Harrison, Lord Goring is it. The actor should have a British accent, should preferably be blue-eyed, sandy-haired, very blasé, the perfect Englishman. But I was so much in love with that part, and so insistent on playing it, that I finally got it.

I immediately started out to turn myself into the typical English aristocrat I was supposed to portray. First, I got hold of an atrocious straw-blond wig, parted in the middle, with a horrid piece of false forehead, as cheap wigs were made at that time. I attached to my upper lip what was intended to be an English brush-type mustache, but was distinctly the "handlebar" variety worn by villains in American barroom melodramas of the eighties. Lord Goring's dress suit should be the creation of one of the most expensive tailors of Savile Row; mine was rented from a second-hand store on 8th Street and in better days had belonged to a waiter in a beer-hall on 14th Street. The suit was too tight for me, too narrow in the shoulders, and the sleeves nearly covered my hands. My cheap patent-leather pumps creaked at every step. For shirt studs I wore some oversized rhinestone buttons which I had discovered in a little junk shop and thought very smart. And to top it all, since I was unsuccessful in holding a monocle elegantly, I stuck it in my right eye with spirit gum. In the scene of the first act with Mabel Chiltern I moved so awkwardly that I still shudder when I see myself in retrospect.

After that glorious performance Father didn't talk to me for several weeks. Cynthia, however, reported that on leaving the Lyceum Theatre he had said to my teachers, "If that son of mine up there insists on taking up the career of an actor, I will personally slap him off the stage with a wet rag. The bastard has no talent whatsoever."

The teachers were more lenient, and let me pass. But it took me years to eradicate the memory of this ghastly evening from my father's mind.

After six months in the senior class of the Academy, I was ready to receive my diploma. This time the graduation exercises took place at the now defunct Empire Theatre on Broadway. We had to act in plays given in their entirety, and the press was invited.

I appeared in two plays, *The Faun* by Edward Knoblock and Ibsen's *Pillars of Society*. Two classmates who graduated with me were Edward G. Robinson and William Powell.

After my graduation the producer Russell Janney, who many years later became widely known as the author of the best-selling novel *The Miracle of the Bells,* wanted to engage me for a tour of open-air performances which he had booked with colleges, high schools, and clubs. Father, however, refused to give his permission. The encouraging notices I had received did not change his mind. I had promised him to attend the Academy only in order to improve my English, and I was not going to be an actor, definitely not. Besides, he would never permit me to start my career in an amateur production. If he ever consented to my acting at all, it must be with a professional company on a legitimate stage.

The "if" gave me a loophole with Father. Grudgingly, he finally agreed to let me appear at the Irving Place Theatre in a German production of a trite but rather effective melodrama by the actor-producer Ferdinand Bonn, *Der junge Fritz (Young Freddy)*. It dealt with Frederick the Great of Prussia and his friendship with Lieutenant Katte, whom Frederick's father, Wilhelm I, executed on a trumped-up charge of high treason in order to break up the close relationship between the two young men. He even forced his son to witness the execution of Katte from a window of the palace "to make a man out of Friedrich."

Friedrich was an excellent part for a young actor, and I received very good notices in both the German and American press. The part of Katte was played by another young actor, G. W. Pabst, who in the postwar years rose to a dominant position in the German film industry and gained worldwide reputation as a director of such outstanding films as *Street without Joy,* starring Greta Garbo, *Kameradschaft,* and *The Threepenny Opera.*

With this performance I finally overcame Father's resistance. He was not at all happy about my new career, but reluctantly he allowed me to sign a contract with Janney to play the juvenile lead in a very good English translation of *The Romantics* by Edmond Rostand, a comedy in verse, frothy, gay, and charming.

7

It was the spring of 1913, almost two years since we had come to America. Soon another summer would have passed, in a few months a new season would begin. What would it bring?

The question did not bother me. To me each new day was the promise of a new adventure waiting just around the corner or at the next party: a girl, a new friend, the great love, a new contract. I was too busy living to think of the future.

Each visit to the theater or the Metropolitan Opera was a discovery, not just of some exciting play or some wonderful performance but, even more thrilling, the revelation of feelings and thoughts of which I had never believed myself capable. Every emotion was unique, each thought had never occurred to anyone but me.

Leo Slezak as Othello, Geraldine Farrar as Madame Butterfly, Caruso in *Pagliacci,* Emmy Destinn in *The Bartered Bride!* After each performance I wandered with friends and colleagues for hours through the night streets, so overflowing with the evening's impressions that had to be shared; unable to separate, determined not to go to bed before we had converted each other to our respective opinions.

There were George Arliss in *Disraeli,* David Warfield in *The Music Master* and in *The Return of Peter Grimm,* Otis Skinner in *Kismet,* Laurette Taylor in *Peg O' My Heart,* John Barrymore in *Anatol,* a play, incidentally, in which Barrymore was billed as John for the first time; until then he had acted only in farces and comedies and used Jack as his first name.

I had seen equally great actors and more important plays

in Berlin, but there I had been part of the audience; now I was "one of them," a member of the fraternity, not merely as the son of my father but as an actor in my own right.

My first professional engagement in *The Romantics* brought me $35 a week. I felt like a Croesus. I was successful, I received good notices, and Kathleen was my lady love—not only in the play.

Kathleen was nineteen years old and had been a fellow student at the Academy. I worshiped her. I dreamed of heroic deeds I would perform in order to prove to her the depth and sincerity of my feelings; I suffered all the pains of jealousy, made the most elaborate plans of how to stage my first embrace, and decided our love must never be defiled—not even by a kiss. Since I had already been initiated into the mysteries of sex, I had come to the conclusion that what I needed now was the experience of "real love." It must be sublime, unselfish, unique. It was all very confusing and romantic.

Torn between my profane lust for Cynthia and my exalted love for Kathleen, I had hardly time to take an interest in Father's professional problems or in Mother's worries.

For Father the question of how to plan the forthcoming season was a very difficult one. His series of unbroken triumphs could not make up for a bitter disappointment. In spite of all his wonderful notices in the New York press, in spite of his international reputation, he had not been able to realize his greatest ambition: to act in English on a Broadway stage. He had been sure that David Belasco would cast him in one of his productions—preferably as Shylock—but, although Belasco never stopped assuring Father of his great admiration and friendship, the offer that Father so eagerly expected did not come. The star of the East Side could never, so it seemed, be a star on Broadway.

And in the Yiddish theater, too, difficulties arose. There was much bickering and professional jealousy, and since the various actor-managers resented Father's domineering position, engagements became rarer and rarer. The German theater, on the other hand, could not guarantee him a long-term contract or a steady income. The financial troubles started all over again. And they mounted from week to week.

Father began thinking of a return to Germany. But where could he go? Since he had reached the height of his career, there were only two theaters in the German-speaking world that could offer him the parts and the artistic home that he wanted: The Burg Theater in Vienna and the Deutsches Theater in Berlin. And he had broken with both Schlenther and Reinhardt. The future looked dark indeed.

Once more a cable changed our whole life. It came from Berlin and was signed by Felix Hollander.

WHEN ARE YOU INTENDING RETURN TO EUROPE QUESTIONMARK THEY DON'T APPRECIATE YOU OVER THERE ANYWAY AND THE GERMAN THEATER NEEDS YOU STOP SEE POSSIBILITY OF RECONCILIATION WITH MAX WIRE ANSWER

Father did not hesitate a moment.

THANKS CABLEGRAM ARRIVING BERLIN BEGINNING OF JUNE STOP GIVE MAX MY LOVE

I finished my tour with *The Romantics,* Mother sold most of her jewelry and our furniture, and we booked passage on the *George Washington.*

At the end of May we left New York.

The days of our crossing were filled with my dreams of Kathleen. With every hour my longing for her grew in intensity. I felt not heroic any more, only stupid. I bitterly accused myself of cowardice. Was she grateful for my noble restraint? In the end she may have taken it as a sign of inexperience or, even worse, of impotence. This thought hurt terribly. My first great love, and what did I get out of it? The memory of a few kisses, and these had mostly been exchanged on stage in the course of a play. I cursed platonic love; I was through with it. Never again, I vowed.

Chapter VIII

1

ERLIN SEEMED so different, and I had been away for
only two years. Two years? Half a lifetime! I had left
as an inexperienced teen-ager; I returned as a mature man,
a professional actor. I had possessed one woman and suffered
because of another. Looking back from the eminence of my
seventeen years at the boy of fifteen, I could hardly believe
I was the same person.

After New York, Berlin at first appeared rather small. But
the moment I entered the Café des Westens I was drawn
into an artistic and intellectual whirlpool that was as fascinating as anything I had experienced in New York. The Café
Royal was after all only a little oasis in the vastness of a big
city; in the Café des Westens one had the feeling that here
the whole future of Berlin and Germany was planned and
molded. The people, including the guests of the café themselves, referred to it as the *Café Megalomania,* but that did
not dampen the self-confidence of the writers, actors, painters,
and musicians whose headquarters it was, nor detract from

the genuine respect in which they were held by the general public. A new book of poetry by Rilke or Arno Holz, a new play by Gerhart Hauptmann, a premiere at the Deutsches Theater was front-page news. The Café des Westens was not merely the hangout of the intellectual and the artists, it was Germany's Olympus.

Immediately after our return Felix Hollander had arranged a reconciliation between Father and the Reinhardt brothers. A new contract was signed and on October 1, 1913, Father resumed his engagement in a revival of *Hamlet*. Since he was not interested in playing King Claudius and had played the First Gravedigger before, he chose the role of the First Actor. According to the Berlin press he played him "magnificently. With his lament for Hecuba he really brought tears to our eyes. And the occasion, we assume, was meant to be somewhat symbolic for Max Reinhardt: his first actor actually played the First Actor."

I had decided to strike out for myself. For the first time I proceeded without Father's advice, without even informing him of my plans. Secretly I went to see Max Reinhardt and asked him to grant me an audition. He was always interested in young actors, and in my case, of course, especially favorably disposed. He agreed.

I read for him a monologue from *Romeo and Juliet*. ("He jests at scars that never felt a wound"), Franz's dream monologue from Schiller's *The Robbers*, and the first-act soliloquy from the Hungarian light comedy *The Highwayman*, which I played in English many years later on road tours in America.

In the audience were the Reinhardt brothers and several of their dramaturgists, amongst them Heinz Herald. Twenty-five years later Herald and I were linked in a different kind of relationship in Hollywood. Herald had written the scenario for *The Life of Emile Zola*, in which I played Captain Dreyfus. The film brought each of us an Academy Award.

The day after my audition Reinhardt offered me a contract. The salary seemed small—175 marks a month—especially when I considered the exchange rate of four marks to
the dollar. But life was much cheaper in Berlin than in
New York, and the contract guaranteed me a steady income
for a whole year. More importantly, I was now a full-fledged
member of the Deutsches Theater.

Father was not at all pleased when he heard about this
new development. However, realizing that he could not
forever prevent me from following a career on which I had
set my heart, he immediately decided he would do everything in his power to help me. "Since you want to be an
actor I will see to it that you will not go through all the
sufferings and humiliations I had to endure," he declared.

He kept that pledge, though Reinhardt often warned him
against trying to make things too easy for me; Reinhardt
pointed out that I had to overcome difficulties and disappointments on my own in order to grow normally as an actor
and a human being. I was much too cocky and conceited
anyhow.

Reinhardt was right. I can only say that, without a large
portion of self-confidence, I could hardly have lived down
the disaster of my first appearance on the stage of the
Deutsches Theater.

I was cast as an officer of the guard in Schiller's *Don Carlos*. It was one of those parts every young actor was given
to show off his stage presence, his elegance in wearing a classical costume, and his ability to recite Schiller's difficult verses.
The officer has a tongue-twisting speech in the fourth act
of the play. It is written in blank verse and must be delivered rapidly, with great emotion:

> "Rebellion! Where's the king?
> Madrid's in arms!
> To thousands swelled, the soldiery and people
> Surround the palace, and reports are spread—

> That Carlos is a prisoner, that his life
> Is threatened. And the mob demand to see
> Him living, or Madrid will be in flames."

I made my entrance as instructed. My costume was beautiful, my excitement touching. "Rebellion!" I shouted. "Where's the king?" And that was all that I remembered. For a second I felt dizzy; the stage, the faces of the actors, the footlights swirled around me; I felt as if I were falling rapidly into a void. Groping instinctively for support, I got hold of some words, formed sentences, and in my confusion plunged into Berlin slang, which was certainly no improvement on Schiller's verse and, to say the least, as bewildering to the assembly of Spanish nobles on stage as to the audience: "Gee, I tell you the people are mad—they got a lot of arms outside, cannons too. Oh, come on, Carlos, get out on that balcony, they want to see you. And if you don't—Oh, everything's just terrible out there. Terrible!"

With that I turned around and made my exit.

No, I did not cover myself with glory at my debut on Reinhardt's stage. I was badly shaken and especially worried about Father's reaction. It was not what I had feared. He who had originally insisted that I should be given some important part immediately, now blamed Reinhardt for assigning "such a difficult role to a mere beginner." Had I been a success, he would certainly have criticized me harshly. But now what I needed most was reassurance, and no one could comfort me as understandingly as Father. Thanks to him, I emerged from this first test scathed but undismayed.

A few weeks later I got a second chance. This time I was cast opposite my father in a biblical legend by Wilhelm Schmidtbonn, *The Prodigal Son*. The play was given in the Kammerspiele, and Max Reinhardt himself directed it.

I felt extremely proud of this new professional relationship with my father. He looked forward to the opening night with an agitation even greater than my own. He had never been so concerned, I am sure, about the reaction of press and public. During the rehearsals he was a changed man. Usually completely immersed in his own role, he was now thinking only of how he could help me, how each scene could be staged so as to show whatever talent I had to its fullest advantage. He wanted to excel in his part, but only to be a more impressive and striking foil for me. Reinhardt was a wonderfully understanding director, but Father was not merely giving me his advice and support—he actually lived my life during those weeks. Every time I stumbled he suffered my pain—and he suffered more than I. In our scenes together he was so preoccupied with my part that his lips formed simultaneously the words I spoke, as if he wanted to transfer to me, by sheer will, all his strength and his talent.

Alas, his efforts were not crowned with the success he had hoped for. The play was warmly received, Father was hailed as usual in the most glowing terms, but I was told that I was not talented enough to play such an important part. The critics implied quite clearly that I was a young man in a hurry, trying to ride to fame on my great father's coattails.

It was a reproach I heard for the first time. I had to hear it often in the next few years.

On the morning after the premiere Father finished reading the reviews at our breakfast table, shrugged his shoulders, and dropped the papers to the floor. "What do they know?" he said disdainfully.

To me the few words were like a knighting. Father believed in me. I would succeed in the end.

2

During the run of this play, at the third or fourth performance, Father's turbulent past caught up with him.

I was in my dressing room, getting ready for my first scene, when an excited stage manager flung the door open. "Where is your father?" he bellowed.

"I don't know. Isn't he in his dressing room?"

"No, he isn't. And curtain call is in ten minutes."

I explained that I had not seen Father since lunch. "Have you tried our home?"

"I just phoned. He is not there. And we have the Crown Prince in the audience tonight. What can possibly have happened to him, for God's sake?"

By now my dressing room was full of people. Actors, stage hands, property men crowded around me, everyone anxious about the missing Rudolf Schildkraut.

Suddenly one of Reinhardt's secretaries pushed through the crowd. "We found him!" he shouted.

"Where? Where is he?"

"In prison."

I looked flabbergasted from one to the other. "In prison? Why?"

As the frantic secretary was finally able to relate, Father had been arrested on his way to the theater. Three years before, the teller of Reinhardt's accounting office had lodged a formal complaint with the police that Father had threatened to kill him because he had refused to give Mr. Schildkraut an advance. An order for Father's arrest had been issued. The man had forgotten to withdraw his suit and the Prussian police in their well-known efficiency had now acted "according to law and regulations."

What were we going to do?

The secretary had an idea: the Crown Prince was a great admirer of Father; his intervention must save the performance! And while he himself rushed out to get in touch with the Crown Prince's adjutant, the stage manager went in front of the curtain to explain the situation to the audience.

The public accepted the news with a burst of laughter. No one wanted to leave; everyone waited anxiously to see what would happen.

In the meantime, Father was in a cell of Berlin's main prison among a bunch of derelicts and drunken bums. No one had told him the reason for his arrest. No one was in-

terested in his entreaties, explanations, and protests. All of
a sudden his cell door was opened and the turnkey, pointing
to him, declared, "The fat one can go home." And not before he arrived at the theater did Father find out the cause
of all this trouble.

The performance started after an hour's delay, but the
public did not mind. They greeted Father's entrance with a
thunderous ovation, a very rare occurrence in the German
theater where applause is expected only at the end of an act.

A large portion of the applause was also intended for the
Crown Prince. Unlike the Kaiser, who preferred light musicals and patriotic melodramas, the heir to the throne was a
constant visitor at the Deutsches Theater and proud of his
friendship with the stars of the artistic world. This, even
more than his dashing appearance in his splendid dolman
and busby, assured his popularity among the upper class as
well as among the workers of Berlin. In Germany before
World War I his interest in the theater was taken as a conclusive proof of his superior intelligence, his liberalism, his
modern spirit, his democratic outlook—when all the young
man really had in mind was to have a good time.

But to find that out the German people had to live
through the horrors of a world war.

3

We spent the summer months of 1914 in Vienna. Father was
starring in a film and I passed my vacation falling in love.
Every few days I met some new girl—or woman—who was
more lovable than the one I was courting. I did not dare
break with the one and I could not let the other go.

We made trips to the nearby mountains and woods, we
drove to little secluded cafés and taverns in Sievering and
Grinzing. Each date demanded elaborate preparations and
was staged with all the trepidations of setting out on a dangerous adventure. Anatol, Julien Sorel, Dmitri Karamazov—
I was each of these heroes in turn, and I acted their romances

in actual life. And the Viennese girls and ladies, whether daughters and wives of aristocrats or shopkeepers, were both willing and gifted partners, firmly believing in the unwritten law of the lovers in prewar Vienna: Why have it simple if you can make it complicated?

How many difficulties we had to overcome: the jealousy of an arrogant husband, the possessiveness of a narrow-minded suitor, the stern rule of old-fashioned parents. Each girl was suppressed, each woman misunderstood, and I her long-awaited liberator and kindred soul. We had to defy the moral order, to hide our passion behind a sophisticated banter, and finally consume it in one of those cozy little apartments, rented by the hour, that were a perfect setting for illicit love. The lady proprietor had the dignity of a duchess and all the discretion of a conspirator in crime.

My "serious" affairs were, as was the custom of those days, with married and much older women of what was called Viennese society. They offered additional problems. One of the most difficult to solve was how to undress these elegantly attired creatures. Their garments, with dozens of buttons and hoops, their corsets, intricate creations of ribbons and laces, demanded from an ardent lover great mechanical dexterity. And they never gave you a helping hand; being respectable ladies, they were not supposed to.

Each of these affairs was full of danger, each caress sweetened with tearful vows of eternal love. And how touching these tears of my paramours were! They made me feel ashamed and unworthy of their great sacrifice and proud of my invincibility: I was Lord Byron, Casanova, and Don Juan, all in one.

At home I was still a teen-ager. Mother would never have believed that I could be involved in more than innocent flirtations, and she looked therefore with indulgence at the continual visits of some *Dienstmann,* bringing billet-doux and invitations to parties, or summoned by me to assist in the execution of my amorous campaigns. Combinations of special messenger, porter, and private secretary, these men in their red caps were important fixtures of Vienna's social life. No love affair was possible without their cooperation. They were wise, cynical, and discreet, masking their insolence with an air of servility. They knew what flowers a certain lady preferred, which tavern in Grinzing served the best heurigen, and what confectioner's shop you should choose to make your meeting with your lady appear strictly accidental. The city had no secrets for them, neither had the human heart. How sad it was that a few short years later this warm, complex relationship was replaced by the cold efficiency of the telephone.

Mother's trust in my innocence received a terrific jolt late one evening when she came up to my room, which was one floor above the apartment of my parents. She found the door locked, and on a chair in the little hall there were a girl's dress and pieces of lingerie. She did not say a word, but picked up all the clothing and threw it out the window into the garden behind our house. Her action was especially cruel since it was raining cats and dogs that night, which was the reason for my sweetheart's staying longer with me than planned. I was soaked through when I retrieved the garments, and my lady love went home in a state of hysteria, shivering in her wet underwear.

The next day Mother acted as if nothing had happened. She did not allude to the incident, nor did she ever tell Father. He was no less determined than Mother to save me from getting involved with "scheming girls" or "dangerous women," but he was much too busy to check on my social activities.

The year before, Father had started to work in films. He was one of the first prominent actors who deigned to descend from the legitimate stage to the low level of this new entertainment, "fit only for the illiterate masses."

The movie theaters of Vienna were primitive halls in ugly office buildings; they smelled of a sweet disinfectant, and the piano player, always hungry-looking and sad, reduced the musical accompaniment to a mechanical strumming. Movies were for teen-agers and lonely women. The few who praised Asta Nielsen, Charlie Chaplin, and Max Linder as serious and great actors were regarded as literary snobs and show-offs.

At first Father had been attracted to the films by his never-ending search for a new source of income. He had not hesitated to act in vaudeville—why not in films? Very soon, however, he found the new medium stimulating and challenging. His enthusiasm proved contagious. The first among his friends to succumb was Felix Salten. He agreed to write an original screenplay for Father. It was *The Shylock of Cracow,* a modern version of Shakespeare's tragedy. The film was produced by the Union Company in Berlin, the predecessor of the world-famous UFA, and met with instantaneous success. Other films followed. From 1913 until our return to America in 1920, Father starred in a dozen films, including *Man and His Demon, The Eighth Commandment, Laugh, Clown, Laugh,* and *The Life of Theodor Herzl* (the founder of Zionism).

From the beginning Father realized that in order to be effective in films he had to adapt his acting style to the new medium. To do that you had to respect it. Whether you acted on the stage of the Deutsches Theater or in vaudeville, whether you were a wandering player, a clown in a circus, or an imperial and royal actor to the emperor, in the end only one thing counted: the sincerity which you put into your characterization. Deprived of speech, you still had your gestures and pantomime to express your emotions: if they were honest and true they had to be convincing. Never believing in style for style's sake, Father approached his film creations with the same realism that guided him on the stage. In contrast to most of the film actors of that period he was rather austere in his acting, shunning exaggeration, always trying to convey a sentiment in the simplest manner, like a sculptor who, working in hard stone, foregoes naturalistic details in the interest of a grand line of design. The result in each case was the emergence of an heroic character, both "true to life" and bigger than life size.

4

Berlin had its Café des Westens and Vienna its Café Central. In its smoke-filled rooms gathered the same kind of people I had met in Berlin, and often they were even the same persons. Yet there was a difference: In the Central the most heated discussion on theater and literature invariably culminated in an even more searching inquiry about who was having an affair with whom.

Also, there were few actors among the habitués of the Central. Only those were welcome who were genuine bohemians or close friends of a writer, painter, or composer. The prominent stars of the "Burg" and the Opera belonged to the upper class in Vienna, and felt closer to the high state officials and noblemen who preferred more dignified cafés and clubs to the back room of the Central.

That back room was strictly for the initiated. Here they sat for hours over a cup of coffee and a glass of water, buried in newspapers from all over the world. The waiters kept bringing more newspapers and every few minutes a fresh glass of water. Everyone knew everyone else. As in a club one went from group to group, conversed from table to table.

One table was an exception, a sort of island. Here Peter Altenberg held court with his faithful admirers.

P.A. was an "original." He wore sandals and no hat, shirts with soft collars, and suits of his own design. He wrote little sketches from daily life in a very personal style; with like passion he preached free love, reform of men's clothing, and a more rational diet. He was always "mortally in love": with the smile of a woman, the legs of a girl, a doll, a little dog. He was a man in his fifties, but with his stubby mustache, his bald crown surrounded by a wreath of sparse hair, he looked much older. Yet this did not disturb the girls who hung around his table like disciples. They wore low-heeled shoes, short hair, and no corsets. Most of them were blond and all were pretty. They were very "modern." I was a little afraid of them.

To Altenberg's circle belonged Karl Kraus, a short, hunchbacked man with extremely expressive hands. His sensitive face was a mask of fanaticism. He was the publisher and editor of a political and literary review. As the most important Austrian satirist of this century, he exerted the same kind of influence on prewar Vienna that H. L. Mencken did on the United States in the twenties.

Then there was Adolf Loos, the apostle of a new style in architecture, characterized by most Viennese as "idiotic": smooth façades, unadorned villas that looked like glass cubes —in a word, insane. Ten years later these "insanities" determined the direction of all modern architecture. Loos was one of the founders of the Wiener Werkstaette (Viennese Workshop), whose aim it was to revive the old Viennese arts and crafts and to do away with *Kitsch*. In Loos's eyes, everything dear to the Viennese middle class was Kitsch, everything that was "sweet," "cozy": bric-a-brac, plush furniture, artificial palms. His closest friend was Oskar Kokoschka, the most modern of Austria's modern painters.

A plump young man with cherubic face and a mane of unruly hair was Franz Werfel, whose successful novels (*The Forty Days of Musa Dagh, The Song of Bernadette*) and widely produced plays (*The Goat Song, Jakobowsky and the Colonel*) later somewhat obscured his great talent as a lyric poet. The poems of his early youth belong to the most beautiful in German literature and mark him as the uncontested master and pacemaker of what became known as Expressionism.

I met all these interesting characters and gifted men in the back room of the Central. There was also Franz Blei, who looked like a French abbé and through his excellent translations probably did more than any other single man to acquaint the German-speaking world with the works of the great French novelists. Egon Friedell, a living encyclopedia and author of important works on the culture and history of western Europe, witty as well as erudite, was twenty years later one of the first to commit suicide when the Nazis came to take him to a concentration camp.

Behind the Central's back room lay the holy of holies: The chess room. Here one went about on tiptoe. No sound could be heard but the tapping of chessmen and from time to time the soft exclamation of a kibitzer.

I knew all the famous players from sight: The melancholy Emanuel Lasker, the phlegmatic Tartakover, and the nervous Russian with the Mephistophelian beard whose real profession was said to be revolutionary journalism and whose name was Leon Trotsky. He was the first to leave Vienna for Switzerland when Austria delivered its famous ultimatum to Serbia. A few months later, when the Austrian cabinet discussed the possibility of a revolution in Russia, Count Leopold von Berchtold, the Imperial Foreign Minister, made the famous remark, "Revolution in Russia? Ridiculous. Who could lead it? Perhaps Trotsky, who spent all his time playing chess here in the Café Central? Nonsense." All the other ministers agreed.

Father was a rare visitor at the Central. He preferred other diversions. When he had a free evening, I had to join him on a culinary expedition. In Vienna a good meal attracted him almost as much as a card game, the races, or an accommodating girl.

In contrast to Hamburg or Berlin, it was not just roast pork that tempted Father to desert Mother's cooking. There were many restaurants that served Father's favorite dishes. Much as he liked Berlin, he never forgave it the weak coffee and the mortal sin of pouring gravy on a Schnitzel. In Vienna, coffee-drinking was a veritable ritual; one could order coffee in a dozen different styles and shades, with or without whipped cream, in a glass or in a cup. Schnitzel, Backhuhn (breaded chicken), and boiled beef were "as good as at home" —you could not give higher praise.

The mecca of our excursions, however, was some kosher restaurant in the Jewish district of the city. Wandering through the narrow and filthy side streets of the Praterstrasse, one had the feeling of being in a Polish ghetto. On the Lower East Side of New York the Jewish immigrants, though adhering to their customs and religious beliefs, made a definite effort to dress like Americans. Here in the Leopoldstadt most of the men still wore long kaftans, broad-brimmed black velvet hats, beards, and earlocks. It was like a scene from one of the Yiddish plays in which Father had played in New York.

As I remember, our first visit to the most famous of these kosher restaurants was not a success. As soon as we sat down, Father ordered his favorite *Sholet*. This was a dish made of beans and barley in a thick gravy, kept for twenty-four hours in the oven, and served with pot roast or chicken.

"No more Sholet," the waiter explained.

"No more Sholet?" It was like the cry of a wounded animal.

"No. Sorry."

"Let's go, Joseph. If I cannot have Sholet, I don't want to eat at all."

We had reached the door when Father suddenly stopped as if struck by an important thought and returned to the startled waiter. "Tell me," he said in a tone of a mourner who wanted to inquire about the last hours of a dear departed friend, "tell me, the Sholet, was it fat?"

5

I was with my parents in a charming sidewalk café in the outskirts of Vienna, enjoying a Sunday afternoon Jause, when I first heard the cry "*Extraausgabe*" (special edition) echo through the crooked and sleepy streets.

It was a glorious day in July. The air was balmy and fragrant, the sky above the old lime trees a cloudless, intense blue. From where we sat we had a commanding view of the Schönbrunn, the emperor's castle; its noble yellow façade gleamed in the afternoon sun. Behind it on a hill rose the Greek pavilion of the Gloriette like a little poem in marble. The peace, the beauty of this sight made your heart ache.

A small orchestra was playing a medley of Schubert melodies. Suddenly the music broke off and intoned the Austrian national anthem. People jumped up, glass and chinaware cracked and crashed. Boys came running up to our terrace, distributing a single sheet of a newspaper, the print still wet and smelling badly. "War!" the headline screamed.

In the next four years I was to hear that dreadful cry over and over again: *EXTRAAUSGABE!* The headlines announced ever greater victories, the annihilation of Serbian, Russian, French, British armies. But from victory to victory the misery grew, the faces of the readers became more pinched and sallow with hunger, the newsboys turned into tattered and torn orphans—and always the same piercing cry and the same bad smell of fresh newsprint.

I had been so immersed in my personal problems during the previous weeks that I had hardly noticed the mounting political crisis. The Balkans were far away, Serbia was "a little nation of swineherds"; even the Austrian ultimatum and the saber-rattling of the German Kaiser did not spoil my amorous play.

"It's good we'll clean up that mess once and for all!" I said in an outburst of youthful patriotic fever. "At least we'll be through with it fast."

Father was shocked and called me an idiot. Mother was worried. He went into a long dissertation on the dangers of the future and the problems of international politics; she wanted to know how to meet the problems of tomorrow, whether the banks might not be closed and what would happen to the film in which Father was currently working. In the end he might not even get paid. She always expected the worst.

Work on the film was stopped the next day, the studio was closed, and Father did *not* get paid. We returned to Berlin. It took us about a week to reach the German capital. Military transports had priority and were blocking the tracks. Our train stood for days on a siding somewhere in the country; we had no food, there was no water. We arrived in Berlin completely exhausted. By now Mother's pessimism had affected Father's spirit. I was too excited about this strange adventure "war" to really suffer from the discomfort. Would I too have to enter the Army? The thought gave me a pleasantly creepy feeling.

All the theaters in Berlin were closed, but in a short time the government ordered that they open again. Would there be an audience? Every family had a son or husband in uniform, millions of them hourly facing death; who could possibly be willing to buy a ticket to the theater? Contrary to our expectations, the public came; in fact, the theaters played to capacity, and experienced a boom as never before.

To be sure, the quality of the theater declined lamentably, especially during the first year of the war. The great British, Russian, French, and Italian authors and composers were banned. Obnoxious ultra-patriotic melodramas glorifying war and the Kaiser, and cheap farces designed to bolster the domestic morale by caricaturing and deriding the enemy, dominated the repertory. Even some of the leading German writers succumbed to the hysteria, and even Reinhardt cooperated by producing some of these questionable concoctions. Very soon, however, a change took place. Most of the contemporary writers were unable to create during this hellish period of war, hence the producers turned once more to the classics. They proved as timely as ever—if not more so.

Food and clothing were scarce, and so were the canvas, wood, and paint needed to build scenery. The material difficulties imposed a new style on the scenic designer and director, and gave birth to the *Illusionsbühne* (illusion stage): lights, a few structural pieces, platforms and steps, and black burlap curtains replaced the lavish sets, the expensive costumes. And Shakespeare and Goethe emerged even more real than in the most realistic productions of the naturalistic era.

The new style in direction and scenic design antedated the expressionistic works that came after the war. By that time the dramatists found a framework ready for their ideas; it influenced and impregnated their inspiration and writing.

My induction into the Austrian Army was repeatedly deferred and I continued to work, first at the Deutsches Theater, and then at the Lessing Theater, which was under the administration of Victor Barnovsky. Here I met the man who more than anyone else, including my father, had the greatest influence on my acting style and technique. That man was Albert Bassermann, "the last gentleman of the German stage," as Father always called him.

Bassermann was of imposing stature, tall and lean, not handsome in the usual sense but a striking personality. His body was like a Toledo blade. He walked like a dancer, and his innate elegance stood him in good stead in classical dramas as well as in drawing-room comedies. Very versatile, he was at home in both. His husky voice had a pronounced Swabian tinge, which added a distinctly individual flavor to his speech.

Father never instructed me in my parts. He was afraid, I assume, of involuntarily forcing me to copy him. Bassermann had no such qualms, probably because his whole approach to acting was basically different from Father's. He was all brain, first and last a marvelously skilled craftsman of the stage. His theory was that when you read a play for the first time you had to see and feel your part completely, not just in its outlines. Afterward you worked out patiently and coldly the technical details of how to recreate the emotions you had originally felt. On stage you must never be governed by your own feelings, never lose control of yourself, never completely submerge in the character you act; he must remain a creation apart from you. Bassermann calculated carefully and fixed in his mind every pause and inflection before appearing for the first rehearsal of a play.

Once during a performance of Goethe's *Egmont*, when the tenseness of the dungeon scene was interrupted by the loud sobs of the audience, he turned to me and said under his breath, "They'll have high laundry bills, listen to them blowing their noses," and immediately continued with his emotional speech, seemingly completely carried away by it. And near the end of the scene, before my exit he turned aside and said softly, "Call up my wife and tell her I'll be half an hour late for supper." In the next second he faced the audience and was again a heroic and magnificent Egmont, in bearing, speech, and gesture every inch a Flemish nobleman.

Bassermann first became interested in me when he found out about my musical background and my love for the violin. He himself was an excellent cellist. We often played chamber music in his villa in the Grunewald—Albert, his wife Elsa, and I. He considered me, he said, "a very talented young actor who lacked technical know-how and polish." He decided to help me.

He insisted that I play Ragnar opposite him in Ibsen's *Master Builder*, as well as the young Duke of Alba in *Egmont*. That was one of the outstanding productions of the war years, with a sixty-man orchestra playing Beethoven's overture and incidental music.

Then Franz Werfel adapted Ibsen's rarely played *Emperor and Galilean*. He compressed its two parts into one, so that it could be presented in one theater evening. Even so the play lasted for nearly six hours. But the Berlin public was used to such marathon productions. Reinhardt's presentation of *Don Carlos* took over five hours, and his version of Goethe's *Faust, Second Part,* nearly nine.

In 1916 I was called into the Austrian Army. I left Berlin

and went to Vienna for my induction. But my military service was of short duration.

One day I ran into a good friend and colleague, Fritz Kortner, who was just emerging as one of the most promising and original actors of the new generation. After the war he became an outstanding exponent of the expressionistic school. In the twenties many of his creations in modern and classical plays made theatrical history.

When I met Kortner on the Ring he was working at the Volksbühne (People's Stage), a kind of avant-garde theater that specialized in plays of contemporary young writers and in experimental productions of the classics. Kortner with his usual determination decided that I could do better than guard some barracks or depot; I would not change the course of the war one way or the other, anyhow. He felt the Volksbühne could gain by my services and convinced the manager and director Arthur Rundt to ask for my exemption. It was granted.

At last I was no longer merely the son of my famous father. In Berlin, even in my successful roles, I had never been able to make the audience and the critics forget this relationship.

The newly won independence must have been one of the reasons for my sudden decision to get married. I had been in love so often and so continuously that I felt it was time for a change. Sylvia was a very young and beautiful actress. She looked like an Arabian princess, and, in fact, played the part of one in a fairy play, *Aladdin and the Wonderful Lamp*, when I first saw her. She came from a very respectable family. This was not just another affair; this was "serious."

We became secretly engaged and then decided to let the whole world know about our happiness. I had an announcement card beautifully engraved. The first one I sent to my parents.

A few days later Father arrived at my dressing room during intermission. I didn't know he had been in the audience.

He looked me over and before I could greet him said very quietly, "And your tie I don't like either." It was the most devastating criticism I have ever heard from Father about a performance of mine.

He then declared that I was not going to marry Sylvia. "You are not even twenty-one. We have enough heartaches and troubles with this damned war. You don't need to make your life and mine still more complicated and miserable."

I could not argue; the intermission was over, and I had to go on stage.

Father, as I found out a few hours later, did not return to the audience. He went to my apartment, collected all the intimate objects that Sylvia had left there—some lingerie, her nightshirt and pajamas, stockings and toilet articles—no, he did not throw them out the window, as Mother had done in a similar case, but wrapped them all up carefully and had the package delivered that same night to Sylvia's parents with a simple note: "I think your daughter forgot these in my son's apartment."

The shock of Sylvia's parents was as great as Father expected. They forbade her ever to see me again. Sylvia was outraged and held me responsible for Father's action. My manly vanity was deeply hurt. I fumed and vowed I would never give in, but in my heart I knew Father was right. I was so young, and marriage would mean settling down, renouncing the free, adventurous life I enjoyed so much. Probably I had already doubted the wisdom of our engagement, but I was too proud to turn back once we had made that decision. In any case, the opposition of both families was too great a strain for our love. Our engagement was broken. We parted.

6

The opening weeks of the season of 1918 brought me three big successes in a row. There was the world premiere of Stefan Zweig's *Jeremiah,* a new play by Georg Kaiser, *The*

Coral, and *Shadow's Dance,* the drama of a musical child prodigy. I received glowing reviews, and was hailed as a discovery.

And then the curtain fell—not merely on the play in which I was appearing but on my whole world, the world I had been brought up in. The Austro-Hungarian Empire was no more.

The death of the monarchy was not a pretty sight. It was not even tragic or heroic, just ugly and sad.

The war had lasted for so long, its imminent end had been predicted so often, that people came to believe it would go on forever. Nothing is definite except the provisional, was a favorite Viennese saying. Everyone realized that the Hapsburg empire suffered from an incurable disease, and still no one was actually prepared for its death.

The revolution was no more a revolution than the new Austria was a nation. The monarchy had simply fallen apart. Czechs, Poles, Hungarians proclaimed their independence. Italians and Serbs, Croats and Slovaks joined their brother nations, and the German-speaking Austrians stood alone and forsaken amid the ruins of a thousand-year-old empire. They had retained a little country with six million inhabitants, a lovely little country with beautiful mountains and lakes, a tiny industrial section, and a modest agriculture which could nourish not more than a fraction of the population. They had kept Vienna, a city which for centuries had been the administrative and cultural center of an immense empire, the commercial hub of southeastern Europe. Now the city, with its two million people, sat like a head bloated with dropsy on the bloodless, deformed body of a dwarf.

The storekeepers on the Graben took down their signs, "Purveyor to the Imperial and Royal Court." The black and yellow flag was removed from public buildings, and the new red-white-red flag was hoisted. This was called "revolution."

The months that followed were like a single week, and the nights were powerless to absorb the noise and the feverish haste of the day. There were throngs at every street corner, red flags, meetings, demonstrations. Worker councils took over our theater. They were radical but they were also Viennese. They hailed the dictatorship of the proletariat, but they never forgot to address everyone by his proper title, and according to the tip you gave you were called "doctor," "baron," or "count" even if you were nothing of the kind. And there was no question that actors must continue their careers undisturbed. Vienna could do without bread and milk but not without the opera and the theater.

Revolution? Yes. But in the Prater and Stadtpark music and dancing went on. On the Ring invalids in their tattered uniforms shuffled along hopelessly, while ladies promenaded in fine dresses. Professors, high state officials, the middle-class intelligentsia, flocked to the pawnshops and sold the jewels, silverware, china, and furniture inherited from their ancestors. Since the value of the krone declined rapidly, farmers stopped delivering their produce to the city, and profiteers and smugglers were the new ruling class.

Vienna took all this in its stride. It suffered from hunger, it shivered with cold, it sank every day a little deeper into an evil morass of misery and hopelessness, while the newsboys shouted, "*Extraausgabe!* Bloody street battles in Berlin! Red terror in Munich!" In Germany revolution was surely something different.

The Café Central, where Peter Altenberg had once preached love and Adolf Loos the new architecture, was now a headquarters of the radicals. They fought for futurism and proletarian art.

Many who returned from the battlefield had lost there a leg or their eyes, many more their faith. Expressionism was born in the trenches. It was born of human suffering and of our impotence to prevent it. It was a cry of despair.

Naturalism had substituted scientific knowledge for mysticism, statistics for visions—but knowledge had been powerless to prevent the mass slaughter; and the truth which the naturalistic poets and playwrights had taken as their highest law turned out to be madness. Amid the roaring guns the writers had lost the power of speech. They could only stammer and scream. That was the new style of the postwar drama.

In Vienna it could not supplant the popular plays of yesteryear. Father came as a guest star to the Deutsches Volkstheater and, revolution or no revolution, played *The Merchant of Venice, King Lear, The Kreutzer Sonata.* I was in the cast of each of these plays.

Albert Bassermann followed Father and we played together Ibsen's *A Doll's House* and *The Wild Duck.* The Noras and Helgas, the Helmars and Ekdals and Gregor Werles of Vienna had long ago shed their inhibitions and moral principles, and love had become a round game with everyone cheating everyone else. That, however, did not detract from the impact of the old masters on our audiences. They clung to the illusions which the theater supplied and which seemed much more real than the nightmarish reality. During the two years of my engagement at the Deutsches Volkstheater from 1918 to 1920, I played no less than a hundred and twenty-odd parts, classical as well as modern. No dramatic school can give a young actor this kind of training and experience. It is one of the major assets of the European repertory theater.

Whereas Vienna, in spite of the revolution, freed itself only slowly and gradually from the traditions of the past, clinging to the old repertory and frowning upon modern experiments in direction and stage design, the theater in Berlin changed with the times. New directors, Leopold Jessner, the head of the Staatstheater (State Theater), and Erwin Piscator "revolutionized" the classics. Jessner turned *William Tell* into a fanfare of rebellion and *King Richard III* into a modern study in morbid psychology. Piscator unfurled the banner of a "political theater," declaring war on "art for art's sake." They were very interesting experiments. In the next two decades they greatly influenced the drama, the scenic design, the style of playwrights, novelists, directors, and actors in Europe and America.

Neither Father nor I found an inner relationship to this new theater. We both worked steadily, but life became more and more difficult and frustrating.

In the fall of 1920 when the four horsemen of the Apocalypse galloping over Germany were reinforced by a fifth—inflation—Father received another offer from the United States. Maurice Schwartz, manager and director of the Jewish Art Theatre in New York, offered him a forty-week engagement. He guaranteed five performances weekly at $250 a performance, plus ten per cent of the weekly gross receipts exceeding $15,000. Schwartz was willing to arrange and pay for Father's transportation.

Father immediately accepted on condition that Mother and I accompany him, and that our visas and transportation would also be provided. He would not come alone. Schwartz agreed.

Once more we left for New York. This time, however, I was sure that in five months I would be back in Vienna. I took merely a leave of absence for one season from the Deutches Volkstheater, where I was under a long-term contract. In my luggage were the various parts I was to study, so as to be ready to resume my work at my return.

Chapter IX

1

I<small>T WAS LIKE</small> stepping from a dark and dingy room into the splendor of a ballroom, ablaze with light, swarming with a gay and carefree crowd. The lights were dazzling; for a while everything seemed to swim before your eyes, and you did not know where to turn. Such was New York after the misery of Vienna.

Never before had I felt the impact of New York so strongly: its bigness, its wealth, its vitality, its comforts.

At the same time I could not get rid of a vague feeling of remorse. I would not have been able to put it into words, and I was actually not conscious of it; it was a fleeting sensation like a throbbing tooth: it didn't really hurt but it bothered me. How easy and rewarding life was here and how difficult and drab over there. What the people of New York considered mere necessities of life, my friends in Vienna would have looked upon as fantastic luxuries. I had a bad conscience when I thought of the colleagues I had left behind, shivering in unheated theaters, chasing for hours after a cup of "real" coffee or a pound of sugar. From the distance and the security of rich New York I felt a new kind of sympathy for poor Vienna.

But this sentimental feeling did not last long. New York overwhelmed me and in a few weeks Vienna was no more than a vague memory. The thought of going back seemed more and more incongruous.

Maurice Schwartz had rented two apartments for us on 27th Street, right opposite the old Madison Square Garden. One was for my parents, the other, a smaller one on the floor above, was mine.

The Jewish Art Theatre was the former Garden Theatre in Madison Square, which had been famous for David Belasco's productions. Here he had presented *Zaza* with Leslie Carter, an American actress of great popularity.

Schwartz had brought his troop uptown from the Lower East Side and installed it close to the center of the theater district. In the ten years since our last visit the Yiddish theater had come of age. It had lost much of its wildness and exotic exuberance. A new generation had come along, the young people tending to free themselves from the life and customs of their fathers; movies and Broadway lured them away. The Yiddish theater tried to hold them by offering a lighter fare, mixing English into the Yiddish dialogue to make the plays and operettas more easily understandable to second-generation Americans.

The new actors and playwrights, too, were more interested in America's future than in the Jewish past, more concerned with artistic problems and theatrical style than with the preservation of ancient traditions. Whenever Yiddish authors looked back on the history of their ancestors, it was to tap Jewish folklore as an inspiration for modern parables.

The repertory of Schwartz's Art Theatre reflected these trends. He presented on the one hand Shaw and Strindberg, Wedekind and Schnitzler, and on the other hand dramatizations of stories by I. L. Peretz and Sholem Aleichem, plays by David Pinski and Ossip Dymov. A very gifted director and actor—especially effective as a comedian—he had gathered around him a group of talented young men and women who a few years later gained important places on the Broadway stage: Jack and Luther Adler, Jacob Ben-Ami, Paul Muni, Celia Adler, Mollie Picon, and many more.

Father opened in a new play by the French dramatist Henri Bataille, *Les affaires sont les affaires* (*Business Is Business*). It had been a vehicle for famous actors in many European countries. Lucien Guitry had played it in France, Emil Jannings in Germany, Bowmeester in Holland. It had the same success in Yiddish, and the response of press and public to Father's performance was as enthusiastic as ever.

One evening I was in the audience, standing in the rear of the theater, when a gentleman tapped me on the shoulder. "Aren't you Schildkraut's son?" he whispered.

I nodded.

Presently the curtain fell and the stranger introduced himself: "Kenneth Macgowan."

The name meant nothing to me.

"You're an actor yourself?" he said.

"How do you know?"

"I saw you a few months ago in Vienna in several plays at the Deutsches Volkstheater. I liked particularly your Cassio in *Othello*."

I bowed and thanked him for the compliment.

"Would you like to play in English on Broadway?"

I looked at him stupefied. Would I? "Certainly!" I almost shouted it. And then I explained that I had been in the United States before, that I had graduated from the Academy of Dramatic Arts.

"Splendid," Macgowan said. "I am the drama critic of the *Globe* and on the advisory board of a new and interesting dramatic group. They call themselves the Theatre Guild and have quite a few successful productions to their credit. Would you like to meet them?"

There and then we made a luncheon appointment at the
Harvard Club for the following day.

After lunch Macgowan took me to the Garrick Theatre on
West 35th Street. Otto H. Kahn, the noted banker and art
Maecenas, had turned this theater over to the Guild; he was
sure they would never be able to pay him a cent for rent. But
he was wrong. For the first time in American theater history
the Guild had succeeded in organizing a loyal following of
subscribers by offering them six new plays each season. It was
a hard struggle, the actors, managers, and directors were far
from becoming rich, but the Theatre Guild had already survived a difficult three years and gained a firm foothold on
the American scene. And that was all the more surprising
since the guiding spirits of this enterprise were anything but
professionals.

I met all six of them: Lawrence Langner, a patent lawyer
by profession who had conceived the idea of this venture;
Theresa Helburn, a writer turned dramaturgical adviser;
Lee Simonson, a very gifted painter who had taken up scenic
design by accident, as it were; Philip Moeller, a writer of
talent who later became a successful stage director; Maurice
Wertheim, a banker; and the excellent actress Helen Westley.

The introductions were made and Macgowan went into a
graphic—and most flattering—description of the performances he had seen me give in Vienna. His report visibly impressed the board. My appearance and bearing—I was rather
good-looking in those days—enhanced their interest.

"What would you like to play?" Langner finally asked.
"Have you any particular play in mind?"

"Yes," I answered, without hesitating for a moment.
"*Liliom* by Ferenc Molnar."

None of them had ever heard of this work, which was not
surprising. It was the only play by the distinguished Hungarian dramatist that was a complete failure when first produced in Budapest in 1909. Later it was revived and fared a

little better. But it had never achieved the success of the other Molnar plays, except in Vienna, where it had been produced during the war by an excellent actor, Joseph Jarno, with his actress-wife Hansi Niese in the part of Julie. Both enjoyed great popularity in Vienna; "the Niese" was much beloved and admired as a natural and earthy comedienne. They won for the play a permanent place in the repertory of the Viennese theater. The other cities, including Berlin, reacted to *Liliom* in a rather lukewarm way.

Inquiries by the Guild brought forth the information that several American producers had at one time or another taken an option on Molnar's play, only to drop it as too big a risk. At that particular moment Arthur Hopkins was interested in it; he had planned a production with John Barrymore in the role of Liliom. But when Theresa Helburn approached him, Hopkins gave up the rights gladly. "I don't think the public will go for it," he said.

In all of New York there was only one copy of *Liliom* available, and that was in German. Therefore it was decided that Lee Simonson and another board member of the Guild, who both knew German very well, should meet with me at Simonson's place in Long Island. There I would read the play to them and they would give the other members of the board a report on their impression.

The reading lasted late into the night; I barely made the last train back to New York. I must have been quite successful in impersonating the various characters and in bringing Molnar's script to life, for a few days later the Guild called me to discuss the terms of my contract. Just on the strength of Simonson's report, without even waiting to read the play in an English translation, the board decided to produce it. They offered me a long-term contract at a weekly salary of $250.

The late Benjamin F. Glazer, at that time connected with a literary agency, had lent me the German copy of *Liliom* for my reading. I had promised him that if something came of it, I would suggest that he be asked to translate the play. I kept my promise, and he was engaged for the job. It led him into a very successful career as a translator of plays, and in quick succession he became a playwright, film scenarist, and finally one of the top motion-picture producers in Hollywood. He passed away a few years ago, a fine and kind man. That copy of *Liliom* brought us together and was the first link in our lifelong friendship.

When I told Father that I was going to play *Liliom* in English, he looked at Mother in dismay and said sadly, "Erna, we have a crazy child. A Hungarian barker of a merry-go-round who kills himself in the middle of the play and then goes to an imaginary police station in heaven and returns to earth again—that stuff he wants to play for an American audience. A crazy child we have."

But I was so sure of myself that even Father's sarcasm could not shake my confidence.

Since my conversational English was quite rusty, the Guild thought I would prefer a director with whom I could, if necessary, discuss matters in German, and they brought Frank Reicher from Hollywood. The gifted son of the well-known German actor Emanuel Reicher, Frank had been in America since his early youth, had won recognition as an actor on the legitimate stage, and was at that time a successful film director. Lee Simonson designed the excellent—by now historic—sets.

The casting of the part of Julie presented a special problem. The Theatre Guild had a number of actresses in mind, but I insisted that there was only one girl right for that part. I wanted to play with no one else. I had seen her a few months before at the Booth Theatre in a light comedy by Arthur Richman. She was beautiful, and I was impressed by her great sensitivity and the honesty of her acting. She had a strange French name: Eva Le Gallienne. The Guild bowed to my wish.

Eva herself told the story of how she came to play Julie in her autobiography *At 33:*[*]

I had met Joseph Schildkraut for the first time while playing *Not So Long Ago*. After a matinee he had rushed backstage in his usual whirlwind fashion, and had almost bowled me over with his enthusiasm over my work, which was expressed with all that colossal vitality of which he is the enviable possessor. It had apparently not been idle praise, for here he was insisting that I play opposite him in *Liliom,* and would hear of nothing else. I asked to read the manuscript and walked home with it under my arm.

I knew nothing about the play except that it was translated from the Hungarian and the name of the author was Molnar. I was surprised on opening the manuscript that the name of the part was Julie. For a few years before a director had given me a play entitled *The Daisy,* translated from the Hungarian by an Englishman. The setting of the play had been transferred to London and the characters were mostly cockney. I was fascinated by the play. The part of Julie cast a spell over me, and I longed to have the chance of playing her. It was a type of play far superior to anything I had hitherto worked on; one might almost call it a great play. Everything was arranged for the production and then the project fell through, for financial reasons, I believe. To everyone's sorrow *The Daisy* was abandoned. It was a sad blow; apart from the practical end of things, it was the first play I had been connected with that had interested me deeply from an artistic angle.

And now I found again a part with the name of Julie. I thought it merely a coincidence until I started to read the play. Was it possible? I thought I had taken leave of my senses! But no—it was true! The play was *The Daisy* and Julie was *my* Julie, to whom I had bade a sorrowful farewell four years before. This was a different adaptation, keeping close to the original in title and locale. Of course there was no doubt in my mind that I must play it. The next morning I started rehearsals at the Garrick Theatre.

[*] New York: Longmans, Green, 1934.

We were to open around the middle of April. However, the day before the premiere it looked as if we would not open at all. For the dress rehearsal was sheer catastrophe.

It so happened that the red and white candy-striped sweater I wore as Liliom was not yet ready and I had to play my part in a conventional Arrow shirt. As insignificant as that change in my apparel may seem, it was enough to ruin my performance. I simply could not get the right feeling for the character. I knew I was terrible and my helplessness affected the other actors.

After the last curtain Theresa Helburn, who was the executive secretary of the Guild, came into my dressing room. She was terribly upset and, trying to appear calm, she spoke with a forced flippancy. "Mr. Schildkraut, you are lousy, the play is lousy, nobody out front, none of the invited guests likes it— let's terminate our contract and not open tomorrow night. Just let's forget about this play, it's not for America."

I felt completely crushed. I just stared at her. I did not know what to say.

Fortunately, at that moment Father came in. I had seldom seen him as pleased and confident. He offered Miss Helburn his charming, mischievous smile like a soothing candy. "I know why everything went wrong tonight," he said. "That's just the traditional bad dress rehearsal. Tomorrow, I'm sure, everything will be all right. We will open as planned. But you have my word, Miss Helburn, if the play or my son fails you will not have to pay him one cent of his salary and you can tear up the long-term contract you gave him."

Then he put his arm around my shoulder and hugged me. "Don't worry, Pepi," he said. "You win, and I was wrong. It's a fine play and you'll be really good—it's the best you have ever done. And you know it." He gripped my arms and shook me. "Don't you? Don't you?"

"Yes, Father," I stammered. All of a sudden my doubts seemed petty, my apprehension, my fear was gone. "Don't worry," I said.

Now we both laughed.

The opening night of *Liliom* made theatrical history. The reaction of the audience was extraordinary. They screamed, they yelled, they whistled, they jumped upon their seats, they would not leave the theater.

After the performance we went to Child's at the corner of 33rd Street and waited for the notices—Father, Mother, various relatives on my mother's side from Brooklyn, and Cynthia, the English teacher of my youth.

I felt exhausted, completely spent. The crowd, my parents and relatives, seemed strangely unreal. Was that elderly lady across the table really the Cynthia I had loved so passionately? Here I was drinking coffee, talking, laughing, but in fact I was somewhere else, far away. While Mother, all excited, was stuffing me with sandwiches and pies, one single question was running through my head like a nagging refrain: What will the critics say?

At last the morning papers arrived. I was afraid to open them.

Father handed them to Cynthia. "Now let's hear the verdict," he said with a broad grin. Then he settled himself comfortably in his chair, squeezed my hand, and did not let it go while Cynthia read the reviews aloud.

They reflected the reaction of the public. Just one quote from Alexander Woollcott's review in the *Times:* "When something like this happens in the American theater, all we critics can do is to sit back in awed silence and reverently raise our hats."

Overnight Eva Le Gallienne and I were stars. When we came to the Garrick the next evening, the workers had put up our names in electric lights. We stood hand in hand in front of the theater, like children staring at a Christmas tree.

There were some excellent performances in that *Liliom* production. Hortense Alden was an unforgettable Marie. And never have I seen Mrs. Muskat, Wolf Berkowitz, and

"The Sparrow" played better and more convincingly than by Helen Westley, Henry Travers, and Dudley Digges.

Yet *Liliom* was more than a hit, notable not merely for its fine production and the good performance of many actors. At a time when the New York stage was dominated by frothy and superficial melodramas and nonsensical cheap musicals—*Up in Mabel's Room, Tickle Me, Ladies Night in a Turkish Bath*—*Liliom* exploded with the force of a bombshell. It brought a new spirit, artistic integrity, the force of real drama, to Broadway.

And it started a trend. Breaking as it did with the traditional form of the three- or four-act drama, written in a prologue and seven loose scenes *Liliom* set a pattern and used a technique that was to inspire many of the rising playwrights of the new generation.

2

A few weeks after the opening night I was approached by an agent. Would I be interested in playing an important part in a film? When I pointed out that I could not leave *Liliom* to go to Hollywood, he explained that the film would be made nearby, in a studio at Mamaroneck on Long Island, and that it would not interfere with the theater.

A film company with studios in Long Island? I was sure it would be a minor one, amateurs probably, and was ready to refuse when the agent informed me that the great D. W. Griffith was producing and directing the film and wanted me for a leading part. The picture was *Orphans of the Storm*. Lillian and Dorothy Gish were the orphans and the storm was the French Revolution. Griffith had me in mind for the part of the Chevalier de Vaudry, a nobleman at the Court of Louis XVI.

Of course I was most eager to work with Griffith. I had seen some of his extraordinary films, which were rightly regarded as new and startling forays into the realm of a new art, such as *Broken Blossoms, Way Down East,* and *Birth of a Nation,* and I was greatly impressed by his work. He made a screen test with me which turned out to his satisfaction, and I was engaged.

This was my first American motion picture and my longest film engagement—it lasted eighteen months. I saw the seasons come and go, come and go. I worked every day, except Wednesday and Saturday when I had to appear at the matinees of *Liliom.*

The film was a landmark in the development of the cinematographic art. The heartbreaking plight of two little girls, the sordidness and squalor of the slums of Paris, contrasted with the splendor of Versailles, with Danton, Robespierre, and Louis XVI, the upsurge of the desperate masses, directed with all the mastery Griffith could command—*Orphans of the Storm* had really everything the public could wish: color, passion, a stunning historical panorama bursting with life.

What impressed me most was Griffith's sense of pictorial rhythm, his simple, untheatrical, and human approach. The love scenes he directed with great delicacy but also with honest realism. He had an invaluable support in his cameraman, the unforgettable Billy Bitzer. Today it is difficult to realize how revolutionary Griffith's invention of the medium shot and the close-up was. Actually, it established the film as an independent art form, giving each scene a new dimension and depth. Film ceased to be photographed theater.

A fanatical perfectionist, Griffith was at the same time one of the most patient directors I have ever worked with. There were scenes between Lillian Gish and me on which we worked for six weeks at a stretch before he was satisfied. And he never lost his temper; in all those eighteen months he did not raise his voice once. Tall, lean, kind, soft-spoken, Griffith was the typical Southern gentleman, so different from the flamboyant and extravagant directors whose showmanship was a trademark of Hollywood. He was a genius without ever attempting to prove it—except in his work.

Orphans of the Storm was a huge success. Lillian Gish, a lovely elfin creature and an enchanting actress, conquered the hearts of the public everywhere. My performance was singled out for special praise. Soon I came to regret it.

The publicity department of Griffith's company thought to enhance my popularity by billing me in newspapers and posters as "the handsomest man of Europe." The slogan proved to be very harmful to my career. It had taken me years to make the audiences in Europe forget that I was the son of a famous father; it took me years in America to live down the notion that I was nothing but a very handsome young man who owed his success not to his acting ability but merely to his physical endowments.

The New York public could see me both at the Fulton Theatre, where we had moved from the downtown Garrick, and at the Apollo Theatre, where the film was shown, and it had an opportunity to realize the range of my abilities. But the rest of the country, where I became known for the first time as a rococo lover with a white court wig and beauty patches on my powdered face, fell for the campaign of Griffith's publicity agent. Hollywood producers, too, came to believe this horrible advertisement. I had become a "type," labeled as "the handsome and effete juvenile." For three years Hollywood had no further use for me.

3

After a long run at the Fulton, *Liliom* had moved to the old 44th Street Theatre.

One evening during intermission the stage doorman brought me a note from my friend, the well-known producer Archibald Selwyn. He wrote in behalf of a young actress, praising her highly for her good looks and her talent. She had appeared in a number of plays under his management, and Archie asked as a personal favor that I audition the girl for the part of Solveig in the Theatre Guild's forthcoming

production of *Peer Gynt*. The play was scheduled for the
next season.

I told the doorman I could not see the young lady since
the intermission was too short for a serious talk. I suggested
that she come back after the performance.

I had taken off my make-up and was changing from the
barker's costume into my own suit when there was a knock
at the door and my dresser announced Miss Elise Bartlett. I
had already completely forgotten the appointment. My life
at that time was marked by the constant entrances and exits
of pretty women, and I was not too eager to meet another
one, not that evening. However, I could not refuse my friend
a favor. Wearily I told the dresser to show the lady in.

She was beautiful. The pallor of her small face was heightened by her Titian-red hair; her features were as delicately
chiseled as in a cameo; her green eyes had the cold fire of
perfectly cut emeralds. It was the face of an exotic idol. I immediately noticed her exquisite and expressive hands. She
was slim but her figure had not the boyish look that was the
rage of those days. She had the deliberate poise of a mature
woman. Botticelli would have loved to paint her. She moved
with grace and walked in a cloud of "Narcisse Noir." I was
stunned.

"Good evening," she said. Her voice was soft and husky.

"Good evening."

I was conscious of my embarrassment and chagrined at be-
having like a tongue-tied adolescent. Or was it her mocking
smile? Haughtily I said, "I will be very happy to audition
you for the part of Solveig."

"Thank you, Mr. Schildkraut."

I bowed slightly.

"And when will that be?" she asked.

"Tonight."

"Oh!" For a moment she had lost her air of superiority.
She looked bewildered. "Where? I mean—now? On this
stage?"

"No. In my apartment."

She threw her head back and laughed, again in control of the situation. "So, you're really as crazy as people have told me?"

Her laughter goaded me on. "Crazy or not—you will audition for me tonight at my apartment, or not at all."

She had stopped laughing. But otherwise her face showed no expression.

"To put your mind at ease," I snapped, "I have no intention of raping you. You are not my type, anyhow. I don't go for snobs."

The mocking smile lighted her face again. "All right, let's go."

Was it to appear eccentric, to impress her with my originality? Instead of taking a taxi, I hailed a hansom cab and ordered the coachman to drive us to my apartment on 27th Street.

While the cab rumbled down Broadway we spoke very little. She was in every way the well-bred conventional young lady, and I tried to hide my antipathy behind formal conversation. The conversation dragged and finally stopped.

Forgetting my manners, I had not asked her to have supper with me, and now I was annoyed at myself for this negligence. "Are you hungry?" I threw the question at her as if I were still on stage acting Liliom.

She did not mind my rudeness. "And how!" she said simply, with the same inscrutable smile.

"Well, then, let's grab a couple of hot dogs over there at the hamburger stand and take them home. Oh—but say, can you cook? I mean, can you make a cup of tea?"

"Yes. I think I can manage that."

"Fine."

I stopped the cab and bought the hot dogs. A few minutes later we were home.

We settled in my library, she made tea, I served the hot dogs, we began to chat. Gradually our conversation lost its stiffness, became animated; we spoke about the theater, about music, I found out that Elise was the only child of a very wealthy businessman, that her family lived a stone's throw away from me at 36 Gramercy Park. She had been educated at the Sacré Cœur in Paris; she was an excellent linguist, spoke Italian, Spanish, and German fluently. Later she sat down at the piano and started to play and sing a little song; her voice was charming and she played exceedingly well. But the theater was her real ambition. She was fanatically determined to succeed as an actress; she was sure she would. And she was witty, with an almost dangerous sense of humor. Highly educated and worldly-wise, she struck me much more as a sophisticated European than as an American girl.

Suddenly it was close to four o'clock.

"When are you going to audition me?" she asked.

"Right now. Are you familiar with *Peer Gynt?*"

"Indeed I am."

"Very good—here—read the Solveig part. I shall cue you as Peer."

I let her do several scenes, some of them, at her request, twice.

I watched and listened with rapt attention. The casting of this part was of utmost importance; it would determine the success or failure of the play. I forgot the circumstances that had brought us together, the place where we were. I was not looking at Elise Bartlett, I was listening to Ibsen's lines. Was it Solveig who spoke them? Did she conjure up the vision of that Nordic girl?

An hour later we had finished. Elise relaxed in an easy chair, smoking a cigarette. I walked up and down, deep in my thoughts. Finally I stopped in front of her.

"I know you will hate me. But, please, believe me—you are no Solveig. Solveig must have blue eyes and blond hair —and I mean that not just in a physical sense. Solveig is the personification of Nordic girlhood, simple, earthy—no, that's not a part for you. I'm sorry. I really am, Miss Bartlett. But will you marry me?"

She rose slowly, she smiled—always the same mocking smile—and said softly, "Yes, of course, why not? Sometime, sure. And now, will you take me home, please?"

I helped her into her coat, took her downstairs, hailed a taxi, and escorted her to Gramercy Park. While the cab waited I accompanied her the few steps to the main entrance of the old-fashioned mansion. At the door I stopped her. "When we are married, I don't want you to wear these large hats," I said. "I dislike them."

"Right, Mr. Schildkraut. I will wear small ones. Good night." And she was gone.

"Good night," I said to the closing door.

Then I went home, picked up the telephone, and rang up every newspaper in town. I had some news for them. It made the early afternoon editions: "Elise Bartlett, young actress, engaged to star of *Liliom,* Joseph Schildkraut," the headlines blared.

At ten o'clock I phoned my fiancée, introduced myself to my future mother-in-law, who proved to be a most charming lady, and was invited for lunch.

In our conversation the night before, Elise had mentioned that she disliked diamonds but had a passion for emeralds. In fact, her favorite color was emerald green, and with a few exceptions her entire wardrobe, including hats and accessories was in various shades of green. I used to call her "the green-clad woman," after the character of the same name in *Peer Gynt,* and in Hollywood some years later I topped the green mania of hers by presenting her, as a Christmas gift, with an emerald-green Cadillac and a new chauffeur in an emerald-green uniform.

On my way to the Bartletts' I had stopped at Tiffany's, and I appeared at Gramercy Park like a living advertisement of an elegant bridegroom, carefully dressed for the occasion and with an engagement ring in my pocket: a diamond-cut emerald.

The engagement luncheon was very pleasant. I took an immediate liking to Elise's parents. They made me feel like one of the family.

Father and Mother were at that time in Lakewood for a rest and I had to inform them by telephone about my engagement. I was too late. They had read it in the New York papers and were anything but pleased. Mother took my hasty decision as a personal offense. The only child, running away from the paternal home and marrying outside the Jewish faith, and not even asking her for her consent! Father was hurt. He would have been jealous of any woman I married, regardless of her faith and background.

A week later we were married in City Hall in Philadelphia where *Liliom* was playing in the old Lyric Theatre. I made Elise wear a Hungarian peasant costume, and when she walked on stage in the prologue of the play the audience greeted her with a hail of rice and old shoes. She looked really ravishing.

Although my parents had still not fully recovered from their shock, they joined us at the wedding ceremony and at the subsequent reception at the Ritz Carlton.

The first meeting of Father and Mother with Elise's relatives was not a complete success. To the Southern aristocrats —Elise's family came from Kentucky—my parents must have seemed strange: natives of the jungle of Europe, they did not even speak English correctly. The Bartletts tried hard to put them at ease, which made things still worse. Mother withdrew coldly into her shell and Father, determined for my sake to gain Elise's love at any cost, was all sweetness and generosity. I was touched by his brave efforts, but they were not convincing to the others. I was glad when Elise and I could repair to our suite.

When we entered our drawing room I nearly fainted. On

every table, in every corner of every room in our suite, there were huge bouquets of gardenias. Somehow Father had found out that this was Elise's favorite flower, and, perfect cavalier that he was, he had spared no expenses to please her. There must have been hundreds of gardenias. To me their fragrance is always reminiscent of death. I shall never forget the horrible thought that struck me when I walked with Elise into that drawing room: Mystery in a Mortuary. It was just a fleeting sensation, for I was passionately in love, but for a few moments my romantic ardor was chilled—not a very auspicious beginning for our honeymoon.

The first thing we did was open all windows to let some fresh air in and to get rid of this sickly odor. Then we gathered all the flowers and asked the porter to take them away and distribute them to various hospitals.

Thus started the first day of our marriage.

It lasted eight years.

4

Those were bitter and exasperating years. From the very beginning we quarreled constantly, tormenting each other with recriminations. Elise was a bad actress, but got it into her head that out of professional jealousy and selfishness I purposely frustrated her career. In spite of her intelligence she simply could not realize the limitations of her talent. I needed warmth, a companion, the moral support and understanding of a loving wife; Elise was a precious object of art. And we both were terribly self-centered, both lacking in emotional maturity. We should never have married.

And the era in which we lived did little to help us find ourselves or each other. From the whirlwind courtship to its tragic end our marriage was typical of the "roaring twenties."

Foolish were those years, hectic and out of focus but also, so far as theater and literature was concerned, of a vitality and creativeness never since surpassed. While the Theatre

Guild broadened its scope with each new production, presenting to the American public the best of Europe's dramatic art, down in Greenwich Village Eugene O'Neill emerged as the first authentic American dramatist of world stature. Avant-garde theaters sprang up everywhere. Overnight a whole new generation of playwrights, directors, and actors had come of age and clamored for attention. My professional life was rich, full to the brim with new plans and projects. My personal life was barren and meaningless.

The first major crisis in our marriage occurred when, during the tour of *Liliom*, Eva Le Gallienne suffered a nervous breakdown and Elise forced me to insist that she take over the part of Julie. She was completely miscast and terribly bad.

In the fall of 1922 rehearsals started for *Peer Gynt*, and Elise could not forgive me for not being asked to play Solveig. Instead, she was cast as Ingrid, the bride, and proved so impossible that at the dress rehearsal the Guild had to replace her; to mollify her, she was given the small part of one of the three Saeter girls with whom Peer Gynt sleeps in the mountains. Elise raged and held me responsible for her humiliation, and I was humiliated by the half-sincere, half-ironic compassion that my colleagues showed for my predicament as a harassed husband. My success as Peer Gynt was no consolation.

The production of this play was outstanding. Theodore Komisarjevsky had come especially from Russia to direct it. An orchestra of forty men under the baton of Laszlo Kuhn of the Budapest Philharmonic Society played Edvard Grieg's score. There were excellent performances, especially by Louise Closser-Hale as Aase, Dudley Digges as the Mountain King, and Edward G. Robinson as the button moulder. Solveig was played by a Nordic girl, Selena Royle. Her success was well deserved. Again, as in the case of *Liliom*, the response of the audience was so enthusiastic that we had to move from the Garrick Theatre uptown to the much bigger Shubert.

It was during the run of *Peer Gynt* that I first met Stanislavsky, who, at that time, played a guest engagement with his entire ensemble at the old Jolson Theatre.

During the intermission of a matinee performance Komisarjevsky came breathlessly running backstage, lined up our whole company, and excitedly informed us that the great Russian director was in the theater and wanted to greet us. After the performance he appeared. He was magnificent in stature, of truly majestic bearing, and his face was like a Russian landscape: wide, wistful, strong. His snow-white hair topped like a gleaming cap his powerful skull; his eyes were of such an intense blue that they reminded one of a glacier.

He approached me, kissed me affectionately on both cheeks, looked deep into my eyes, and said with his melodious voice, *"Ah, votre père est un grand artiste!"*

I was quite taken aback by what I felt was a rather left-handed compliment. But some time ago I came across a book, *Stanislavsky: a Life** by David Magarshack, in which I found a letter written by Stanislavsky from New York to his partner Nemirovich-Danchenko in Moscow. This letter sheds such an important light on Stanislavsky's impressions of the American theater and is, incidentally, so flattering to me that I may be forgiven for setting it down here:

It is certainly a great thing to be successful in America. But anyone who has seen their theatrical managers or knows anything about their theatrical trusts, which are all working for the benefit of the owners of the theaters, will understand what a terrible thing it is—what a ghastly catastrophe it is—not to be successful here. I tremble to think what Gest, Shubert, or Otto Kahn would have done to us if we had not been successful and if we had incurred losses. Having realized it both with my brain and with my heart,

* New York: Chanticleer Press, 1951.

I should like to warn everybody against the danger of being unsuccessful here.

It is a great mistake to suppose that they don't know good actors here. They have seen the best that Europe could give them. Perhaps that is why America values personality so much. . . . Such an actor as David Warfield, whom I saw in the part of Shylock, we have not got. And Belasco's production of the *Merchant of Venice* exceeds in sheer lavishness anything I ever saw, and as for its technical achievements, the Maly Theatre could envy them. John Barrymore's Hamlet is far from ideal but very charming. Such a Peer Gynt as Schildkraut we have not got in Russia. And they have many more well-known actors we have not seen yet. The opera, as far as voices are concerned, is incomparably better than any theater in Europe. Nor will you be able to find in Europe such conductors or such symphonic orchestras as they have here.

I value this praise from Stanislavsky all the more since he himself had staged a famous production of *Peer Gynt* with his star Kachalov in the title role.

5

Toward the end of May 1923 I received an offer from the Samuel Goldwyn Company in Culver City. They wanted me for their film *Isle of Man*. Although the Theatre Guild protested my leaving *Peer Gynt* in the midst of a successful run, they finally gave in and Elise and I left for California.

I had signed the contract without looking at the script. But on the way to Los Angeles I read the novel on which the film was based, and I immediately realized that I was completely miscast in that part. They wanted me just to get a "name." The director, Victor Saestrom, shared my misgivings. The dark-haired, dark-eyed, Balkanese-looking Schildkraut as a blue-eyed, blond, very reserved British judge! It did not make sense. The company had engaged me without consulting even the director.

We went on location to San Francisco. From day to day I felt more unhappy. I knew I was bad and wooden. To tell the truth, I never liked working in silent films anyhow. I needed the spoken word to express myself.

When we returned from San Francisco I was asked to come to the studio, and was shown the "rushes," the scenes that had been shot so far. To put it mildly, I was just horrible— a gawky, awkward, swaggering guy trying to pass himself off as a British judge.

By mutual consent I withdrew from the picture and was replaced by Conrad Nagel. He was a perfect choice.

Since I had gone to Hollywood much against the Theatre Guild's will and to the accompaniment of a lot of publicity, I did not want to return without any film to my credit. Fortunately, there was a part for me in Norma Talmadge's picture, *The Song of Love*. It was a trite, conventional story, the saccharine love affair of an Arabian dancing girl and a French officer. At least I could look the part and the uniform was very becoming. But that's all I could say for myself. The film was not much of a success, for either Norma Talmadge or me.

During my six weeks' work on that film, the conflict between me and the Theatre Guild sharpened and finally came to a head. We had previously agreed that they would put on Shakespeare's *Richard II* as their next production. That was a part I had dreamed of playing for years. Now the Guild informed me that they had changed their minds and wanted me to take the lead in Molnar's *The Guardsman*. They reminded me how much I owed them: they had given me my first great chance, they had accepted all my suggestions, but now they felt I should show myself to the American public in a different light, as a drawing-room comedian, the kind of character I had played so successfully in Europe. *Richard II* would come later.

I hit the ceiling. My replies to the Guild's letters and telegrams were, I am sorry to admit, rather nasty. They were motivated, aside from my disappointment about the postponement of *Richard II*, by my strong aversion to *The Guardsman*. I disliked the play heartily, and I still dislike it. It is well written and witty, granted, but phony, and I have never been able to stomach its preposterous premise.

The Guild remained stubborn; I remained stubborn. We had a long-term contract, and now under Elise's pressure I made the worst mistake of my career. When the Guild's lawyer notified me that they would consider my refusal to appear in *The Guardsman* as a breach of contract I took my wife's advice and answered, "All right, it's a breach of contract, let's cancel it." And so it was done.

The rest is theatrical history. A brilliant young actor and his wife were engaged to do Molnar's comedy: Alfred Lunt and Lynn Fontanne. They were magnificent and the play was an outstanding success. Subsequently they were signed to a long-term contract by the Guild, and all the parts that I would have played if I had not acted so foolishly were now given to their new star, Alfred Lunt.

To restore my badly damaged self-esteem I had to prove myself in another play. I hoped I had found the right one in a light comedy by the Hungarian author Lajos Biro. *The Highwayman* had its premiere at the Playhouse in Chicago. I doubled as director and star, and Elise insisted on playing the feminine lead. In spite of a successful run in Chicago and on the road and excellent notices everywhere, I was smart enough to close the play before it reached New York. This time I heeded the advice of Father, who—rightly—found the comedy old-fashioned and criticized my performance in these words: "A very good-looking but unpleasant, conceited, and arrogant race-track tout." He hated me in that part and I shared his feelings. And the presence of Elise did not help matters any. She looked like a heavenly apparition and acted like the bloodiest amateur.

Immediately after the closing of the play we separated. We

saw each other occasionally, we met sometimes for dinner
and at parties, but we did not live together any more.

6

Looking back at the years that followed, I have the impression of a wild ride in a roller-coaster: the sensation of a dangerous race over a winding and tricky road, the childish
satisfaction of scorning all prudence and reason, and the
sickening feeling of emptiness. The "lost generation" tried to
find itself in speakeasies and drowned its doubts in whisky and
jazz. I have never been a drinker or a gambler, and night-
clubs always bored me. I drowned my aching loneliness in
women.

There was no romance, not even sexual passion. I rushed
from one woman to another, a succession of faces and bodies
which meant nothing to me; I could hardly remember the
names of my bed companions. Each "conquest" merely in-
creased the intensity of my emotional hangover.

My friends—and how many I had!—saw me only as the
great charmer, the woman-chaser, the irresistible braggart.
To a large extent my success as Benvenuto Cellini had something to do with this image. Women especially were inclined
to take the character I played on stage for my real self.

The play was *The Firebrand* by Edwin Justus Mayer. An
amusing historical comedy, it was played against the pic-
turesque background of medieval Florence. Woodman
Thompson designed brilliant sets and costumes, emphasizing
the sensuous atmosphere of that period. The men were attired in heavy silk tights that ended under the lowest rib.
We wore short Italian boleros, proudly parading our mascu-
linity, and some critics maintained that its strong sexual
flavor more than any literary merit accounted for the play's
great popular appeal.

Up to the dress rehearsal the play was quite different. It
even had another title—*The Golden Key*. Our director had
staged it as a stodgy, slow-moving historical drama. When

Father, who had read the script and liked it very much, saw it during the rehearsals in Brooklyn's Shubert Teller Theatre he was furious. "The play should have the taste of French champagne and the gaiety of Offenbach," he complained. "Instead it tastes of stale beer and bores you with its pretentiousness." Despite this scathing criticism, we would have taken the play to Broadway and to a certain and swift death, had it not been for an incident that occurred during the dress rehearsal.

That evening Mr. Mayer brought me a woodcut of Cellini, showing him partly bald with a full beard adorning his face. "You don't look right," the author complained, "not at all historically true, as you can see from this portrait. At least put on a beard, please."

I did not wish to be difficult, so I agreed. I sent my valet across the street to a make-up shop and had him buy a few lengths of crepe hair. Out of it I fashioned a glorious beard in the style of the eighties. It hid my cheeks and my mouth and ended in the middle of my chest. I knew I looked ridiculous and only hoped the director and author would finally agree and sacrifice this piece of historical authenticity. I did not reckon on my father's impetuosity.

The house was packed with invited guests. The curtain rose. Benvenuto Cellini made his first entrance attired in a smart velvet bolero and burnt orange tights—and the wild beard. He had just committed a murder and was leaning against the door of a palace, dagger in hand, panting heavily.

At this tense moment Father's resonant voice boomed out: "Beard, beard, where are you running with my boy?" And while the audience roared with laughter, Father swiftly walked up on stage, tore off my beard, and sent me to my dressing room. I had to remove the remaining fringes and stubbles of the crepe hair.

For a few moments I was terribly embarrassed, like a schoolboy reprimanded in front of strangers. I felt ashamed of Father's lack of civility. But then I succumbed to the comicality of the situation and joined in the general laughter. After all, was Father not right?

The director was less understanding. When we resumed the rehearsal he had left the theater. Father took over the direction of the play. He changed it into a naughty French bedroom farce and even changed its title. He turned it into a "hit" that ran on Broadway for a year.

Father did not accept credit for his work, or any remuneration. The previous director received all the praise. Father did not mind remaining anonymous—as long as he could help me in my career. He was not too particular about credits anyway. When he first came to America in 1911 and was asked how large he wanted his name printed over the title of the play on the advertising posters, he answered, not being used to the custom of star billing in repertory, "I don't really care. Put it any size and any place you want to." And with a little modest smile he added, "They'll find me."

Chapter X

1

IN THE FALL OF 1922 Father at last realized his great ambition: he was given an opportunity to act in English. The play was Sholem Asch's *The God of Vengeance*. It was presented at the Provincetown Playhouse, Eugene O'Neill's original showcase.

I never doubted that Father's personality and talent would shine in an English-language production as brightly as they had on the German and Yiddish stage. But what surprised everyone was how he mastered the English language. In his daily life he spoke English haltingly and with a strong accent. On stage, however, there was no German accent, merely a slight foreign intonation that fitted the character he portrayed. And he had not only studied his own part; he knew the whole play so well that he often cued the other actors in their own roles.

The strongest memory I have of the opening night is a scene in Father's dressing room after the performance: John Barrymore and Marjorie Rambeau pushing through the crowd of well-wishers, and actually kneeling down, with tears in their eyes, to kiss Father's hands. The tribute was so sincere and touching that the gesture did not seem at all theatrical.

To attract bigger audiences, the production was soon moved uptown to the Apollo Theatre on 42nd Street. And here something happened that made the play front-page news and turned it into one of the biggest sensations of the season. The Society for the Suppression of Vice lodged a complaint against the drama, denouncing it as "obscene, indecent, disgusting, and tending to the corruption of the morals of youth." After a Sunday matinee the entire company was arrested and taken to prison. A long and bitter court battle ensued.

The God of Vengeance is the story of a Jewish brothel-keeper in a little town of Poland. He is a former pimp who has married one of his girls and become wealthy and "respectable." Now he has only one aim in life: the happiness of his daughter Rifkele. She is the only person he has ever loved sincerely and unselfishly. She must never be soiled by the world in which he moves, and he guards her innocence with fanatic zeal. At the opening of the play she is about to be married to a decent young man. But "the sins of the father are visited upon the children." The girl is seduced by a prostitute in her father's brothel, is paired off with one of the customers, and runs away from home in search of glamour and excitement. When the father discovers Rifkele's fate, his whole world collapses; he denies God, curses his wife and daughter, and chases them into the brothel. His evil past, in the end more powerful than all his good intentions, destroys him. He cannot escape God's vengeance.

To bolster their accusations the "moralists" presented as witness a policeman who testified that the girls in the brothel scene had performed in the nude—which was an outright lie; that the daughter and the prostitute were "openly flaunting their lesbian relationship"—another lie; and that the final scene, in which the raving brothel-keeper turns the rabbi out of his home and curses God, was sacrilegious.

The leading lawyers of the day, among them Oswald Garrison Villard, sociologists such as Professor H. A. Overstreet, Doctor Henry Neumann, a prominent leader of the Ethical Culture Society, and dramatists and politicians came to the defense of Sholem Asch. They maintained that the play had the realism and inherent ethos of an ancient Greek tragedy or biblical legend. Nevertheless, the Appellate Division of the Supreme Court of New York confirmed the verdict of the Court of General Sessions and condemned Father to a fine of $200. The manager and producer had similar fines to pay.

Incidentally, two actors who have since gained an enviable position on the American stage stood their first test of fire in that play and, so to speak, graduated under Father's auspices: Sam Jaffe, who played the matchmaker, and Morris Carnovsky, who had the part of the rabbi.

The triumph Father had scored in *The God of Vengeance* finally brought him the fulfillment of his dearest wish: the Theatre Guild offered him the part of King Lear, of all parts the one he regarded as his greatest accomplishment, in a new and excellently cast production. The contracts were prepared. I was to play the Fool; Helen Chandler, Cordelia; Moffat Johnson, Kent; A. P. Kaye, a fine English actor, Gloucester. Lee Simonson designed simple but impressive sets. And then, at the last moment, just before the contracts were to be signed, Father had to beg off. The reason? He was simply physically unable to play eight times a week one of the most taxing parts of the world's dramatic literature. Since the Theatre Guild was dependent upon its subscribers, no solution could be found; they would not even accept six performances a week and have somebody else play the two matinees. The production was called off. It was a dreadful blow to Father from which he never really recovered.

After the closing of *The God of Vengeance,* Father acted once more in English, at the Longacre. Warren P. Munsell,

As Benvenuto Cellini in *The Firebrand* (New York, 1924)

(*Left*) In *The Garden of Alle*
with Marlene Dietrich and Hen
Brandon (1935)

(*Below*) In *Marie Antoinet*
with Tyrone Power and Norr
Shearer (1938)

With Marie

on our tenth anniversary

. . . and today

As Death in *Everyman,* a television production (1954)

As the German Crown Prince Wilhelm in *Lancer Spy* (1937)

With Eva Le Gallie in *Uncle Harry* (19

Captain Dreyfus in Warner
others' *The Life of Emile Zola*
37)

Father in the last year of his
(1930)

Max Liebermann's portrait
Father, which Goebbels orde
burned publicly

Otto Frank

in real life

. . . and on the stage

With Susan Strasberg in *The Diary of Anne Frank* (New York, 1955)

General Manager for the Theatre Guild, had branched out on his own to produce a play by the noted Viennese author Hermann Bahr, *The Mongrel.* Elmer Rice adapted it for the American stage. Despite Father's highly acclaimed performance and a fine cast, it did not appeal to the general public and closed after eighty-odd performances.

Between *The God of Vengeance* and *The Mongrel,* Father sporadically returned to the Yiddish stage. And on his birthday I presented him with his own theater, a chamber playhouse at 180th Street in the Bronx. Its distance from the heart of the theater district did not deter Father's admirers —and they were numerous. Here they could see him once more in his whole repertory from Shakespeare to modern farces. His greatest artistic success there was August Strindberg's *Sheet Lightning,* which, incidentally, I directed for him. I liked the play very much and had seen it in an excellent production by Max Reinhardt in Europe, which made my task pleasant and easier. The greatest financial success was Ossip Dymov's comedy *Bronx Express,* which ran for nearly a full year. Later Father appeared in this play in many American cities, and everywhere this clever satire on American business and advertising was a huge success. Everywhere but on Broadway. There it was presented with Charles Coburn in Father's part and failed.

2

Cecil B. de Mille had seen me in *The Firebrand* and offered me a contract. After his break with Paramount the famous director had established his own independent company. His first film in which I was to star was *Road to Yesterday,* based on a popular American play and adapted for the screen by Janie McPherson, who wrote many of de Mille's scenarios.

At the same time Carl Laemmle, the head of Universal, engaged Father for one of his pictures. *His People* was the story of a Russian Jewish emigrant in New York and of his struggle to find a new foothold. It was a simple, almost primi-

tive little story. The entire picture, produced by Paul
Kohner, who today is one of Hollywood's best-known agents,
cost about $90,000, which included my father's salary. It
was an outstanding success all over the world, grossing over
$1,000,000.

Road to Yesterday did not fare nearly so well. The film
had many interesting features; the photography was excellent, the sets stunning, and from a technical point of view it
was flawless. But the audience could not follow the two or
three parallel story lines; it was like sitting through a mam-
moth performance of a three-ring circus. The film was a
"flop," and de Mille lost a fortune. He recouped it very
soon, and many times over, with a single film which to this
day is still shown, especially at Christmas and Easter times,
on television, in schools, universities, and churches the world
over: The King of Kings, the story of Christ. Both Father
and I played in that film. He was the high priest, Caiaphas,
and I was Judas.

De Mille engaged both Father and me under a five-year
contract. As a director he was the opposite of Griffith. A
great showman, he always went for the spectacular—mass
scenes with thousands of extras, earthquakes, train wrecks. I
think he turned to the Bible for his most famous films, not
out of a deep religious feeling but primarily because biblical
figures have the larger-than-life dimensions, because primitive emotions and violent passions can be splashed on the
screen in a grand manner. De Mille is always aiming at
sweeping theatrical and pictorial effects, and not only in his
work. On the set he is never merely the director guiding the
actors; he performs the role of a director, sitting on his chair
in a Caesarian pose, shouting through the megaphone, every
word, every gesture calculated to impress onlookers and invited guests with his importance and power.

One of the few persons he failed to impress was my mother.
We were shooting the big train-wreck scene in Road to
Yesterday. It was a night sequence and the accident was

staged in the yards of the Southern Pacific Railway. I sat in a compartment of a car looking out of the window at the supposedly passing landscape, while in back of me a steam locomotive was to crash through my car, stopping just one foot behind me.

It was not a pleasant feeling to sit there and wait for that crash, hoping the engineer would stop in time. He did stop at the prearranged spot, but we had not thought of the hot steam escaping from the engine. It scorched my face and hands. In spite of my pain I did not move, according to the script presumably dead, until de Mille whistled the all-clear signal and I could climb out of the car. A physician and nurses rushed to my aid. Fortunately, I had not been hurt badly.

My parents were among the guests who had been invited to watch this spectacular scene. But not until days later was I told about Mother's reaction. When the locomotive started to move, Mother suddenly picked up a heavy stick of wood and hid it behind her back. Father looked at her stupefied. "What are you doing?" he asked her.

"If something happens to Pepi in this scene," she said quietly, without raising her voice, "I'll kill that guy." And she pointed at de Mille. No, she was never impressed by his domineering pose.

Besides *The King of Kings,* Father and I also acted together in other de Mille films, none of them particularly successful, nor did they further Father's or my career. But even though the stories were mediocre, they could not dim Father's performing power.

There was *The Country Doctor,* in which Father portrayed a typical New Hampshire small-town country doctor. In *A Ship Comes In,* he was a Czech immigrant. And he was equally convincing as one and the other.

I, on the other hand, suffered from the impossible parts in which I was cast. De Mille was determined to force me upon the public as another Valentino or Navarro, a sentimental-romantic hero, though my real talent does not lie in this field. And so I was hardly outstanding in de Mille's pictures.

There was only one part I really liked. In *He and His Dog*, based on a story by Alfred Payson Terhune, the famous breeder of Scotch collies, I played a drunken, dissolute bum who finds a crippled dog in the street. Under the influence of this fine and noble animal the tramp turns into a decent human being. I gained satisfaction from this part, and great acclaim for my performance, but the film was not popular and proved a financial failure.

Disappointing as my artistic experiences with de Mille were, they did not diminish my respect and warm feelings for him. I love de Mille for one reason above all: he regarded Father as the greatest actor he had ever seen, and he says so to this very day. Although he is at times tyrannical, willful, and impatient, de Mille has one thing in common with D. W. Griffith: a generous heart and a great kindness which he hides behind an aloof and sometimes unapproachable attitude. We have remained very close friends. Yet I suspect that it was not so much my talent that earned me de Mille's friendship as his profound admiration for my father.

When we first went to Hollywood, it looked to us more like a spot in the south of France than an American town —a sleepy resort whose main attraction was its wonderful climate, its beautiful vegetation, its charming bungalows, sun, peace. To the world at large it was a hurly-burly of intrigues and sins, the mecca of romance and glamour.

Racial and political persecution had not yet uprooted the European actors, writers, and directors; it was ten years later that the victims of Hitler arrived in great numbers. In the twenties there were few Europeans among the film people. They had come at the urgent request of the big companies and were their top stars: Ernst Lubitsch, unforgettable master of the comedy of manners, a German whose sensitivity and light ironic touch tempted one to swear that he must have been born in the heart of Paris and raised on champagne; Emil Jannings, remarkable for an acting range that encompassed drama as well as comedy, but, unfortunately, at heart the type of provincial and narrow-minded German who easily succumbed to Hitler's blandishments; Greta Garbo, Pola Negri, and Marlene Dietrich, who conclusively proved that sex appeal was not a matter of an over-sized bosom. The shopgirl from Stockholm, the Polish housewife. and the daughter of a Prussian general had one thing in common: style. It cannot be learned or imitated. It was the one commodity that Hollywood with all its wealth could not acquire.

I had bought a house on Courtney Avenue for my parents —one of those charming bungalows complete with palms, orange trees, and avocados. I had a little house of my own on Whitley Terrace. Separated from my wife, I lived alone, a rather quiet and normal life—or, I should say, abnormal, according to the standards of Hollywood. No wild parties, no scandals.

Father spent his spare time mostly at the bookmaker's or at the race track, though he had not yet completely lost interest in pretty girls, while I had a few close friends who shared my love for music and regularly dropped in to listen to my latest records or to idle the evenings away in pleasant conversation. Mostly they were people who were not connected with the film industry—doctors, lawyers, professors. Foremost among my actor friends were Charlie Chaplin and Erich Von Stroheim.

I had first met Chaplin during the run of *Liliom* in New York and we became very fond of each other. Soon Father was the third in this union. When Chaplin did *City Lights* there was not a day when Father and I were not on the set. Watching this unique artist perform was one of the greatest experiences of my life. Amazing as he was in the studio— actor, director, camera man, author, and composer, all in one —I could appreciate his genius even more in the confines of a small gathering at his home, when he would suddenly pro-

ceed either to improvise on the organ or, better still, to play
a whole Japanese drama, acting the part of the lover, husband, and wife in Japanese, without actually uttering a
single Japanese word.

This all-round clown—one of the greatest of all time—is
a very complex person, full of contradictions. On the one
hand, he is imbued with a genuine compassion for the little
man, the helpless victim of society. There has never been a
false sentimental note in his presentation of the outcast, for
he himself had been one in his early days. On the other hand,
he surprises one by his selfishness and incredible stinginess.

Some people after gaining fame and wealth can overcome
the memory of their humiliating past because they achieve
a sense of self-confidence and serenity. Others never outgrow
the fear of their inadequacy; one day they may be thrown
back into the gutter again. I think Charlie is unconsciously
hounded by this fear. Hence his selfishness, his greed, his
never-ending, pathetic attempts to prove himself, as lover, as
conqueror, as an equal to the shrewd captains of the film industry. Besides, there is something very feminine in Chaplin's psychological make-up. It explains his extreme vanity,
his nebulous radicalism, his frequent hysterical outbursts.

I remember one night when I was awakened by the ringing of the telephone and heard Chaplin's excited voice:
"Come at once, something terrible has happened."

I dressed in frantic haste, jumped into my car, and rushed
to Chaplin's house.

I found him almost paralyzed with fear. "What happened?"

A skunk had found its way into Charlie's bathroom and
he did not know how to get it out. Since our clothes, once
contaminated by the skunk's secretion, would have to be
burned or buried, we stripped naked and finally succeeded
in shooing the animal, which was as frightened as Charlie,
out of the house. The whole incident was really grotesque,

our antics so comical, that I could not stop laughing. Chaplin, however, was a nervous wreck.

As a comedian Charlie is, in my opinion, unsurpassed to this day, and there are few men, indeed, who have done as much as he has to turn the medium of the film into great art. As a man he has many foibles. As a friend to Father and myself he was always loyal and affectionate. One of his birthday gifts to me, sixteen-millimeter prints of *The Gold Rush* and *City Lights,* is among my treasured possessions.

One can hardly imagine two men of greater contrasts than Charlie Chaplin and Erich Von Stroheim. And yet they were in some respects kindred souls. The "lovable tramp" and "the man you love to hate" were both fanatical perfectionists. And Erich, too, was hounded by his past. He drew the most devastating and bitter portraits of the German officer and at the same time was passionately in love with uniforms and with all the manners, customs, and pomp of the military caste. He loathed sentiment and was an unbelievable sentimentalist, ridiculed Vienna and could never forget it. He gloried in his cynicism, shocked millions of people by expressing contempt for moral standards while he was, in fact, firmly bound to middle-class morality. Rude and gruff, he was at the same time a considerate and loyal friend and a perfect cavalier of the old school. He squandered money in a manner that staggered even the most extravagant film moguls, and thus he was the terror of every producer. They saw in him only "a gifted lunatic"; very few realized that there was no one whose feelings and personal interests he spared less than his own. And he recognized and respected real talent without envy wherever he saw it, serving his art with complete dedication and without compromise.

No Stroheim film was as bitter and cruel as his own life was, and his tragic end in Paris: paralyzed, dying bit by bit, without a franc to his name, the creditors like a pack of hounds besieging his villa—which was his then no longer—

and the French government coming to his rescue by . . . bestowing upon him the officer's cross of the Legion of Honor! He could not move his body, but he had the medal pinned to his pajama coat and the photographers were there to immortalize this historic moment.

Stroheim won great fame as an actor, but as a director he showed his true genius. *Greed* will, I am sure, always remain one of the great film classics. His *Wedding March, Foolish Wives, Merry Widow*—chaotic and uneven as they are—are lasting monuments to his art.

3

When de Mille's company was dissolved in 1928, I received an offer from New York to star in the adaptation of an Italian play, *Death Takes a Holiday*. I packed my bags and was ready to leave for rehearsals in New York when somebody told me that Universal Pictures was about to do *Show Boat* by Edna Ferber. The film was based not on the successful musical then running on Broadway, but on the original novel. I read the book and decided then and there that I and nobody else would portray Gaylord Ravenal.

This part was the dream of every actor who had gained screen fame as a lover and romantic hero; Gilbert Roland, Rod La Rocque, John Gilbert, among others, were being tested for the role. At that time I was not much in demand; the pseudo-romantic parts I had played under de Mille had not enhanced my artistic reputation or my popularity, and I was sure Universal would not think of asking me to take a test.

Therefore, I decided to strike out for myself. Without informing my agent I drove out to the Universal lot, found out on which stage Harry Pollard was shooting tests for *Show Boat*, walked right on the set, and cornered the director.

"You don't know me, Mr. Pollard," I said, without any introduction, "and I don't know you. But you probably know me by name and I know you by name." And then, putting my hand on his shoulder, I said in a quiet voice, emphasizing every word, "I am Joseph Schildkraut, the only actor who can play Gaylord Ravenal."

Pollard took his pipe slowly out of his mouth, looked me over with his cold, watery-blue, and alcoholically blurred eyes, and said softly, "I don't think so."

"You will, Mr. Pollard!" I said, and left.

I had come to the studio, rather foolishly, in old sport clothes and had not even shaved that morning. My physical appearance must have shocked Pollard. That little shrimp wanting to play the glamorous Ravenal? Preposterous! I had, of course, hoped he would know me as an actor and not judge me by my looks. I realized my mistake.

But was it too late to rectify it?

A few minutes later my mind was made up. At my own expense, I had Eddie Schmidt, then the foremost tailor in Hollywood, and the Western Costume Company go to work and make for me the proper elegant clothes for the Mississippi gambler, complete with built-up Congress gaiters which brought my height to six feet two. A smart pearl-gray top hat of the period made me look even taller. For good luck Father bought me the cane, which Ravenal constantly pawns when he finds himself in financial difficulties. It was made of Brazilian snake wood and had an ivory tip, and a hand-carved seventeenth-century ivory skull which Father had purchased separately was attached to the cane for a handle.

I donned this elegant outfit, put on the top hat, took cane and gloves, and drove out to the Universal studios. Again I walked on the set where the tests for *Show Boat* were in progress. At this moment John Gilbert was before the camera. Twirling my cane and with the most sarcastic Ravenal smile I could manage, I stepped in front of Pollard.

The effect was sensational. Pollard jumped up from his director's chair and yelled, "Who's that? But that's Ravenal!"

"No, it's Joseph Schildkraut," I said. "I told you **you** would change your mind, Mr. Pollard. Didn't I?"

An hour later my agent signed a long-term contract with Universal. My first role: Gaylord Ravenal.

When the film was finished I went to the hospital for an appendectomy. In the meantime the first talking picture was released, and it was decided to re-shoot half of *Show Boat* in sound. When it was finally shown at the Biltmore Theatre in Los Angeles—and simultaneously all over the country— it was the second talking film, or rather semi-talking film, in motion-picture history, a triumphant success for both Universal and myself.

Now, at last, I had repeated my American stage success on the screen, and my future in films seemed secure and promising. But all too soon my great hopes were rudely shattered.

Carl Laemmle died and his son, Carl Laemmle, Jr., became president in charge of production. He was all of twenty-one years old. I did not hold his age against him—Irving Thalberg or Mervyn Le Roy certainly proved that age in itself is not an essential prerequisite for a successful film producer— but Laemmle, Jr., had nothing to his credit. It was his idea to capitalize on my success in *Show Boat* by putting me into a gangster film, *Night Ride*, in which I was cast as, of all things, a Kansas City reporter by the name of Jack McGrew. I looked much more a revolutionary from the Balkans than a Midwestern journalist.

Another actor, however, found in this film the start for a great career. There was the part of an Al Capone-like gangster in the picture and I suggested my good friend and former classmate at the American Academy, Edward G. Robinson, for the role. Young Laemmle had never heard of him, and it took all my persuasion to make Universal engage him. Robinson was magnificent and, perfectly cast, he "played me right off the screen," as the saying goes. His performance earned him his next part, *Little Caesar*. I, on the other hand, lost, with this and similar films I did for

Universal, much of the prestige I had gained with *Show Boat*.

It was a low point in my career, and a frustrating and sad period in my personal life as well.

Immediately after my success in *Show Boat* Elise returned to me. Material considerations played an important part in her wish to live with me again, but she also wanted to share as my wife the excitement and luxurious social amenities of Hollywood's "nobility." But again our life together was spoiled by quarrels and bitterness. In my depressed state of mind, discouraged by my latest professional disappointments, I was not much interested in parties. Elise resented my preoccupation with my work, and felt cheated of the glamorous life she had expected to enjoy. She had started to drink heavily; my attempts to stop her headlong flight into self-destruction proved futile and only exacerbated our relationship. We decided on a divorce.

We made an out-of-court settlement. It was very one-sided: Elise set the terms and I had to accept them, for she had entered the negotiations heavily armed. Through private detectives she had collected information about my affairs with various women and threatened to turn over to the press names and facts if I did not agree to her demands. With my prestige at a low point anyhow, I could not brook a public scandal. I said Yes and Amen to everything she wanted, and she walked out with nearly a quarter-million dollars. I was left with the house on Whitley Terrace and its furniture. Fortunately, I could keep my beloved library; she had also wanted to take that away, but on that point I put up my strongest fight and finally won.

I saw Elise again only three times.

A few years later she married the publisher Horace Liveright, a good friend of mine. At that time, I, too, had been married again and was staying with my present wife, Marie, at the Essex House in New York. On her wedding day Elise appeared in our apartment magnificently gowned, bejeweled, and dead drunk. Waving a revolver, she threatened to kill my wife and me. A few moments later she stormed out again and was married the same afternoon. The marriage did not last long and soon afterward I learned that she had married a nightclub owner in Florida.

The last time I saw her was in 1944. During a matinee performance of *The Cherry Orchard* at the National Theatre in New York, in which I was co-starred with Eva Le Gallienne, some evidently drunk person kept interrupting the second act by muttering, talking, and applauding every second line or so. There was commotion in the audience, then quiet returned. After the final curtain we were informed by the stage manager that a raving drunken woman had been the cause of the disturbance. She had insisted that "the guy on stage" was her husband and that she wanted to talk to him. The house police had thrown her out.

When I returned to our hotel room I was confronted by a strange and pathetic scene. Here was Elise, bitterly crying and hysterically apologizing to my wife for her behavior in the theater. Marie's soothing words were of no avail. Elise insisted that as a penance she had to give my wife a present, a beautiful jade necklace which she had received from me on our honeymoon. Since there was no other way to calm Elise, Marie finally had to accept it. Whereupon Elise kissed us good-by and left.

That same evening Elise's father arrived from Florida in search of her. He appealed to the police for help. In the hope that Elise would show up again in our hotel, a detective was assigned to have dinner with us; Elise's father and a physician friend of ours joined us in the dining room. Sure enough, a little later Elise staggered in. She was in a stupor. Babbling incoherently, she asked her father for money. He gave it to her, begging her not to spend it on liquor.

Elise got furious and banged the table. "Stop ordering me around!" she screamed over and over again. Then she turned to the detective and said, "You seem a nice guy, come along and buy me a drink."

The detective rose at once. "Yes, of course," he said softly, took her arm, and escorted her politely out of the room.

The rest I was told by mutual friends. The detective took her to the nearest police station and from there she was committed to an institution. She escaped and was found a few weeks later in a horrible condition, somewhere in Florida. All her jewels and expensive wardrobe were gone. My emerald engagement ring she had given to a sailor in Miami for a drink of whisky. Soon after, she died of delirium tremens in a Florida hospital.

Were the failure of our marriage and her tragic end to some extent my fault too? A close friend of Elise's told me once that it was my lack of faith in her acting talent that eventually drove her to drink and self-destruction. It is probably true that vanity and frustration destroyed this beautiful and brilliant woman. And the chaotic times through which we lived, the milieu in which we moved, were certainly not helpful in providing her with the necessary emotional stability. It was true, also, that another man might have given her the confidence and self-discipline she needed. I was not that man. In bringing us together fate played a cruel trick on us both.

4

In 1929 Father's health began to fail. Diabetes and cardiac asthma developed. Despite his tremendous vitality, the wild excitement of his past life had taken its toll.

He had an important part in RKO's production of Arnold Zweig's famous novel, *The Case of Sergeant Grischa*. During the shooting of the film he became gravely ill and had to be replaced. He recovered and MGM engaged him for the German version of Eugene O'Neill's *Anna Christie*. He played the old sea captain, with Greta Garbo as his daughter Anna.

Frank Reicher, who had directed me in *Liliom*, was in

charge of this film. One day in July 1930, Frank brought
Father home from the studio. It was a very hot afternoon,
the air heavy, stifling. Father looked pitiful; his face, deeply
lined, was the color of yellow paper and seemed terribly
small. His eyes had lost their luster and looked like clouded
glass.

Father was then living with me in my house. That had
been doctor's orders. "If you want this wonderful man to
live a little longer, for God's sake, under one pretext or
other, get him away from your mother's poisonous food,"
the doctor had said to me. "Your father needs a strict diet.
Your mother simply doesn't understand how serious his condition is." I had a difficult time convincing Mother that
Father should stay with me. The doctor's arguments did not
impress her. How could her cooking be bad for Father? Nonsense. He had enjoyed it all his life. But in the end she
agreed. Since Maxl and Pepi wanted it that way . . .

And so Father had moved in with me. He had part of the
house all to himself, and now a trained nurse took care of
him day and night. And, of course, I had a special telephone
line installed—to his bookmaker.

During the long weeks of his illness Father did not suffer
severe pain, even though the recurrent asthmatic attacks
often made him feel quite miserable. But he never complained, never lost his wonderful humor.

The 15th of July began with a visit of a young physician
who had been sent by MGM to check on Father's illness for
the insurance company. Sitting in a comfortable chair by his
desk, Father was in the best of spirits. He had just placed a
bet of $5000 on a horse in the Kentucky Derby. Gallant Fox
was a sure winner, he explained to me—a wonderful horse;
it would certainly live up to its name.

The nurse ushered the physician in. He examined Father
thoroughly. As the doctor bent over his chest, applied the
stethoscope, and listened to his heart, Father looked over the
doctor's head at me and said with a faint smile which had

not yet lost its mischievous charm, "You see, Pepi, they have already sent me the angel of death." There was no bitterness in his remark; in fact it sounded rather flippant. No, Father would not let himself be pressured into leaving this world. Immediately I felt more hopeful than I had been for a long time.

I had promised to attend a performance that evening of an English play, *Interference*, at the Hollywood Playhouse. A dear friend of ours, the actor Fritz Feld, was to keep Father company while I was out.

When I returned, around midnight, the two were enjoying themselves thoroughly. Father was in bed, laughing heartily at Feld's jokes and American and German songs which the young actor sang to the accompaniment of his ukulele. Fritz was really good at it.

Since I had to get up early in the morning for my work at the studio I kissed Father good night and went to my bedroom, leaving him in charge of Fritz and the night nurse.

I don't know how long I had been asleep. Someone shook me, I heard a voice calling my name; the next moment I was wide awake. I saw Fritz standing at my bedside. He looked grave. "Please, call the doctor," he said softly. "I think Papa has had an attack."

I jumped up, ran to Father's bedroom, took one look at him, and knew: This is the end. But instantly I banished the thought. No, it could not be, not yet. Not tonight. As soon as the doctor came—the doctor would save him; he had to—just another of his attacks—he had weathered so many of them. I ran to the phone and called the doctor.

I felt terribly helpless. If I could only do something! The doctor—where was he? I ran out into the street in my pajamas, ran to the next corner, as if I could thus hasten the doctor's arrival. The street was deserted. It was close to four o'clock.

Why did it take the doctor so long? God, God, make him come, quick—now!

The headlights of a car blinded me. Here he was. It had not taken him more than ten minutes.

We ran to Father's room. The doctor had not even reached the bed when he turned to me and said softly, "He has made his last exit, Pepi."

At that moment the triteness of this sentence did not shock me; I hardly heard his words. But a few minutes later I felt the banality of his remark like a slap in the face. The doctor was a great admirer of Father and loved him dearly, and I know he was not aware of how silly and theatrical the words sounded. "Leave me alone, please, go!" I mumbled, "all of you—go."

I don't know how long I stood at Father's bed, staring down at him. The doctor had said something and was gone; the nurse had tiptoed out of the room. I have to call Mother, I thought. But how should I tell it to her? No, I could not do it, not over the phone.

"Fritz!"

"Yes, Pepi."

"Please, drive out to Courtney Avenue and bring Mother here."

"Yes, Pepi."

"And send the nurse home."

Now I was all alone in the big house. The silence was so complete—not a single sound. I sat on the bed, holding Father's hand. I felt as if I had never been so close to him in all my life.

I looked at Father's face, absorbing every little detail, but I did not see it, not really. I saw our whole past together: Father as a young man and I, a little boy, listening to his stories; I kneeling at his feet in the premiere of *The Prodigal Son;* our walks through the Wurstelprater; Father in my dressing room after the rehearsal of *Liliom;* a wholly insignificant little joke he had once made at our dinner table in Berlin; his entrance in *King Lear*. There was no sense or logic in this progression of scenes; they flitted like shadows over his face, while I heard his voice fill the room with words, laughter, laments. No, he was not dead. He could not be.

I bent over him and took him in my arms. I lifted him up. How light he was. Not heavier than a child. And what a heavy man he once had been. In the last two years he had lost over a hundred pounds. I picked him up and carried him in my arms from the bed to the window, from the window to the opposite wall, as if he were a baby. I am with you, Father, I don't let you go. Sleep, Papa, sleep. . . .

A car stopped with screaming brakes in front of the house. I put Father back to bed, covered him carefully with a blanket. The next moment Mother burst into the room. She threw herself over Father, crying, sobbing hysterically. If I could only cry, I thought. If I could only cry . . .

5

Father had always wished to be cremated, but for some reason or other I could not bring myself to carry out his wish. Neither could I stand the thought of having him buried. And so he rests in a vault of a mausoleum in the Hollywood Cemetery.

Cecil de Mille spoke a truly magnificent eulogy. The entire company of the Jewish Art Theatre, which happened to be playing in Los Angeles at that time, was present. Thousands of people lined the streets from the chapel to the cemetery.

I had to say the Hebrew death prayer—the Kaddish—which is spoken by the oldest son of the family over the body of the father. Since I cannot read Hebrew the prayer was written out for me in English letters. I read it quietly and calmly. Everyone admired my self-control. Only our doctor, standing next to me, knew the truth. He expected me to collapse any minute.

I still had not shed a single tear. My knees trembled violently. This was the only sensation I was conscious of.

I had arrived at the end of the prayer. The bronze casket was placed in the vault.

On the bronze tablet two words only are inscribed: Rudolf Schildkraut.

Condolences poured in from all over the world. Among them was one from the German ambassador in Washington. In the name of his government he expressed the deep sorrow the whole Reich felt over Father's death.

That was in July 1930.

Three years later Propaganda Minister Goebbels ordered my father's life-size portrait to be destroyed publicly. It had been painted by Max Liebermann, one of Germany's greatest painters, and hung in the "honor gallery" on the first floor of Max Reinhardt's theater. There, in the courtyard of that theater, it was burned.

But as one of Father's closest friends, Eduard von Winterstein, a great actor and a wonderful man, who all through the Nazi regime never wavered in his devotion to the other Germany, wrote me at that time in a letter smuggled out of the Teutonic brown hell, "Don't worry. He would no longer have wanted to have his portrait hanging here. Nor should he."

Chapter XI

1

WEEKS PASSED—one month, another month. The pain remained, an agonizing numbness. I could not shake it off. I did not want to. I felt utterly lost, too tired to work, too tired to think.

I had moved into Mother's house at Courtney Avenue. There I sat on the porch for hours, staring into the blue and cloudless sky. My head was empty, I felt as though I had lost control of my limbs, as though all my blood had flown out of my veins.

I knew Mother suffered too. Sometimes I reproached myself for not trying to comfort and distract her by taking her for a walk or a ride. I could not. With a bitter obstinacy I clung to my own grief, hiding in my stupor as in a dark cave.

September came. Suddenly I decided to break out of that cave. Escape! It was not easy, it took a lot of effort. The concern for Mother, my bad conscience over having neglected her for so long, spurred me on. I put Mother and myself on a boat, and we went to New York via the Panama Canal.

New York was even more depressing to me than Holly-wood. The economic crisis enveloped the city like a poisonous fog. Everyone was haunted by fear—fear of losing his job, of going out of business. The present was bleak and the future full of uncertainty.

I knew I was not yet emotionally stable enough to go on the stage, but I also realized that the only solution for me was work. If I could only get an interesting part in some show . . .

My secret thoughts must have reached Herman Shumlin. As soon as he heard I was in town, he sent me the German script of a play he had just bought. It had had a very suc-cessful run in Germany. The author: my dear old friend from Vienna, Vicki Baum. The American adaptation was to be presented under the title *Grand Hotel*. I was offered the part of the Baron.

Was it my subconscious resistance against going on again with my professional life "as if nothing had happened," or was my judgment warped by the shattering experience of the previous months? However it may have been, I refused the part. I thought the play inept, boring. I remember driv-ing to the theater in a taxi a few weeks later with three friends whom I had invited to the opening. I apologized for the "turkey" we were about to witness. "I don't think the play will run for more than a couple of days," I predicted. I certainly was as wrong as one could be.

The play was a sensational success. My part was played by Henry Hull, and Eugenie Leontovich, who for years had struggled in vain for recognition, became a star overnight in the role of the ballerina.

The New York climate did not agree with Mother, and she went back to her house in Hollywood. I settled in a small apartment on Central Park West. I waited for—I did not know what.

And then the producer Bela Blau decided to present Schnitzler's *Anatol* and offered me the title role. For years I had wanted to play that part in New York. Jo Mielziner designed truly beautiful sets, Marc Connelly directed with great sensitivity, and the cast was excellent: Miriam Hopkins, Dennie Moore, Patricia Collinge, and the wonderful comedian Walter Connolly. Everything seemed fine until, on the day of the opening at the Lyceum Theatre, I caught a bad head cold. I ran a high temperature, and, weak-kneed and tottering, was in no condition to play an elegant and sophisticated man-about-town.

The opening night was real torture for me. I felt a terrible loneliness. Memories buzzed around me like hundreds of gnats that could not be chased away. I knew I could have been really good under different circumstances, and that thought depressed me more. Beyond this, I suddenly felt that the magnificent sets were much too massive for this fragile comedy, which should be light as a soufflé. The performance dragged. I felt the evening was much too long. Nevertheless, the notices were good—quite undeservedly, in my opinion—but of course not as good as we all had hoped.

After a few weeks the play moved to the smaller Booth Theatre. We all took salary cuts and tried hard to keep the show alive. It improved considerably, but it was too late. We closed after about ten weeks.

And so there I was in New York in the middle of the season of 1930-1931 with nothing to do. A dreary and sad winter it was.

I had never been in England. And so when I received an offer from Herbert Wilcox, the British film director, to appear in two pictures to be produced in both an English and a German version, I accepted. I could hardly wait to escape from New York. On May 1, 1931, I landed in England.

2

My cousin and close friend, Herman Goldner, met me as planned in Southampton and remained with me as my secretary. The company had rented for me the house of Richard

Hughes, whose novel *A High Wind in Jamaica* was then being talked about everywhere. It was a beautiful house in Lloyd Square, which reminded me of New York's Gramercy Park. I was instantly captivated by its congenial atmosphere.

On the other hand, the pictures I worked in did not please me at all. My parts were the usual run-of-the-mill pseudo-romantic trifles: in the first film I played an Italian officer; in the second a Hungarian gypsy fiddler. I was not particularly good or particularly bad in either of them. The only satisfaction was my very handsome salary.

London disappointed me. The eternal rain and fog were exasperating. Also, I found the speech of the English a bit difficult to understand at first. It seemed to me affected, phonetically strange, and irritating. I was surprised at the cordial, even enthusiastic, reception of the London press. The reason for my popularity was the great success of Father's films, especially *His People* and *The Country Doctor*, and de Mille's *King of Kings*. Besides, *Show Boat* had been recently released in England and my performance had been highly praised.

One day I received through the studio's publicity office an invitation to a tea party given by a prominent and politically influential personality. I went with Herman.

Drifting through the crowd, I saw a blond girl enter the room on the arm of a very distinguished-looking elderly gentleman. Instantly my interest was aroused. The girl had blue eyes and a cute snub nose, and her hair was the color of ripe wheat. She was dressed simply, yet with perfect taste. She was not stunning; there were more beautiful girls present, but none with more natural grace and dignity.

I found out that the old gentleman was Judge Strauss, who held a high position in the London Courts. The girl was his niece and her name was Marie McKay.

After I had maneuvered myself into a seat next to her, I tried desperately to make a favorable impression on her. My efforts at spirited conversation were ineffective. With a chilly aloofness she looked at me and said finally—just a bit disdainfully, as it seemed to me—"You know, you've got a rather interesting face. You ought to try to go on stage, or be in pictures or something."

"My name is Joseph Schildkraut," I answered with a little ironic smile.

"That doesn't matter, you can always change your name," she said consolingly.

And with that our conversation stopped.

Later on, Marie was told by her uncle and other people who I was and what an important part my father had played in the European and American theater. The following week I received an invitation to a high tea she gave. I went with great expectations, but again my self-esteem was dealt a heavy blow. In introducing me to her guests Marie said most charmingly, "And this is Mr. Schildkraut. You know, his father was a great actor."

And yet, these two incidents, aside from her strange aloofness and her beauty, deepened my interest in her and my determination to win her friendship.

Friendship? It was the first time that I had met a very attractive girl without thinking how and when I would succeed in steering her into my bed. I was surprised at myself. It was not that Marie lacked femininity; on the contrary, she was very desirable. Though her background and upbringing excluded the kind of affair in which I was usually involved, that in itself would not have prevented me from trying to make love to her. It was just that I would have felt silly trying to impress her as a charmer and man-about-town. And I was actually grateful to her for giving me a chance to establish our relationship on a higher and more mature level. I was tired of the game of pursuit and conquest, I was in need of understanding, comradeship, warmth. Marie had it to an astounding degree. All the women I had loved had been objects of my whims and desires; Marie had to be met on her own terms. For once I was not the master of the situation. I had felt lost; now I had someone to hold on to.

But what could be the outcome of our relationship? I was so happy in Marie's company that I did not want to complicate matters by plans for tomorrow. The thought of proposing to her scared me. Another marriage? Was I really made for married life? Would it be fair to Marie? Could I ever give her what she must want most: stability, the harmonious life she was accustomed to?

In my confusion I decided to "think things over." The two films were completed, I had no other professional commitments in England, and so I thought of a trip to Austria. An absence of a few weeks would give me a chance to take stock of my own feelings.

For days I hesitated to tell Marie. How would she react? She would certainly feel slighted; she might try to hold me back. I loathed the thought of one of those scenes I had lived through with other women under similar circumstances.

But when I finally informed Marie that I intended to leave for the Continent with Herman she did not seem to mind at all. I wanted to visit Austria? Why not? Austria is a beautiful country. I would certainly enjoy the trip. Now *I* felt hurt. Did she care so little for me? She could at least show her disappointment. Her attitude, so sensible, so matter-of-fact, gave no indication that I meant more to her than a passing acquaintance. And I thought she might be in love with me! Fool that I was! If my trip to Austria was originally conceived as a kind of flight, I saw it now as a gesture of defiance. I could do without Marie at least as well as she without me.

Vienna welcomed me with open arms. It had not forgotten me, and I was touched by my warm reception. To be sure, after a few days I realized that the Viennese who swarmed around me, flattered and feted me, were not motivated exclusively by their fond memories of my previous performances. Almost everyone wanted something from me. The something was American dollars. Everyone tried to sell me something: a movie script, a play, clothes, jewelry, a house. I was even offered the ownership of the Deutsches Volkstheater, where I had scored my greatest triumph before I had left for America.

It was not difficult to perceive behind the outbursts of sympathy and admiration the more material considerations that prompted my Viennese friends to make me such generous offers, but I did not mind. Not really. Vienna was poor, life was hard and difficult; that explained and excused much. In spite of everything Vienna had not lost its old charm and I succumbed to it. There were my old colleagues, so many pretty girls, the opera, as excellent as ever; there were the cafés and heurigen. The memories of the happy years I had spent here overcame me, and I decided to accept the offer and to buy the majority share of the Deutsches Volkstheater. After all, it was a beautiful theater and I could buy it for less than $18,000—a real bargain.

I phoned Mother in Hollywood. Our conversation was short and to the point:

"Hello, Mama—"

"Yes, Pepi?"

"I'm calling from Vienna."

"Hurry up then, that call will cost a lot of money. What happened?"

"Nothing happened. I can buy the majority shares of the Deutsches Volkstheater for eighteen thousand dollars. Please make the necessary arrangements and have the money transferred from our joint account—"

Mother did not let me finish. "Look, Pepi, I am glad you woke me up, I just noticed I forgot to turn off the radio before I went to bed. That costs too much electricity. So I can turn it off now. For the rest, please don't drive me and yourself crazy. Good night, Pepi."

And she hung up.

No, I did not buy the theater.

3

Summer came. Vienna was hot, the theaters and the opera closed. In a few days the city seemed to have lost half of its population. The streets were deserted; in the glaring sun you could see how dilapidated the houses were, how much in need of repair. The leaves of the chestnut trees on the Ring had turned brown; in the parks the lawns and flower beds were gray, covered with dust. Even my favorite café was no refuge. The room with the curtains drawn against the sun was in semi-darkness, the air stifling; the waiter was dozing in a corner, looking as if he had gone to sleep on his feet. Fat flies were buzzing around the tables. Time stood still and I thought I would suffocate.

I left Vienna. We went to St. Wolfgang, Herman and I. The little old village with its quaint houses and lovely lake, guarded by pine-covered mountains—it is one of the most enchanting places I know.

We stayed at the White Horse Inn. Viewed from our balcony the scenery was as unreal as a stage set for an Austrian operetta and as real as a beautiful dream. Gradually I drifted into a state of inner contentment, a soothing lassitude.

Came the 15th of July. The first anniversary of my father's death hit me with the force of a bodily blow. The peace and serenity of St. Wolfgang only deepened my misery and hopelessness. I hated the dazzling colors of sky, lake, and mountains, they were such an incongruous contrast to my dark and somber mood.

Herman became alarmed at the violence of my despair. He was afraid I would lapse into a complete nervous breakdown. Was there no one who could help me? Then he thought of the answer: Marie. Without informing me, he called her on the phone in London.

The next evening Marie arrived.

Herman and I shared a suite on the third floor of the hotel. Marie found accommodations two floors below.

That first night a bizarre incident occurred.

It was about four o'clock in the morning. Herman and I were sound asleep when we were awakened by a pounding at our door. It was Marie, clad in a dainty nightgown, trembling with fear, at the point of hysteria. She stumbled into our room.

She had slept with her windows open. A bat flew in and frightened her to death. Unable to speak German, unable to summon help, she had fled to us.

As Marie explained later, a week or two before she was born, her mother had an unfortunate experience with a bat that flew into her bedroom and got entangled in her hair. That story, which Marie had heard as a child, made a lasting impression on her. She wore her hair in the old-fashioned way; when not set in a coiffure, it hung down below her waist. The thought that the bat might attack her scared Marie out of her wits.

She was afraid to go back to her room. But in our suite there was only one double bed, which I shared with Herman, and not a sofa or couch that would accommodate any of us. And so Marie installed herself in the middle of the bed between us. She was soon sound asleep. Herman and I on either side of her did not close our eyes. It was indecently platonic and most irritating, to say the least.

From that day on, Marie and I never separated again. She became my wife. But she has also been mother, friend, nurse, adviser, and business manager all in one. I owe her a great debt for her kindness, understanding, and unwavering love. That we have no children was nature's will. This great wish of ours has not been fulfilled. It has been the only imperfection in our union.

Fortunately, two years ago Marie and I discovered a little boy to whom we could give some of the love and support that we could not give to a child of our own. Albert Lotto was ten years old when he was introduced to me as a very promising pianist. At first I was skeptical; I am not keen on child prodigies. But Albert, who looked as Franz Schubert might have looked at his age, proved to be a sensitive, well-bred, well-behaved youngster, intelligent without being precocious, not at all the usual *Wunderkind*. When I heard him play—from Mozart's Coronation Concerto, from Schubert, some Beethoven and Bach—I was enthralled. His musical maturity was really astonishing. Marie shared my enthusiasm. We immediately decided that this talent deserved all our support. We found him an excellent teacher, and in September 1957 he passed his examination for the Juilliard School of Music with flying colors. Today, a student of Miss Frances Mann, he is the pride of this excellent school; a few months ago he won a scholarship for composition.

Often Albert spends his vacation with us. During his last one he gave a superb performance of Beethoven's B Minor Concerto with the Merenblum orchestra of Los Angeles, which has been in existence for about thirty years. But what makes me even more happy than his successes is to see how Marie has found in this boy an outlet for her deep understanding and love of children. She watches over Albert's artistic and intellectual progress as if he were her real son.

4

We were married in Vienna, where I played at the Deutsches Volkstheater in Erwin Piscator's dramatization of Theodore Dreiser's *An American Tragedy*. My leading lady was a talented young actress who later won two Academy Awards for her film performances: Luise Rainer.

One afternoon the manager of the theater, Dr. Rudolf Beer, called me on the telephone and suggested I should not play that night. Another actor was ready to replace me. He explained that it was an election day, that pro-Nazi and anti-Semitic feelings were running high, and he feared violent demonstrations against me.

I refused to be intimidated. The evening performance

passed without incident, except for a standing ovation at the end of the play by which the audience expressed not merely its appreciation for my work but also its contempt for the propaganda of the Nazis.

That was in May 1932. Hitler had not yet come to power in Germany, but in Austria too the brown flood was rising dangerously. Most of our friends did not take the menace seriously. To them Vienna was a bulwark of socialism and democracy, and the Nazis in Austria were an insignificant minority, "a bunch of derelicts and bums." To Marie and me the young and not-so-young hoodlums in their white stockings, which, since they were not permitted to wear uniforms or badges, they had chosen as their party insignia, looked dangerous enough. Their *Juda Verrecke* ("Death to the Jews") echoed equally ominously through the streets of the rich and poor districts of Vienna.

From day to day the change became more noticeable. You could see it in the faces of many people: a bitter line around the mouth; distrustful, angry eyes. Their voices grew hard. An uncertainty appeared in their gait, they carried their heads between their shoulders. They began to look like haunted fugitives.

"Death to the Jews!" First you saw it scrawled on the walls of telephone booths or urinals, then painted in tar on the sidewalks. Next it was neatly printed on stickers, pasted on advertising pillars and shop windows. And finally, slips of paper bearing the words floated down from the sky. Four words replaced Beethoven and Mozart, Goethe and Schiller, knowledge and reason—Death to the Jews!

The Austrian "patriots" yelled them at the top of their lungs.

One more summer we spent in my beloved St. Wolfgang, Marie and I. But even there I could no longer escape the feeling of doom. Austria was ready for Hitler.

That was the last time I saw the land of my birth.

5

At the end of the summer we returned to America.

Before leaving Vienna I had received a cable from Eva Le Gallienne informing me that she was about to stage a revival of *Liliom* at her Civic Repertory Theatre on 14th Street. She could not conceive of the play without me in the part and asked me to join her company for the forthcoming season.

I accepted at once, not only because I had no other commitment either on Broadway or in Hollywood, but primarily because of my great friendship and admiration for Eva. She had founded the Civic Repertory Theatre in 1926 against terrific odds. Every "expert" had "proved" conclusively that a repertory theater in the European sense could not exist in America: the popular prices she charged were too low; the public would look upon her productions as cheap, not up to Broadway standards. Many ridiculed her ignorance of the average theater-goer, who expected entertainment, not Chekhov and Ibsen.

Eva, a real pioneer, stuck to her convictions, and she succeeded. Now, after six seasons, the Civic Repertory Theatre was definitely established as an important artistic center of New York. Some of her productions had failed, but most of them had not only met with great critical acclaim but had played to sold-out houses. In six years Eva had produced thirty-four plays, of which she personally had directed thirty-two—a truly remarkable accomplishment that indicates Eva's talent and her incredible energy.

We opened the theater's sixth season with a road tour, alternating *Liliom* and *Camille,* Dumas' sure-fire drama in which I played Armand opposite Eva's Camille.

At the end of October we brought *Liliom* to New York once more. Ten years had passed since that first memorable presentation of the Theatre Guild. Eva and I had both changed, and we knew that the change had been for the better; critics agreed that our performances had more depth and maturity.

One of my great joys during that season was playing the Queen of Hearts in Le Gallienne's outstanding production of *Alice in Wonderland*. Special features of this show were the costumes, masks, and scenery which were exact replicas of the original Tenniel drawings. Richard Addinsell furnished an enchanting musical score.

And then, suddenly, the crash. President Roosevelt closed the banks.

The intake at the box office had climbed to a high average, but the theater still needed a yearly subsidy of approximately $75,000 to be able to continue. Overnight Eva Le Gallienne's financial backers found themselves unable to fulfill their promises. We were rehearsing Galsworthy's *Loyalties*, with myself in the part of de Levis, when Eva had to admit defeat. The Civic Repertory Theatre ceased to exist.

6

Once more I was back in Hollywood. At first, Marie and I took up residence in Mother's house. Immediately I was confronted with the painful problem of Mother's violent animosity toward Marie.

Mother had always been jealous of every woman to whom I became attached. Since Father's death her possessiveness had become stronger than ever. She looked upon Marie as an intruder who had robbed her of her son's love and loyalty. I tried constantly to convince her that her fears were unfounded, but to no avail. Marie's efforts to win her love, or at least sympathy, proved futile. It was a very trying situation for all three of us.

It took years for Mother to change her attitude toward Marie. Only in her last years, while she was gravely ill, did she turn to my wife and actually become more and more dependent on her. Before she passed away in the spring of 1940, she would not let the nurses touch her unless Marie was present, and no one but Marie could cajole her into following doctor's orders and taking the prescribed medicine.

As for me, I tried hard to give Mother full credit for her good intentions but I could not control my inner resentment against the stubbornness with which she clung to her middle-class prejudices. After Father's death I grew away from her more and more. Intellectually and as an artist, I had little in common with her. Looking back, I have a clearer realization of her great qualities than I had at that time: her strength, her common sense, her natural modesty. It was just that, though we lived only a few streets away from each other, we lived in two separate worlds. No, with all her love she could never be to me what Father was: a guiding star, my artistic conscience. Instinctively I blamed her for her shortcomings, though it was not her fault that throughout her life, which took her halfway across the world and into the society of famous people, she remained to the day of her death the same simple and unsophisticated person she was when Father met her at the delicatessen store in Vienna. If she had changed she would not have been true to herself. Therein lay her strength and her limitations. Maybe if I had had more patience and understanding I could have overcome my irritation, but I could not find much time for Mother.

Those were very busy years for me. One film followed another, and in between I appeared in plays on Broadway. There was *The Garden of Allah,* a film in color produced by David Selznick. Marlene Dietrich and Charles Boyer were the lovers and I, for the first time in my film career, played an all-out comedy part as the Arab guide, Batouche. I loved the part and I particularly enjoyed working under that excellent director Richard Boleslavski, a former member of the Stanislavsky theater.

I will never forget our days on location in Yuma, Arizona, where it was so terribly hot that Marlene had fainting spells right on the sand dunes. The company was sent home, and tons and tons of desert sand were shipped to Hollywood where all outdoor scenes were shot indoors at the Selznick studios in Culver City. In that film the Viennese dancer and dear friend of mine, Tilly Losch, did an Arabian belly dance which I remember to this day as one of the most sensuous exhibitions I have ever seen.

Then followed *Viva Villa,* another David Selznick picture which he produced for Metro. As Pancho Villa Wallace Beery gave what I believe was the finest performance of his career.

The part of General Pascal had been especially written for me by Ben Hecht, one of my closest friends. Years before, as a drama critic in Chicago, he had been one of my "discoverers," and we had become very fond of each other. We still are. No one who has seen the picture will ever forget Pascal's end, one of the most dramatic and harrowing scenes in this excellent film. Pancho Villa had his adversary's, General Pascal's, body smeared with honey and stuck, head first, with his hands tied behind his back, into an ant hill. The camera then moved up into the sky and focused on a couple of vultures circling the fields.

Other films in which I starred during the next few years were *Lancer Spy, Slave Ship, The Man in the Iron Mask, Marie Antoinette, The Rains Came,* and *Idiot's Delight.* And in 1937, as I have mentioned earlier, I was Captain Dreyfus in *The Life of Emile Zola.*

When the Academy Award dinner was held early in 1938, my agent discouraged me from going to the affair, which was staged at the Biltmore Bowl in Los Angeles. He had heard the award for best supporting actor would go either to Ralph Bellamy, for his part in *The Awful Truth,* or to Thomas Mitchell, who had scored a great success in *Stage Coach.* So we stayed home.

I was already in bed when the telephone rang. The excited voice of a man who did not even bother to introduce himself bellowed at me. "Where in hell are you? Why aren't you here?"

"Where?"

"Here at the Bowl."

"What for?"

"The awards are about to be handed out and you are not here."

"Did I get it?"

"Never mind. We can't tell you that. Just come down here. At once."

I could hardly think straight. Was this some practical joke? "If you don't tell me, I won't come," I blurted out.

"Yes, you son of a gun," the man shouted. "You won it. Get down here!"

We dressed in haste, ordered our car, and went in style to the Biltmore Bowl. I arrived just in time to be seated at the Warner Brothers' table and to accept the "Oscar" for my portrayal of Dreyfus from Frank Capra.

A typical sidelight on Hollywood: I won that award for Warner Brothers in 1938 and have not worked on that lot since.

7

During the next two years the atmosphere and social climate of Hollywood changed considerably. Every day new victims of Hitler arrived, actors, directors, writers, musicians from all European countries—an army of intellectuals and artists whose past accomplishments were their patent of nobility but whose names, in most cases, meant nothing to the rulers of Hollywood. Most had saved only a fraction of their worldly possessions; many were destitute. However, they suffered less from their financial predicament than from the recurrent request to "please spell your name." They had thought themselves world-famous; they found out that they were just refugees.

Many of them were friends of my youth and former colleagues. They suddenly made the horrors of Nazism a living reality to all of us. Overnight self-centered, extravagant Hollywood became socially conscious, politically minded.

To be sure, there were some die-hard Communists among the actors and writers, some drawing-room Bolsheviks who embraced Communism because it seemed "the wave of the future," a fashionable fad. But most of those who developed leftist leanings were motivated by their personal concern for Hitler's victims. Well-meaning, though politically immature, they saw in the Communists not the propagandists for the Red dictatorship, but the most energetic fighters against the Nazis. Never interested in politics and always averse to joining a party or a movement, I remained as aloof from the radical rage of the thirties as I had been an outsider during the crazy days of the twenties.

In the film *Shop around the Corner,* which Ernst Lubitsch directed, I played a light, humorous part for the second time and was again "discovered" as a comedian. I had hoped this success would lead to similar parts in which I could show my talent, but Hollywood continued to cast me in worn-out pseudo-romantic roles or as villains, in pictures that had no merit whatsoever except that they made money. Why did I complain? Was I not paid well for my services? Very well?

And then, at the beginning of World War II, Michael Kanin, Garson's brother, called me up and asked me if I would be interested in a film version of Edgar Allan Poe's *The Tell-Tale Heart.* It was to be a short film, and there was not much money in it, but at last here was a chance to escape the run-of-the-mill parts I was offered all the time. Besides, Michael and his charming wife, Fay, have been close friends of mine for many years, and I have been an admirer of Poe since my early youth. I found the screenplay excellent.

Poe's story is merely the monologue of a mentally deranged man, and the film was to a great extent in pantomime, accompanied by music and various sound effects. In fact, I did not speak more than about four short sentences in the whole picture. As the weaver apprentice who is mistreated by his employer, a fear-ridden, stingy man, and finally murders his tormentor, I could create an interesting character with a minimum of words, a challenge that has always fascinated me.

The Tell-Tale Heart was truly a brilliant psychological film and it won an "Oscar" for the best short dramatic subject of that year.

8

One evening Stella Adler, Harold Clurman, and Boris Aronson were my guests for dinner. Later when we had settled in the library the talk led to Billy Rose's production of Clifford Odets' new drama, *Clash by Night*, for which Aronson was to design the sets. Tallulah Bankhead was to play the wife, Lee Cobb the husband. Odets and Lee Strasberg, the director, were desperately looking for an actor to play the third part, a motion-picture projectionist from Staten Island.

In the middle of our animated conversation Harold Clurman, whom I regard as one of the really great directors and an excellent theater critic, suddenly pointed at me and said with a quizzical smile to Stella, "Earl Pfeiffer?"

Since I had never heard of *Clash by Night* before, I did not understand. "Who's Earl Pfeiffer?" I asked.

Clurman explained. Pfeiffer was the third character in Odets' play and it had just occurred to him that I may be ideal for that part. On the spot he sent a wire to Odets.

For a long time I had cherished the hope of some day appearing in one of Odets' plays. I admire his work; in my opinion he did for modern American drama what Ibsen did in his time for the European theater. My disappointment therefore was great when a few days later I received Odets' answer. Much as he would like to have me in one of his plays, he could not quite see me in that particular part. And that was that, I thought.

But I was wrong. A fortnight later I received a second wire, asking me to fly immediately to New York and to read a scene or two of Earl Pfeiffer's part for Billy Rose, Clifford Odets, and Lee Strasberg. All my expenses would be paid, of course.

What was there to lose? I could only gain. So I accepted.

I took the night plane to New York. It was my first flight and I frankly admit I was frightened. After the take-off the pilot, walking through the plane, came over to me and said, "Welcome, Mr. Schildkraut. I understand this is your first flight. Is there anything we can do for you?"

"Yes," I said, "please, fly low and slow." And I really meant it.

The next day I had dinner with the three gentlemen at Odets' home on Sutton Place. After dinner I was asked to read a scene with Lee Strasberg giving me the cues. But I had hardly read two or three lines when Odets and Rose interrupted me. "Oh, nuts, how much do you want?"

The next morning I signed the contract.

A few months later I returned to New York, and the rehearsals began.

Lee Strasberg was a very considerate director though for my taste somewhat puzzling. I was not used to the jargon of the Group Theatre, nor to this day do I understand the lingo of the Actors' Studio. Maybe it's all very good and important, but it's just not the world of the theater in which I was brought up. This constantly misinterpreted and misunderstood Stanislavsky "method" infuriates me. The great actors and actresses I have seen in my lifetime, I am certain, never used "inner motors" or "images" and "obstacles." Imagine Eleonora Duse using an "obstacle" or my father "making like a hat rack"!

I was once invited to a so-called modern-drama class. Some very talented youngsters appeared in a number of scenes from various plays, and after two or three hours of this I heard the instructor—and he is a big name in the American theater—discuss the students' performances with them. I was puzzled and shocked at what I heard.

Later I was asked to say a few words. All I could think of was a parable by the classic German writer, Gotthold Ephraim Lessing. "Ladies and gentlemen," I said, "once upon a time there was a beautiful fig tree standing by a river's edge somewhere in India. In the crown of that tree there lived a graceful, beautiful artist, a centipede. Every morning at sunrise, that centipede would slither down from the tree and dance in the sand and do beautiful pirouettes. It was indeed a perfect exhibition of his art.

"Under a dried-up bush near a swampy pool of stagnant, evil-smelling water lived the charming centipede's neighbor, a slimy, ugly, warty toad. This limping and hobbling Mr. Toad was terribly jealous of that exquisite artist, Mr. Centipede. And so one day he sent his neighbor the following letter:

" 'Your Excellency of the fig tree across the way. You are beautiful, you are a born artist, and your morning dances are a delight to all my senses. I am just a slimy, ugly, limping toad. But permit me to ask you a question: How do you do it? What does foot number 719 do when number 68 is stretched out, or where is number 16 when number 540 is about to bend? In which position is the knee of number 8 when number 95's toes are about to touch the sand? Where is foot number 2 and what does it do? Respectfully yours. The Toad.'

"The centipede read the letter and from that day on he could not move a leg.

"And that's how I feel about the entire idea of modern instruction for actors."

The rehearsals of *Clash by Night* were indeed clashes by day and night, and not through my fault, either. I really behaved like a lamb. But between Miss Bankhead's obstreperous and condescending manner of rehearsing, Mr. Cobb's introverted and monosyllabic approach to his role, and Lee Strasberg's well-meant but to me vague stage directions I felt utterly lost. I nearly went crazy. I was always careful to be extremely polite to Miss Bankhead, as one is cautious in approaching a tigress. Had I ever lost my temper, even for a few minutes, I think I would have killed her.

Lee Strasberg frequently invited me to his home. I recall most vividly his magnificent library with hundreds of books about the theater, the many glass tanks filled with tropical fish, and a little baby in a crib called Susan, Lee's and Paula's daughter, who, fifteen years later, would be my co-star in *The Diary of Anne Frank*.

When *Clash by Night* closed after about eight weeks, I sent Miss Bankhead a box of roses with a polite good-by note. On stage, after the last curtain-fall, she turned to me and thanked me for my gift with these words: "You're a gentleman but I don't like you. I still like your wife." And she left me standing there gaping after her.

The failure of *Clash by Night* came in the middle of the 1941-1942 season. But this time I was determined not to return to Hollywood until I had found a play with an interesting part for me and the possibilities of commercial success and a long run. I read dozens of plays. Nothing. Some were, in fact, quite good and subsequently proved successful on Broadway, but the parts were not right for me.

This is one of the curses of our American theater. Once you are a "star" you must have a "starring" part; you cannot afford to step down from that billing in favor of a supporting role in a play, however excellent it may be. And so it happens that a star can count himself extremely lucky if during his entire career he finds four or five parts which are really "right." If I remember correctly, it was the famous actor Joseph Jefferson who actually played only one part through his entire career: Rip van Winkle. And after his death, his son and later his grandson continued in the same role.

A grotesque dilemma: On the one hand, we all look for a play that may prove both artistically important and commercially successful; on the other hand, when we find such a rare script we get pretty much fed up with it after playing the same part day after day and month after month. The only exception to this general rule for me was my part in *The Diary of Anne Frank*. But that play was a very special case, and my association with it meant to me more than just playing a role.

One day a script was mailed to my hotel. It bore the colorless title *Uncle Harry*. The author, Thomas Job, was unknown to me. There was a note attached to the script signed by a certain Clifford Hayman who introduced himself as stage manager and nephew of Max Gordon, the well-known New York producer. He asked me please to read the script as soon as possible.

I started reading reluctantly, without much hope or interest. But by the end of the first act I knew I had found my play. Immediately, I so informed Mr. Hayman.

A few days later Mr. Hayman sent me a very apologetic letter. He was sorry to have imposed on my time but the author, a teacher of playwriting at Carnegie Tech in Pittsburgh, could not see me in that part at all. Maybe it was his fault for not having described the character clearly enough: a sandy-haired, blue-eyed, slightly pot-bellied Welshman. He had thought of Charles Laughton or Claude Rains in that part. In spite of his great admiration for my work, he could not offer me his play.

What Mr. Hayman did not tell me was that *Uncle Harry* had already been tried out on the road with the able actor Russell Collins as Harry, and had failed. Half a dozen producers whom I talked to considered the script "old hat" and unhesitatingly declined to put it on.

But that did not dampen my interest in *Uncle Harry* or my conviction that here was the part I was looking for. I got in touch with the author and explained to him how I conceived my role. I suggested that he rewrite some scenes, have the drama play in French Canada instead of Wales, and move the action into the late eighties or early nineties. Thus the play would benefit from the colorful costumes and the atmosphere of that period. Mr. Job reluctantly agreed to my suggestions.

Mr. Hayman wanted Pauline Lord, a very gifted actress, for the leading feminine part. I had my own ideas. Though I did not even know whether she would be interested, I insisted on Eva Le Gallienne. Unfortunately she was very ill at that time, confined to a hospital with pneumonia. When I visited her she was in an oxygen tent and we all feared the worst. But my wife was confident. "By the time you are ready for rehearsals," she said, "Eva will be well and able to play." And Marie was right. Eva, thank God, recovered, and finally gave in to my constant pleading. She consented to take the part of Lettie on one condition: as soon as *Uncle Harry* finished its run, I was to play Gaev opposite her in Chekhov's *The Cherry Orchard*. That was a promise I most gladly gave.

Since no reputable Broadway producer was interested in *Uncle Harry*, Marie and I decided to raise the money for the production on our own. Eva wanted Margaret Webster to direct the play, but I had already offered that job to a young director who had just scored a notable personal success in *Brooklyn U.S.A.*, though the play itself had failed. I had met Lem Ward and I was very much impressed by him. He was a slender young man with a burning passion for the theater. He came from Philadelphia, where he had directed all sorts of plays, and was an excellent dancer and choreographer.

We finally succeeded in raising practically the entire amount for our production. But when we started the dress rehearsal we were as good as broke. Our bank account was somewhere in the neighborhood of twelve dollars, and we had to open "cold," without a tryout out of town. To add to our worries, the author was greatly displeased with our show. We had decided not to present his play as a typical British melodrama, the way he had conceived it, but to give it a good measure of humor and romance. Tom Job was horrified. He was almost ready to withdraw the play.

My exasperation reached its climax when after the rehearsal Marie came into my dressing room and said calmly, "I wouldn't give you a dollar fifty for the whole play. The end was terribly anticlimactic. For heaven's sake, cut out the epilogue."

I almost choked with fury. "But the epilogue is precisely why I wanted to play the part in the first place!" I shouted.

Of course, my wife was right. Her instinct of a nonprofessional theater-goer was correct. We did cut the epilogue. Job also rewrote the prologue, and the invited guests who had left the dress rehearsal disappointed were quite amazed to see *Uncle Harry* emerge as a genuine hit the next night. With all due respect to the author, the director, and the cast, it was Marie's suggestion that saved the play.

It ran for over a year in New York alone. Lem Ward became, as I had predicted, one of the most sought-after directors. It was mainly his sensitive work that carried Maxwell Anderson's *Eve of St. Mark* to its big success. Sad indeed that this highly talented and sensitive artist had to die so suddenly, so young. In the middle of the rehearsals for Sidney Kingsley's *The Patriots,* pneumonia, complicated by a heart attack, cut short a career that held so much promise for his future. His death was a great loss to the American theater.

On the road *Uncle Harry* was, if possible, an even greater success than it had been in New York. But after a few months Eva Le Gallienne grew weary of her part and of the play, magnificent as she was in it. She wanted to quit. The management hoped I would continue the tour with another actress, but I declined. Just as I never played *Liliom* with any other actress but Eva Le Gallienne, so I could not see myself playing *Uncle Harry* with anyone but her. And so both of us left the play. Two other actors took over, and in

three weeks the play closed; it had become too closely as-
sociated with our names. After all, while it was a clever and
effective drama, it was no important literary work.

Eva and I returned to New York and immediately plunged
into the rehearsals of *The Cherry Orchard*. Margaret Webster directed the play, Motley designed the sets, the rest of
the cast was excellent. Outstanding were Edward Franz as
the eternal student Trofimov and Ann Jackson as my young
niece. Though Eva Le Gallienne was really wonderful as
Madame Ranevskaya—in some scenes simply superb—I have
a feeling that she herself was never really satisfied with her
performance. At least she kept telling me all the time how
great Alla Nazimova was in that part when Eva had directed
the play in the Civic Repertory Theatre. Be that as it may,
Eva's production enjoyed the longest run this great play had
ever had in America.

When we closed for the summer I went back to California
to work with John Wayne in a film for Republic Studios—
from *The Cherry Orchard* to *Flame of the Barbary Coast*.
It was then that I made one of the major mistakes of my life:
I let Herbert Yates, the president of Republic Pictures, talk
me into signing a long-term contract with his company.
True, I was to receive a very high salary and I was promised
that I would act in pictures of real substance and importance
—two films a year my contract called for—but, as I should
have foreseen, that promise was never fulfilled.

I cannot say that I was not forewarned. When Mr. Yates
saw *The Cherry Orchard* in Chicago, he came back stage and
scoffed. "What kind of lousy play is this? Where were the
cherry trees? Where was the orchard?" Eva Le Gallienne
passed us in the corridor at that moment and gave me a look
I shall never forget. It predicted everything that I was to experience at the Republic Studios in the next three years.
Alas, I did not heed Eva's warning and I had nobody to
blame but myself for the disappointments that followed. No-

body forced me to sign the contract. And when later on I asked Mr. Yates to release me, he chose rather to pay me a lot of money and to put me into Western horse operas, though these parts could have been played for far less money by a score of unemployed actors specializing in that kind of performance.

Chapter XII

1

WHEN AT LAST, in March 1948, my contract with Republic expired, my mind was made up: I would not accept any part that was silly or superficial, or act in a film that did not have some merit and significance. Since, unfortunately, such parts were not offered to me I turned to other activities. I worked in television. From 1949 to 1955 I appeared in over eighty-five live television shows, some for Omnibus, such as *The Last Night of Don Juan* by Rostand and *Everyman,* others on my own program, *Joseph Schildkraut Presents* for the Dumont network.

There were two theater ventures during those years which I really enjoyed. I played the father in Pirandello's *Six Characters in Search of an Author* at the Brattle Theatre in Cambridge, Massachusetts. This theater, founded and run by a group of talented young Harvard students, had always interested me. Its contribution to the theater in America should have been an inspiration to all similar companies throughout the country. It truly represented the spirit of the European repertory theater. The six weeks I spent with this group of enthusiastic youngsters belong to my nicest memories. Today the Brattle Theatre is—should I say, "of course"?—a garage or a second-run movie house.

One of the members of that company, Albert Marre, later made quite a name for himself on Broadway. In January 1953 he staged a revival of Shakespeare's *Love's Labor's Lost* at the City Center in New York. I played Don Adriano de Armado, the wonderfully tragic-comic hero, whom I conceived as a mixture of Chaplin and Don Quixote. Though the critical opinion about Marre's production was divided, I thought it brilliant, one of the best interpretations of Shakespeare I had ever seen. Marre recreated most charmingly the period of Edward VII, with hammocks, croquet games, and old-fashioned phonographs, using effectively incidental music from the works of Schubert, Mendelssohn, and Delibes. To be part of that show was a lovely experience and I would not have wanted to miss it, even though the play ran for only three weeks and my salary was all of eighty-five dollars a week.

Some time during the winter of 1953-1954 a friend called my attention to a book called *The Diary of a Young Girl,* by Anne Frank, a translation from the Dutch. The author was a young Jewish girl, a native of Germany and refugee from Hitler, who had lived in hiding in Holland for almost two years before she was arrested and deported. She died in a concentration camp.

Extremely interested in everything pertaining to the Nazi era and the tragedy of the Jewish victims, I read the book and was deeply touched. I had to share this moving experience with my wife, and so I read it aloud to Marie from beginning to end.

When I had finished, Marie said softly, with tears in her eyes, "This diary would make a great play."

I looked at her flabbergasted. I was really outraged. "Are you crazy?" I shouted. "How can this book ever be adapted to a play? And, even more important, who the hell would pay six bucks to come and see it? Nazis and Jews—everyone wants to forget about those events. The Jews do not wish to be reminded of their terrible suffering under Hitler, and the majority of the Gentiles don't give a damn one way or another. Not to mention the official attitude of the State Department and most of our newspapers, playing up to Germany and coddling the former Nazis. Really, it is as if you were living on the moon!"

Marie remained very calm. "All right, it won't be a play."

A few months later, in December 1954, we had guests for dinner—the comedian Sig Arno, his talented actress wife Kitty, and the film director Fritz Lang. The telephone rang. It was my New York representative, Jane Broder. She wanted to know whether I would be interested in appearing on Broadway and free to start rehearsals in six weeks.

"A play? What kind of play? I hope, not again one of those—"

She interrupted. "Tell me, Pepi, did you ever read a book called *The Diary of a Young Girl?*"

"*The Diary*—" I yelled so loud that my guests in the dining room across the hall almost dropped their knives and forks. "Why do you ask? Is this the play—"

Jane explained that the Hacketts—Frances Goodrich and Albert Hackett—had adapted the diary, Kermit Bloomgarden was going to produce it, Boris Aronson would do the sets, Garson Kanin would direct.

I was so excited I could hardly contain myself. This was too good to be true. I was a friend and admirer of every one of these people. Though I had never met the Hacketts, I had liked very much their play *The Great Big Doorstep* and, of course, their "Thin Man" films, and the charming comedy *Seven Brides for Seven Brothers,* for which they won an Academy Award. I regard Boris Aronson as one of our best set designers and a wonderful person. He did his first stage design in America for my father's so successful production of Ossip Dymov's *The Bronx Express.* I had followed

Bloomgarden's productions with respect and admiration, and an old friendship linked me to Garson Kanin and his family.

Jane confided in me that Kanin, at that time in England, had cabled Bloomgarden that he wanted me for the part of Otto Frank and had no second choice. But for some reason or other Kermit Bloomgarden could not quite see me in this part. He still thought of me as a flamboyant and dashing character—he remembered me as Liliom, Peer Gynt, Benvenuto Cellini, Uncle Harry. Otto Frank was a simple, unassuming, quite ordinary businessman. How did I feel about that part?

Before answering the question I had to read the play. Jane promised to send it immediately.

When I told Marie and our guests the content of my telephone conversation everyone agreed it was a most interesting and worthwhile project, but, with one exception, all felt it was more than doubtful that the play could ever be a commercial success. The exception was Marie. "If Garson Kanin is really going to direct it," she said, "this 'Diary' will be a smash hit."

We all looked at her ironically. How could she say that? She had not even read the play yet. And she must admit the topic was tragically unpleasant, not at all the stuff of which popular successes are made.

Marie did not budge. "I don't care what you all say. If Kanin directs, it will be a smash hit." It was no use arguing with Marie. I dropped the subject.

A few days later the script arrived. I read it once, I read it a second time. I went into the garden, sat in a secluded corner, and read it a third time. For two days I did not speak with Marie about it. And when my friends, the Arnos and Lang, called and asked me what my impression of the script was I evaded an answer.

Marie became worried. This had never happened before. Through all the years of our marriage, whenever I read a play I had no difficulty in making up my mind. Why was I walking around like a mute? What was the matter with me?

The truth was, I found the script sincere and moving, really beautiful, but I was not sure that it was theatrically effective. Was it not too drab, too didactic for Broadway? It was certainly free from cheap sensationalism, but could it grip an audience, hold their attention, excite them? It was a work of literary value, but was it good theater?

I discussed my doubts with my good friend Dore Schary, at that time production chief of MGM. He too had read the script. He was blunt. "You must play Otto Frank," he declared. "This is a powerful play, extremely well written. Garson Kanin is sure to direct it superbly. Whether the play will be a success—who can make such a prediction in regard to any play? Yes, it is a difficult subject but you must play that part."

The same evening I finally read the play aloud to Marie and Fritz Lang. Lang still had his doubts but shared Schary's opinion that I must act in it, even if it should run for only a short time. Marie stubbornly defended her previous prediction, though she added this time, "The success depends entirely on Garson Kanin's direction. If for one or another reason someone else should direct it, don't do it."

There remained the question whether Bloomgarden would change his mind and agree with Kanin that I was right for the part of Otto Frank. On December 20 I was in New York. I had dinner with Bloomgarden and his wife. We had not yet been served our main course when Kermit turned to me and said, "Garson is right. I wouldn't want to do the play without you in that part." Two days later I signed the contract. Rehearsals were to start on January 17.

Next day came a cable from Kanin in Europe: If he was to direct the play, rehearsals must be postponed until August and the *Diary* opening in New York set for the first week of October. There were two reasons for this. Kanin wanted more time to prepare the production and he was afraid that a March opening would give too short a run before the hot weather. Summer might prove too great a handicap for this kind of show.

We were all disappointed about the delay, but Kanin was right. In fact, he was right in every single suggestion and decision he made in regard to the production. That Bloomgarden chose him as director was sheer inspiration. I don't think anyone else could have led this play to its great artistic and popular success.

So we waited for nearly eight months. I used the time to familiarize myself thoroughly with the diary. I read it in French and also in the excellent German translation which Otto Frank sent me.

That started a correspondence which Otto Frank and I have kept up to this very day.

Frank is really an unusual man. There are thousands of men and women who have lived through the same harrowing experiences and miraculously survived the tortures and agonies of prisons and concentration camps. What distinguishes him is his humility, his unwavering optimism—or perhaps I should call it serenity. After he was liberated and found out about the tragic death of his wife and daughters, he remarried. His present wife is a Viennese whom he met in the concentration camp of Auschwitz. At that time her head was shaved and they were both marked for the gas chamber. The Soviet Army freed them just in time and took them to Odessa. From there a British boat brought Frank to Marseilles. He made his way on foot across the Continent to Amsterdam.

It was during his first visit to the warehouse on Prinsengracht where the family and a few friends had lived in hiding for two years that Frank found Anne's diary, the Dutch original which is now displayed in a museum in The Hague. The prologue of the play describes this discovery as it actually occurred.

Frank lives now in Basle, Switzerland, but when the Hacketts and Kanin went to Amsterdam to gather local color and additional information for the play, Frank joined them and took them many times on tours of the city and through the now historic warehouse and its secret attic. Hundreds and hundreds of photographs were taken and sent to Aronson to assist him in the designing of the set.

Incidentally, the first time Kanin entered Anne's tiny cubicle in the attic, his eyes fell on a Dutch poster advertising a new film. It hung on the wall over Anne's bed among many other pictures of movie stars which the girl had collected. The poster read: *"Tom, Dick and Harry*—starring Ginger Rogers, directed by Garson Kanin."

Among the many letters I received from Otto Frank, the following seems to me especially significant. It illuminates his character and his outlook on life:

> I have a request today. When you portray "me" on stage, Mr. Schildkraut, please don't play me as a "hero." Believe me, I am not a hero. Nothing happened to me that did not happen to thousands upon thousands of other people. Being an optimist and having an optimistic outlook on life, I consider myself happy that I have at least lived those two years in the midst of my family—even under those dreadful conditions and even in the face of what happened to all of them in the end. It is this optimistic viewpoint which made me remarry and try to pick up the threads of my life where they were so brutally cut off. So please, do not weave a completely undeserved halo of heroism around my head.

2

On August 19, I arrived in New York for the rehearsals. First I had an appointment with Garson Kanin at his home. We had not seen each other for a number of years, and when I walked into his living room, he looked at me in dismay and exclaimed, "Oh, my God, too handsome and too young looking!"

Kanin was right. I certainly did not resemble the simple, sedate businessman from Frankfurt. During the rehearsals this discrepancy worried Kanin more and more. And one day he took me aside and said, "You know, Pepi, I think I have finally found out what bothers me. You act Otto Frank but you don't give the impression of being Otto Frank. That won't do." And so we decided that I was to make myself look as much as possible like Otto Frank. "He is partly bald," Kanin pointed out. "Please shave the center part of your head."

I indignantly refused. I suggested a compromise. My make-up consultant provided a can of nicely perfumed rose-colored wax which I used to smooth down the center part of my hair and then painted over with a liquid make-up. Now it really looked as if I were partly bald; at least, that's what I thought. But Kanin was not satisfied.

I had played in that make-up for about three weeks, and we were near the end of our Philadelphia tryout, when he came into my dressing room and said, "Pepi, you look like a painted actor. Who do you think you're kidding? You look phony, especially when you step from an amber light into a blue light. Then the trick is given away. Please, shave your head. You owe that to your performance and to Otto Frank. God damn it, you owe it to the memory of little Anne Frank. Shave your head."

I still refused.

Some time later, three days before we left Philadelphia for New York, we were in my dressing room, Kanin and I. A heavy rain lashed the city, my room was hot and muggy. I was sitting in front of my make-up table and Garson, who had been working eighteen hours every day since our opening, was resting on my couch. Absent-mindedly I scratched at the label on the can of rose-colored wax which listed my make-up man's address. Suddenly the whole label peeled off and underneath appeared the inscription, "For morticians' use only."

I turned to Kanin and said, "Let's shave the head."

He looked at me with tired, bleary eyes. He did not understand.

I showed him the inscription and he burst out laughing.

Ten minutes later we were at the nearest barber shop. "Here, fella, shave this guy's head!" Kanin ordered. The barber obliged. But I will never forget the incredulous, even mortified look he gave me when we departed.

Twice during rehearsals I had formally handed my resignation to Kanin. I knew how that part must be played, and yet I could not get rid of the dreadful feeling that I was not doing justice to the character. I was too theatrical, not simple enough. Kanin, however, disregarded my request to be released from my contract. "Do you believe you can play Otto Frank?" he asked. "Yes," I said. "Then shut up and go back to rehearsals. Just suppress your own personality. Play the part as a supporting actor, not as a star. And you'll be *it*."

That evening, after I had shaved off part of my hair, I knew for the first time that I had solved my problem. This was more than an attempt to look like Otto Frank—the sacrifice, small as it was, somehow cured me of my vanity, my egotism, of my subconscious drive to be brilliant and startling, and helped me to achieve in my acting the simplicity and humility which this part demanded.

We opened in New York on October 5, 1955, a day that I regard as the high point of my career and of my whole life.

Just before I went on stage I found a little note which Kanin had left on my dressing table. It read:

Dear Pepi, thank you for your talent—thank you for your genius—thank you for your patience. When in doubt—*less*. Please!

Love, Gar.

And the next day, after all the reviews were out, each more enthusiastic than the other, I received a wire from Garson:

THEY FOUND YOU DIDN'T THEY LIKE THEY FOUND YOUR FATHER AND I AM SURE YOUR FATHER WOULD HAVE LIKED YOUR TIE TONIGHT.

3

In my opinion, Garson Kanin's contribution to the triumphal success of the *Diary* cannot be overestimated. As Walter Kerr wrote, "He had not so much directed the play with love, as orchestrated it." He had a marked influence on the rewriting of the original script, he mastered the inherent danger of its being static by giving it depth and dramatic power, and it was he who picked every one of the ten actors for the play.

Susan Strasberg's great success made me especially happy. I had known her since the day she was born. That opening night I witnessed her rebirth as a star, but the success did not turn her head. She remained guileless, modest, lovable, a mixture of child and sophisticated young lady that is her special charm.

I admired Gusti Huber's Mrs. Frank, a difficult part, not at all what one would call "rewarding." She turned it into a very moving performance. How eloquent she was, even when she had no words to speak!

Kanin imported from England two actors—Lou Jacobi, who gave an excellent performance in the part of Van Daan, and David Levin, who was a refreshing and convincing Peter Van Daan. He was in London on a scholarship at the Royal Academy of Dramatic Arts when Kanin found him and gave him his first part on the legitimate stage.

A bit of brilliant off-beat casting was to put Dennie Moore, a blond blue-eyed Irish comedienne, into the part of Mrs. Van Daan. Equally right was Jack Gilford as the comical Mr. Dussel, though until then he had been known mainly as a nightclub entertainer and pantomimist. Eva Rubinstein (daughter of the pianist, Artur Rubinstein) as Frank's elder daughter Margot, Clinton Sundberg as Mr. Kraler, and Gloria Jones as the Dutch girl Miep each had a share in the success of *The Diary of Anne Frank*.

4

Why do I regard my work in *The Diary of Anne Frank* the climax of my long career in the theater? Why does this part mean so much to me?

I have appeared in plays of greater literary value and in parts that were not less important. And I had won acclaim and praise before. Yet never before have I felt such an intimate relationship with a play, never such an identification with a part.

In her diary Anne Frank actually wrote the epitaph to a whole period of the history of Europe, the history of Germany, the tragedy of the Jews. That era was marked by the breakdown of the walls of the ghetto and the westernization of the Jew. Germany became his promised land. It turned into his hell.

My father was a symbol of that era. A poor and homeless Jew from the Balkans, he brought to the German people a new and profound appreciation of the great classics. Germany was his artistic fatherland.

Not until he had to leave Germany did he realize in America that he had actually never left the home of his people. Romanian, German, or American, his soul and heartbeat were Jewish.

I had never felt the burdens or the blessings of this heritage. All my life I have been a man of the world. I am proud of my American citizenship, for America is not just another nation to me but a way of life in which I passionately believe.

Came that evening when I stood on the stage of Madison Square Garden in New York to take part in the annual Hanukkah celebration for Bonds for Israel.

This was a special event. A torch had been brought from the new state and with it I was to light the candles and say the prayer exactly as I did on stage in *The Diary of Anne Frank*.

Thirty thousand people filled the arena, a sea of humanity. And like powerful waves the murmurs, sighs, prayers of that mass rose up to me, engulfed me, carried me away. I felt sorrow and exultation. My eyes burned, my heart ached in pride and grief.

For *The Diary of Anne Frank* is not only an epitaph to an era, but also the promise of a new world. Not merely an end, but also a beginning. In her child's wisdom, Anne has left us not only the legacy of her doom but her hope and faith in the future: "In spite of everything I still believe that people are really good at heart." I see in these few words the essence of Anne's work and the real meaning of her death.

The extraordinary success the *Diary* has had in Germany with thousands and thousands of the young people crying their hearts out, not daring to applaud, leaving the theater with bowed heads, is more than a tribute to a gifted author. It is—at least this is what I want to believe—a proof that Anne's voice has reached the hearts and minds of the German youth. In remembering what Germany has done to the Jews they cannot fail to remember what the Jews have given to Germany.

In presenting *The Diary of Anne Frank* the theater, once more, fulfilled its noble mission of a "moral institution." This was the theater that my father served so magnificently, and which I hope to serve for the rest of my life. For what is theater and art if it does not rise above the clamor and confusion of the marketplace and plant in the hearts and minds of the bewildered and frustrated the seeds of understanding, hope, goodness, and humanity?

Index

Index

(The abbreviations *ill.* I and *ill.* II refer to the two sections of illustrations following pages 118 and 182.)

241